DEFINING AND I
DEMOCR

CU00766704

DEFINING AND MEASURING DEMOCRACY

edited by

David Beetham

SAGE Modern Politics Series Volume 36
Sponsored by the European Consortium for
Political Research/ECPR

SAGE Publications
London · Thousand Oaks · New Delhi

Editorial arrangement, Introduction and Chapter 2 © David
Beetham 1994
Chapter 1 © Michael Saward 1994
Chapter 3 © Geraint Parry and George Moyser 1994
Chapter 4 © Axel Hadenius 1994
Chapter 5 © Jørgen Elklit 1994
Chapter 6 © Stuart Weir 1994
Chapter 7 © Patrick Dunleavy and Helen Margetts 1994
Chapter 8 © Nikolai Biryukov and Victor Sergeyev 1994
Chapter 9 © Bhikhu Parekh 1994

First published 1994

SAGE Publications Ltd
6 Bonhill Street
London EC2A 4PU

SAGE Publications Inc
2455 Teller Road
Thousand Oaks, California 91320

SAGE Publications India Pvt Ltd
32, M-Block Market
Greater Kailash – I
New Delhi 110 048

British Library Cataloguing in Publication data

A catalogue record for this book is available from the British
Library.

ISBN 0 8039 7788 3
ISBN 0 8039 7789 1 (pbk)

Library of Congress catalog card number 94-068162

Typeset by Type Study, Scarborough
Printed in Great Britain by Biddles Ltd, Guildford, Surrey

Contents

Notes on Contributors

David Beetham is Professor of Politics and Director of the Centre for Democratization Studies, University of Leeds. He is author of a number of books on political theory, including *The Legitimation of Power*.

Nikolai Biryukov is Lecturer at the Moscow State Institute for International Relations, and joint author of *Russia's Road to Democracy*.

Patrick Dunleavy is Professor of Government at the London School of Economics. His books include *Democracy, Bureaucracy and Public Choice*, *Theories of the State* (co-authored) and *British Democracy at the Crossroads*(co-authored).

Jørgen Elklit is Senior Lecturer in Political Science at the University of Aarhus, and an advisor on elections to the Danish Ministry of Foreign Affairs. He has written on electoral systems, electoral behaviour and political parties and was a member of the Independent Electoral Commission in South Africa in 1994.

Axel Hadenius is Professor of Political Science at the University of Uppsala, Sweden, and author of *Democracy and Development*.

Helen Margetts is Lecturer in Public Policy at Birkbeck College, University of London. Her current research is on local policy-making structures, and information technology in central government.

George Moyser is Professor of Political Science and Director of European Studies, University of Vermont. Publications include *Church and Politics in a Secular Age*, *Les citoyens et la politique locale* (co-authored) and *Political Participation and Democracy in Britain* (co-authored).

Bhikhu Parekh is Professor of Political Theory at the University of Hull, and is currently working on the philosophical foundations of multiculturalism. Recent works include four edited volumes of *Critical Assessments of Jeremy Bentham.*

Geraint Parry is W.J.M. Mackenzie Professor of Government at the University of Manchester. Publications include *Participation in Politics*, *Les citoyens et la politique locale* (co-authored) and *Political Participation and Democracy in Britain* (co-authored).

Michael Saward is Lecturer in Politics at Royal Holloway, University of London and is currently working on democratic theory and green political theory. He is the author of *Co-optive Politics and State Legitimacy.*

Victor Sergeyev is Deputy Director, Centre for the Analysis of Scientific and Industrial Policies, Russian Academy of Sciences. He is joint author of *Russia's Road to Democracy.*

Stuart Weir is Senior Research Fellow at the University of Essex, and joint editor of the Democratic Audit of the UK. He recently co-authored the Audit's first report on executive government bodies, *Ego Trip* (May 1994).

Acknowledgements

The editor's thanks are due to the European Consortium for Political Research, which helped organize and finance the workshop on 'Indices of Democratization', of which this volume is a product; also to the Joseph Rowntree Charitable Trust, which sponsored some of the attendees to the workshop, and which finances the Democratic Audit of the UK, the subject of three of the chapters in the volume. I should also like to thank Charlotte Williams for her work in helping prepare the final typescript, and Ziyad Marar and Rowena Lennox of Sage Publications, for seeing the work through to publication.

David Beetham

Introduction

David Beetham

With the new phase of democratization across all continents since the late 1980s has come a renewed interest in the question of how we define and assess 'democracy' and 'democratization'. By what criteria or benchmarks is the progress towards democracy of a given country to be assessed? How far are comparative levels of democracy subject to measurement, and if so what kind of measurement and with what degree of precision? Can the same criteria be applied to developing democracies as to established ones? Do we need different criteria to assess the durability of democracy from those used to assess its degree? And are the standards used by Western scholars ethnocentric or universal? These questions, at once philosophical, analytical and empirical, are of interest not only to political scientists, but also to governments, which are now using progress in 'democracy and human rights' as a consideration in their aid policies, and to informed citizens who are concerned about the level or quality of democracy in their own countries.

The chapters of this volume were first presented as papers at a European Consortium of Political Research workshop on 'Indices of Democratization' at Leiden, Holland, in 1993. The development of indices to assess the level of a country's democracy has in fact a long pedigree within the discipline of political science. Particularly influential was Robert Dahl's book *Polyarchy* (1971), which distinguished two different dimensions of democracy, those of public contestation or competition, and of participation or inclusiveness, to be assessed according to eight separate institutional guarantees or indices. Later writers, such as Bollen (1980, 1991), Gastil (author of the yearly Freedom House surveys, see Gastil, 1991) and Hadenius (1992), have developed and consolidated these indices, distinguishing in turn between the electoral process, its effectiveness and inclusiveness, on the one hand, and the protection of civil or political liberties, on the other, as the two key dimensions of democracy.

In the context of this literature, the present volume is distinctive in a number of respects. One is its concern to situate the assessment of democratic indicators within the broadest theoretical discussion of democracy and its meaning. Saward's defence of political equality and responsive rule as key democratic principles leads, he shows, to much more stringent criteria for political participation and administrative regulation, as well as the inclusion of key social rights in any list of democratic indices. Beetham's analysis of democracy in turn extends its dimensions beyond those of the electoral process and civil rights or liberties, to include open and accountable government, and aspects of civil or democratic society; and it suggests making the indices of political equality more stringent by examining the degree of effective rather than merely formal equality of political rights and opportunities. Parry and Moyser's chapter demonstrates the complexity of citizen participation as an index of democracy by rigorously dissecting the concept of participation into its component aspects, and deploying evidence drawn from their recent study of participation in Britain to illustrate its complexities. In their different ways these contributions all show the value of conceptual analysis to the assessment of democracy in particular contexts.

A second distinctive feature of the collection is the differentiation it makes between the purposes which the democratic indices represented are designed to serve. One such purpose is an *explanatory* one: to assess how far the level or durability of a country's democracy is determined by key socio-economic variables, such as its degree of economic development or social equality. As the previous literature shows, such a project requires the quantification of a large number of examples for statistical analysis and comparison (see, for example, Bollen, 1979; Jackman, 1974; Lipset, 1959; Muller, 1988; Smith, 1969; Vanhanen, 1984). This is the tradition in which Hadenius' work stands. His chapter in this volume shifts his focus of interest from explaining the *level* of democracy in Third World countries (Hadenius, 1992), to the question of its durability. His treatment is original in embracing both institutional and socio-economic variables, and his analysis of over thirty countries concludes that both the method of selecting the executive, and the degree of economic development, are significant in explaining the durability of democracy.

A different purpose of democratic indices is more directly *evaluative*, and practically or policy-oriented, whether for political actors within a given country or for those outside who wish to know how it stands in comparison with others. Such indices may be aggregated into an overall quantitative scale, as in the Freedom House surveys, or treated as disaggregated and assessed qualitatively. Elklit's chapter offers a detailed comparison of electoral democracy in five countries, and directly addresses the question of what kind of measurement the different indices used are amenable to. He concludes that the only comparison possible between countries is on an ordinal, multidimensional scale of measurement; and that we should avoid aggregating the different indices into a single scale, since the weights to be assigned to each are so contestable.

A novel development of democratic indices is for the purpose of democratic 'audit' of a single country. Three of the chapters in the volume arise from work carried out for the Democratic Audit of the UK. Where Beetham's chapter explains and justifies the concept of such an audit, Weir conducts a systematic comparison between the UK and selected Western democracies across a number of key democratic indices. His comparison helps identify and situate both the distinctiveness of the UK's political system and some of the aspects in which it can be seen to be most defective from a democratic point of view. Following this broad comparative overview, the chapter by Dunleavy and Margetts concentrates on a comparison of electoral democracy in Britain with other countries. Their 'experiential' approach breaks new ground in disaggregating national data into regional and area figures, and in seeking to identify how people themselves experience the different aspects of electoral inequality at these more local levels. When reaggregated at national level, the authors show, these experiential measures produce markedly different results from the standard 'institutional' measures of cross-national comparison.

Dunleavy and Margetts' chapter reinforces the argument made by Elklit, that the basis of any quantitative measurement of a country's performance has to be carefully defined and justified; and that we need to distinguish those indices where quantification can provide a genuine measure of precision and objectivity from those where it cannot. Two rules can perhaps be formulated on the basis of the evidence in this volume. The first is that we should be particularly cautious of quantification where it results from the translation of qualitative judgements, for example about the condition of civil liberties in a country, into precise scores. The second is that the more the primary purpose of any comparison is explicitly evaluative, rather than explanatory, the more important it is to keep the different indices in a disaggregated form, rather than combine them into a single score or ranking order.

Two final chapters offer a more thoroughgoing critique of the whole enterprise of cross-national comparison through the construction of democratic indices by questioning whether there can ever be a culturally neutral concept of democracy to support them. Biryukov and Sergeyev argue that, because democracy is interpreted differently in different cultures, if we wish to assess the 'progress towards democracy' of a given country, it can only be done in terms of the meaning ascribed to democracy by the relevant political agents, not by reference to abstractly defined criteria or indices. This conclusion is exemplified by their account of the Russian political culture, and the way in which, from the standpoint of its conception of the popular will, key elements of the Western political tradition appear undemocratic, rather than the reverse. Parekh's subject is a re-examination of that Western political tradition itself, and a reinterpretation of the liberal element within 'liberal democracy' in the context of societies which are multicultural. Arguing that liberalism should now be understood less as the abstract definition of individual rights, and more as a framework for the ongoing negotiation of differences between different cultural communities in a spirit of mutual tolerance, he concludes that this has significant implications for how any democratic indices should be defined and interpreted.

The overall thrust of the volume, in conclusion, is to raise a variety of questions about the indices that have been developed to date for the comparative assessment and measurement of democracy. From the standpoint of democratic theory and conceptual analysis, some of the assumptions that underpin these indices appear over-simplistic. From the standpoint of a critical evaluation of established democracies, indices which treat their existing practice as the summit of democratic attainment seem unduly self-congratulatory. At the same time a careful assessment of the limits of quantification suggests that we need a sharper analysis of which features of democracy can be measured and which cannot, and of what kind of quantification the former are susceptible to. Finally, from the perspective of non-Western societies, doubts are raised about whether there can be a single entity called democracy as the subject of comparative assessment, rather than a variety of democracies, each to be assessed in its own terms. Together these chapters make a distinctive contribution to the comparative evaluation of political systems in the post-Cold War era, and to its methodological development.

References

Bollen, K. A. (1979) 'Political democracy and the timing of development', *American Sociological Review*, 44: 572–87.

Bollen, K. A. (1980) 'Issues in the comparative measurement of political democracy', *American Sociological Review*, 45: 370–90.

Bollen, K. A. (1991) 'Political democracy: conceptual and measurement traps', in A. Inkeles (ed.), *On Measuring Democracy: Its Consequences and Concomitants*. New Brunswick, NJ and London: Transaction Publishers. pp. 3–20.

Dahl, R. A. (1971) *Polyarchy: Participation and Opposition*. New Haven, CT and London: Yale University Press.

Gastil, R. D. (1991) 'The comparative survey of freedom: experiences and suggestions', in A. Inkeles (ed.), *On Measuring Democracy: Its Consequences and Concomitants*. New Brunswick, NJ and London: Transaction Publishers. pp. 21–46.

Hadenius, A. (1992) *Democracy and Development*. Cambridge: Cambridge University Press.

Jackman, R. W. (1974) 'Political democracy and social equality: a comparative analysis', *American Sociological Review*, 39: 29–45.

Lipset, S. M. (1959) 'Some social requisites of democracy: economic development and political legitimacy', *American Political Science Review*, 53: 69–105.

Muller, E. N. (1988) 'Democracy, economic development and income inequality', *American Sociological Review*, 53: 50–68.

Smith, A. K. (1969) 'Socio-economic development and political democracy: a causal analysis', *Mid-West Journal of Political Science*, 30: 95–125.

Vanhanen, T. (1984) *The Emergence of Democracy*. Helsinki: The Finnish Society of Sciences and Letters.

1

Democratic Theory and Indices of Democratization

Michael Saward

The indices of democratization can only be known within a full theory of democracy. In this chapter I will outline such a theory, focusing on definition and justification, the conditions of democracy, and what these conditions demand of democrats in terms of specific political practices and political institutions.

Problems of definition

Self-evidently, the properties of democracy can only be derived and listed after democracy has been defined adequately. What is the best way to go about this?

First, and perhaps most familiarly, we can look at those countries commonly called democracies and define the concept according to certain features of those systems.[1] This approach, however, is subject to an equally familiar flaw. It is illogical to define democracy by induction from the practice of any one political unit or any one sub-set of political units (this has been called the definitional fallacy[2]). To take the same problem from a slightly different angle, we could argue with Ryan that 'it is no use *defining* democracy in terms of the politics of any particular country, for then we can no longer praise that country for being democratic – we cannot praise a society for qualities which belong to it by definition rather than by political contrivance' (1970: 29). An etymological route to definition serves us little better. The phrase 'rule by the people' is highly ambiguous and is open to highly diverse interpretations (Hadenius, 1992; Held, 1987; Lively, 1975).

A more promising route might be to define democracy according to certain basic principles. Beetham seeks to isolate 'the core ideas or principles embodied in the historical conception of democracy as "rule of the people"' (1993: 6). He takes these to be 'popular control' and 'political equality'. Hadenius adopts a similar approach and arrives at a conception of 'political democracy' which holds that public policy 'is to be governed by the freely expressed will of the people whereby all individuals are to be treated as equals' (1992: 7–9). Lively (1975: 49–51) pinpoints the norms dictating inclusive citizenship and political equality, while Holden (1988: 6) boils democracy down to popular sovereignty.

No doubt each of these core principles speaks directly to 'rule of the people'. Again, however, different writers isolate different (sets of) principles, even among our very limited sample. Should all three elements put forward – equality, sovereignty/control and inclusiveness – be regarded as core principles, or just one or two of them? As Sartori writes, 'there are hosts of characteristics or properties eligible for selection; not only majority rule and participation, but also equality, freedom, consensus, coercion, competition, pluralism, constitutional rule, and more' (1987: 184).

So where do we go from here? I suggest that the alternatives are either to retreat into essential contestability (that is, to give up)[3] or to look for reasons that might justify adopting certain principles as basic. Of the four writers quoted above, only Beetham does so. He writes:

> The first principle [popular control] is underpinned by the value that we give to people as self-determining agents who should have a say on issues that effect their lives; the second [political equality] is underpinned by the assumption that everyone (or at least every adult) has an equal capacity for self-determination, and therefore an equal right to influence collective decisions, and to have their interests considered when they are made. (1993: 7)

Even this effort begs a range of questions. Why does 'self-determination' not require anarchy rather than democracy (or any other centrally organized political structure)? Why – on what basis – can we *assume* that people have an *equal capacity* for self-determination? What version of people's interests is worthy of 'consideration' – real, perceived, revealed, or some other? Is having 'influence' and having one's interests 'considered' inconsistent with those interests being virtually ignored in substantive public policies?

Although in the end this approach is also inadequate, it does provide hints as to how we might proceed. In essence, we need to justify more fulsomely our choice of principles. Defining democracy is a political act; the assumptions involved must be justified explicitly and convincingly to be of real value. What is needed is a definition of democracy which is not forged in theoretical isolation, but which is embedded in a theory which justifies and clarifies the concept of democracy as part of the process of definition. We should not posit a readily refutable, foundational equality as a core principle without an argument about what it is about communities and people that makes such an assumption reasonable (or, more strongly, unavoidable).

Justifying and defining democracy

The most ready way to justify democracy is to start from an assertion that all people are equal in some important respect, since it follows from this that all should be treated equally in certain specific political respects. The most straightforward way to assert such a foundational equality is to say that, for example, we all have an equal capacity for self-determination, or for rationality, or for making life-plans. Once an acceptable principle of political equality is forged, it can be used to define and to justify democracy. Further, it can be used to facilitate the deduction of democracy's logically necessary conditions (and therefore the indices of democracy). This approach, for example, characterizes Dahl's efforts in *Democracy and Its Critics* (1989), where he posits what he calls the 'idea of intrinsic equality' as axiomatic.

The critic of democracy has an equally ready reply, however, to foundational assertions of human equality. He or she can say: 'People are not manifestly equal. It is clear that if they share in rationality, or a capacity for self-determination, then they share in it in complex and unequal ways. People differ in their tastes, their preferences, their outlooks, and the processes by which they form their beliefs.' 'Much better', the critic might argue, 'to ignore pious and unworldly talk of foundational equality and to build political practices and institutions on the manifest inequalities of human beings.' The chances of convincing many people living in societies where a certain structure of inequalities is widely accepted that democracy is the best form of government would be greatly diminished.

Can a satisfactory justification of democracy be built on different – one might say more sceptical – grounds?[4] I believe that it can. The following account is necessarily brief, but I hope at least that it conveys the flavour of the argument.

Claims that one person or minority group should rule a political community – that is, a group of individuals who need to make at least some binding collective decisions – without being democratically chosen can be based upon many foundations, notably sex, age, class, race, religion, military strength and knowledge (see Thorson, 1962: 135).[5] Most of these claims can be reduced to a common form of claim: that one person or group of people, by virtue of some specified characteristic, knows better the proper political course for a community than other people and groups.[6] If some such claim to superior knowledge – whatever precise form it might take – is in principle acceptable, then democracy looks not to have a secure foundation. It is the strength of such claims to superior knowledge of political rightness that need to be examined: does any person or minority sub-group possess superior knowledge such that it can be said that *they* have a powerful claim to rule the rest in perpetuity? Initially, the question can be cast in the following form: are all claims to the requisite superior knowledge necessarily *fallible*?

In philosophy, the claim of fallibilists is that we are never entitled to assume that our knowledge – whether moral or factual – is beyond doubt. As Thorson has put it, the principle of fallibilism 'does not say that we can never know the truth, but rather that we are never justified in behaving as if we know it . . . we are never justified in refusing to consider the possibility that we might be wrong' (1962: 122). In John Stuart Mill's (1912) famous argument, fallibilism is valued for its social consequences, although his argument is rather more ambiguous on the question of whether our knowledge claims necessarily *are* in fact fallible. In Peirce's words, 'fallibilism is the doctrine that our knowledge is never absolute but always swims, as it were, in a continuum of uncertainty and of indeterminacy' (1940: 356).[7]

On the face of it, fallibilism offers an attractive sceptical ground upon which to build a justification for an open-ended polity which thrives on freedom and criticism precisely because no one viewpoint is superior to others. However, the strength of the fallibilist argument applies only to a limited class of claims to superior knowledge, which I will call non-contingent superior knowledge. Non-contingent superior knowledge is knowledge which is *not* confined to any one or any sub-set of a political community's spheres of activity (such as health, education or energy).[8] My argument is based on the fact that politics spans the community, is relevant to the whole community and the understandings and goods that are held to and made within it. Before defending the notion that there is in fact such a sphere of activity, and that the fallibilist principle defeats claims to non-contingent superior knowledge within it, we need to consider how arguments that we ought to recognize *contingent* knowledge claims can overcome fallibilist objections.

We commonly do recognize a variety of claims to superior knowledge, and with good reason. Most of these are in the realm of specialized, technical and therefore contingent knowledge: the garage mechanic knows better than I how to fix my car; the nuclear engineer knows better than I how to build a nuclear reprocessing plant; the social worker knows better than I how to deal with runaway teenagers. We can still be fallibilists and recognize a plurality of claims to contingently superior knowledge – especially efficacious knowledge in certain contexts – since fallibilism is not a doctrine of equal knowledge, or of equal proximity to the truth.

Of course, it is an old argument, going back to Plato at least, that knowledge of how political affairs ought to be conducted is not a type of knowledge qualitatively different from that required for a plethora of other technical or specialized tasks. This argument holds that the realm of politics is a realm of contingently superior knowledge: people with relevant specialized skills will always be better at it than others by virtue of their possession of those skills. If this is the case, then certain claims to superior knowledge in the realm of politics can escape the fallibilist critique. If the principle of fallibilism is to be usable as a justification for political equality – and thereafter of democracy – then we will need to establish that politics forms a sphere of activity where only non-contingent claims to superior knowledge obtain. This means establishing that politics is a distinctively, qualitatively different sphere of activity to others within a defined community, and that claims to contingent superior knowledge in one or other sub-sphere of such a community cannot rightly be carried over into the sphere of politics.

A key part of Michael Walzer's argument in *Spheres of Justice* (1983) is that we can recognize that certain groups of people can legitimately monopolize the control of certain social goods, mostly on the grounds that some social understandings of certain social goods include recognition of special skills or superior knowledge with respect to the particular character and the appropriate distribution of the good in question. However, for Walzer, political power denotes a sphere of social activity qualitatively different from other spheres. He writes that

> political power is a special sort of good. It has a twofold character. First, it is like other things that men and women make, value, exchange and share; sometimes dominant, sometimes not; sometimes widely held, sometimes the possession of the few. And, second, it is unlike all the other things because, however it is had and whoever has it, political power is the regulative agency for social goods generally. (1983: 15)

This suggests that politics is a sphere of activity qualitatively different from others, because it is the 'regulative agency' for other spheres. Does this approach establish politics as a sphere of non-contingently superior knowledge? Ultimately, it fails to do so. We could argue, for example, that health and education are 'regulative' of other spheres of activity, in that both involve conditions that can deeply constrain the capacity of any one group or individual to prosper within other spheres (including politics). The 'regulation' involved may well be informal (or cultural) rather than formal (or legal), but the argument still stands.

Aside from the 'regulative' argument, however, there are three other arguments which go considerably further to establish politics as a qualitatively different sphere of activity. I shall call these the implication, cumulative and temporal arguments respectively.

The implication argument suggests that politics is the only sphere of activity which is implicated in all other spheres within a political community. Whether it be the sphere of distribution of money, social status, education or health care, politics is involved.[9] To show this, we need to take Walzer's argument a stage further than Walzer himself does, since he views political power as something that 'stops' at the boundaries of other spheres of activity.

First, we can argue that insofar as the conception, creation and appropriate form of distribution of social goods is dependent upon social understandings, it is dependent upon social *interests*. Walzer recognizes that claims to monopolize social goods 'constitutes an ideology'. An ideology, in turn, is derived from a conception of interests. The idea that this or that recognized and distinct sphere of activity and understandings exists is itself the product of certain interests coming to the fore. Where interests are concerned, and therefore where the very constitution of spheres (and the precise nature of appropriate specialized knowledge within them) is concerned, so is politics. The 'stuff of politics' – power, conflict and interests – does in fact go *to the heart* of any single sphere of activity, and does not (cannot) stop at the boundaries of semi-autonomous spheres of interest.

In sum, on Walzer's logic (if not in his actual account) politics denotes a sphere of activity which is deeply, and inevitably, implicated in all others. It is not a sphere of contingent, specialized knowledge which is confined to a certain sub-communal domain.

The cumulative argument suggests that the role of politics within all other spheres adds up to more than the sum of its parts. Consider, for example, an effort to understand the complexity of politics at a given time in what Dahl (1989) calls a 'modern dynamic pluralist' society. We could locate, and attempt to characterize, the nature of political battles within a number of separate spheres of activity. Assuming this can be done, we could then 'add' together these characterizations in an attempt to get an overall picture of the nature of political power within the community as a whole. But if we were able to do even this, our picture would be radically incomplete, because we would not yet have taken into account the politics involved in the boundary struggles between spheres in addition to the extra layer of political complexity involved in the interactions between spheres. Politics is not 'just' about the nature of, and the different sorts of political claims within, different spheres of activity constituted around certain social goods; it is also about the multi-faceted relationships between them.

The temporal argument adds the effects of intra- and inter-sphere politics over time to the above points. The dimension of complexity of politics increases greatly over time as the sum total of relationships between and within spheres changes over time. Politics involves not just how spheres and their interactions differ at time t and time $t + 1$, but also information about the transition to the new state of affairs reached at $t + 1$. The need to understand the terms of this transition adds yet more to the complex – and qualitatively different – nature of political power.

Overall, these arguments establish not just that politics is an activity which is qualitatively different in type from all others, but also that it is distinguished by massive differences of degree. My contention is that politics is not a realm where contingent claims to specialized, superior knowledge are legitimate; rather, it is a realm in which only non-contingent claims are admissible in principle.[10] However, since the principle of fallibilism renders inadmissible any such claims to non-contingently superior knowledge, all claims to superior knowledge with respect to politics must fail.

There is implicit in this argument another argument about interests, which needs to be specified. Taking the points made above from a slightly different angle, we can concede (putting it briefly and formally) that a political authority (PA) could have legitimate contingently superior knowledge of what is in the interests of a citizen (C) with regard to an issue (X). However, the *sum* of C's interests at a given time t consist of judgements with respect to not only X, but also $X_1, X_2 \ldots X_N$. It is highly dubious, given the above arguments, to think that PA's knowledge of C's interests can extend to X_N at t. Even if it could, it would have somehow to encompass the extra dimension involved in how, for example, C's interest in X might be affected by his interest in X_1 and X_2. Even granting her super-human knowledge up to this point, PA's job becomes tougher still at $t + 1$; at that point, PA would require, at a minimum, knowledge of C with respect to X_N at $t + 1$ in addition to the original knowledge of C with respect to X_N at t. Further, consider that the claim that PA can know the 'best interests' of citizens generally means that she would need to know the interests of C_N at $t, t + 1, t + 2$, etc. The only reasonable conclusion that can be reached is that those in political authority cannot rightly claim to know the better interests of any citizen, or any group of citizens, beyond narrow considerations with respect to a narrow range of issues. Across the full range of a given citizen's relevant concerns, individuals must be adjudged the best judges of their own interests in the absence of any alternative convincing argument.[11]

In conclusion, no one person can rightly claim to have sufficiently broad or perpetual superior knowledge of either (a) the rightful course for a political community, or (b) the totality of a given citizen's interests. Individuals and sub-groups must be taken to be the best judges of their own interests, not because of some inherent quality which they possess equally, but because of the *absence* of such a quality, or of our capacities to know such a quality.

The equality assumption

If the above arguments with respect to political authority are accepted, then it is imperative upon us to adopt – and to work with – an assumption that all citizens are equal with respect to their right to decide the appropriate political course of their community. I shall refer to this as the 'equality assumption'. The need to adopt the equality assumption arises from the fact that there is no secure ground upon which it can be said that one person or group has better insight in this field than any other. Crucially, it involves the view that legitimate non-contingent claims to superior political knowledge are restricted to those made by democratically elected representatives during their period in office.

The equality assumption is similar to arguments such as that we are equal in our capacity for self-determination or for rationality. It differs from these other conceptions, however, in that it is based on an absence (of certainty) rather than a presence (of some specified capacity or characteristic).[12] As such, it is easier to defend than other assertions of factual equality, since we do not need to argue that we all share a determinate characteristic in equal measure.[13]

Defining democracy (again)

The equality assumption is to be the basis for the definition of democracy within the theory of democracy. The only general rule that can reasonably follow on from the equality assumption is that: substantive policy, and political and administrative actions performed under substantive policy, must correspond to the express preferences of a majority of citizens.

This rule can be reformulated by altering slightly the similar defining rule set out by May (1978): there should be necessary correspondence between acts of government and the equally weighted express wishes of citizens with respect to those acts. On the basis of this definition of democracy – which May calls 'responsive rule', a locution that I adopt – we can construct a continuum. A political system is democratic to the extent that, and only to the extent that, it involves realization of responsive rule.

Why does the equality assumption require us to focus on defining democracy in terms of appropriate outcomes (responsive rule) rather than procedures? Because we have no good reason not to opt for the strongest form in which self-judged interests filter into public policy. If the requirement were instead for responsive procedures, it would be by no means guaranteed that what citizens want is what they will get in terms of substance. Further, focusing on responsiveness with respect to substance involves implicitly the necessary establishment of decision procedures designed to secure such substance. Such procedures may take a variety of forms in different contexts, but their democratic character will be diminished insofar as they are not geared towards maximizing responsiveness.

Why 'necessary correspondence' between acts of government and citizens' wishes? Because anything less than full correspondence suggests either (a) that values other than democracy are taking (at least partial) precedence over the realization of democratic decisions (I return to this later), and/or (b) that procedural inadequacies are affecting the democratic character of policy decisions. With an 'absolute' definition of a separate principle – the principle of democracy – we can see more clearly areas in which democracy is traded off in favour of other values or principles, whether by choice or by necessity.[14]

What 'acts of government' are being referred to in the responsive rule definition? This term must cover administrative acts as well as more clearly political acts. It covers decisions and the structure and activity of institutions whose role it is to implement those decisions. It should be remembered that there is substance in procedures (Dahl, 1989); the precise character and demands of a decision are still fluid to some degree once the decision is authoritatively taken. The realm of, for example, official discretion must therefore be brought into the purview of the responsive rule requirement.

Is not an uncompromising responsive rule definition counter to empirical sense? Should not empirical realizability be allowed to qualify the definition and elucidation of democracy as a political concept (see, for instance, Hadenius, 1992)? Now, on one view, this seems eminently sensible: surely what is realizable should temper our would-be neutral definitions of concepts? It is, however, a far from sensible move, and can only create confusion. Once the floodgates are opened – once a writer's own views of how far (some version of) democracy is actually realizable tempers his or her definition of the term – the task of definition becomes ridiculously subjective.

Arguments concerning empirical realizability depend in large part on the views of individual authors. Much better, I would argue, to define democracy more generally, and on more logical grounds, and *then* look later to arguments as to why it may not, or in a certain context cannot, be realized fully. Among other things, this is an argument for keeping democracy conceptually separate as a political value, which may need to be diluted in this or that practical context depending upon the range of constraints and opportunities which present themselves with regard to the organization of politics in that context.

A couple of further comments are appropriate before we take the argument to its next step. I take it as axiomatic that simple majority rule is superior to any of its alternatives: qualified majority rule, minority rule or unanimous rule.[15] The responsive rule definition, in its as yet unexplored state, makes no acknowledgement of the widely agreed notion that majority rule on its own is inadequate – normally, it is understood that some form of limited majority rule is appropriate to democracy. The important thing for present purposes is that the distinctive nature and value of democratic rule – that it centres on responsiveness – needs to be understood in isolation to be fully appreciated.

Finally, following the idea of responsive rule, it might be thought that direct rather than representative forms of decision-making are favoured, since the former will by definition almost always be more 'responsive' than the latter. This is true (Saward, 1993). The theory – as set out so far, at least – leans heavily towards direct mechanisms rather than indirect mechanisms, insofar as the former are more likely to maximize responsive rule than the latter.[16] This is also a part of regarding democracy as an independent value.

The logic of self-limiting democracy

Responsive rule does not mean unlimited rule, or 'tyranny of the majority'. The basic argument against such a position follows logically and directly from the equality assumption and the responsive rule definition: if (a) responsive rule should operate in political communities so far as this is feasible, and (b) responsive rule may be overthrown in a simple majority rule system, then (c) factors logically necessary to responsive rule's persistence should be taken out of the reach of majority decision procedures.[17]

So responsive rule must be subject to certain conditions. These conditions arise from the internal logic of democracy, and not from limiting values separate from democracy. It follows from these points that there is no justification within the theory for the majority viewpoint not being decisive in terms of substantive policy in cases other than those which threaten the persistence of responsive rule itself.

The logically necessary conditions of democracy

Responsive rule does not come easily. Various conditions must be met before we can say that it is effectively in place. My argument concentrates on what are logically necessary conditions, rather than on empirically necessary conditions (though these two categories no doubt overlap at various points). The conditions largely refer to rights, freedoms and decision mechanisms. Each follows deductively from the equality assumption and the responsive rule definition. The basic freedoms reflect the requirements flowing from the equality assumption. Citizenship and participation conditions reflect the need for minimal rights and specified mechanisms essential to the maximization of responsive rule. The publicity condition is a key background condition making responsive rule possible and helping citizens to develop informed interests. Social rights are included for similar reasons (I shall say more about them below). If the general argument holds, then these minimal conditions taken together form the indices of democratization.

(A) *Basic freedoms*
 1 Each citizen has the right to freedom of speech and expression.
 2 Each citizen has the right to freedom of movement.
 3 Each citizen has the right to freedom of association.
 4 Each citizen has the right to equal treatment under the law.
 5 Each citizen has the right to freedom of worship.

(B) *Citizenship and participation*
 6 The political community must have a common and standardized form of legal membership compatible with the basic freedoms.
 7 Citizens have an equal right to run for elective office.
 8 Citizens have the right to be equally eligible to serve, and, where appropriate, granted an equal probability of being selected for service, in non-elective representative and decisional bodies.
 9 Citizens have the equal right to vote in all elections and referendums.
10 Citizens' votes must be decisive under all decision mechanisms.
11 Mechanisms must be available for citizens to vote directly on substantive outcomes. If elected officials deem a decision inappropriate for direct decision, the burden of demonstrating the grounds of such inappropriateness lies with those officials.
12 There must be a voting system (such as two-stage contests) which

allows for the expression of a majority preference in multi-sided contests.

13 Where votes for representatives are conducted, these votes must be renewed at regular and specified intervals.

14 Regular opinion polls must be conducted by an appropriate agency on all issues of substantive importance, whether or not these issues are to be decided by representative decision. The burden of demonstrating the appropriateness of not following citizen preferences on a given issue lies with elected representatives.

15 There must be a presumption that all issues will be decided by referendums, and clear guidelines as to when a referendum may be forgone.

16 All issues not specifically prohibited from majority decision must be open to majority decision via one of the appropriate mechanisms.

(C) *Administrative codes*

17 There must be appropriate codes of procedure for employees in public bodies.

18 There must be regularly produced evidence that public decisions are being put into effect.

19 There must be appropriate time limits placed on the realization of the substance of public decisions.

20 There must be instituted adequate appeals and redress mechanisms with respect to public bodies and their functions.

21 There must be freedom of information from all government bodies. The burden of proof of demonstrating the inappropriateness of full freedom of information in specific cases lies with the elected representatives.

(D) *Publicity*

22 There must be a constant and formal process of public notification of decisions, options, arguments, issues and outcomes.

(E) *Social rights*

23 Every citizen has the right to adequate health care.

24 Every citizen has the right to an adequate education.

Following the logic of the general theory, in principle each of these rights or freedoms must be guaranteed to each citizen in spite of the will of a majority or minority of citizens, and must be protected by a judicial system which is not itself a part of majoritarian decision processes. In other words, each should be constitutionalized.

Some further comments are needed in order to justify the style and content of the above list. One general concern is that there are various arguments and suggestions to the effect that restrictions on majoritarianism are undemocratic. In particular, many worry about putting power in the hands of unelected judges, whose task it is to interpret constitutional requirements in a democracy. According to Dworkin this is the reason why 'judicial review [in the United States] is generally regarded as undemocratic, even by its sometime friends, and even by its passionate admirers' (1987: 28–9). Pennock likewise notes that the Supreme Court is 'an institution that is often said to be undemocratic' (1989: 30). Discussions of constitutionalism and democracy regularly start from the highly questionable – and normally undefended – assumption that there is an essential tension between the two (see Brennan and Lomasky, 1989: 2; Elster, 1988: 7). Clearly, not all restrictions on majority decision can be democratic; indeed, as I have suggested, those restrictions that are acceptable because logical (deducible) are quite specific and few in number. It is not 'precommitment' that must be endorsed, but democratic precommitments (see Holmes, 1988). Holmes argues rightly that to 'grant power to all future majorities . . . a constitution must limit the power of any given majority' (1988: 226). His argument, though, stresses the good, 'enabling' consequences of certain precommitments, whereas it is more important to stress the fundamental nature of *democratic precommitment*. As Sunstein writes:

> Rights provisions are designed to fence off certain areas from majoritarian control, but they also serve different functions. The protection of some rights is rooted in a desire to protect democracy, however understood. The right to freedom of speech and the right to vote are examples. The fact that majorities cannot intrude on such rights should not obscure their democratic nature. But rights might also be antidemocratic, in the sense that they interfere with democratic processes for reasons that are independent of a desire to preserve the functioning of democracy. (1988: 328)

Social rights

There are various objections to constitutionalizing – and therefore making into rights – any social (or economic) conditions. The first is that constitutions are about negative liberties (like freedom of speech and association), not positive liberties (like the right to a decent education). Kymlicka and Norman write that many constitutional experts 'worry that it would be a radical and potentially dangerous new step to let judges determine the government's positive obligations' (1992: 2). Note, however, that this objection depends upon a rather weak characterization of different rights. For example, a right to an adequate education can be construed as a negative right: the state does not have the right to deprive you of an adequate education. Construing 'civil' and 'political' rights as negative and 'social' rights as positive is optional, a matter of rhetoric rather than substance.

A second objection is that these provisions would place too many cash burdens on governments with few resources at their disposal. That this may be the case does not mean that these social rights should not be constitutionalized according to the logic of democracy. If a government genuinely cannot afford to deliver on these social rights, then it may well be the case that acceptable discounting rules can be used when the theory of democracy is applied to political practice.

A third objection is that constitutionalizing some social rights politicizes the judiciary. If so, so be it; it is a mistake, as noted above, to assume that the role of the judiciary is always to act as a brake on democracy. My argument is the 'interdependence' argument: as set out by Kymlicka and Norman, referring to Marshall's notion of the historical extension of rights from the civil to the political to the social,

> [w]hile this process can be seen as adding new rights, it can be seen as extending the earlier rights. Just as political rights are now seen as a way of guaranteeing civil rights, so social rights can be seen as providing the conditions for effective exercise of both civil and political rights. (1992: 11)[18]

Finally, it might be objected that the interdependence argument opens the floodgates to the constitutionalization of a much more extensive range of social (and other) rights. I have confined the social rights specified here to health and education requirements, since these are distinctively related to a citizen's capacity to exercise his or her other basic rights. I would concede, however, that no clear cut-off point can be specified in a thoroughly non-arbitrary manner. This concession involves accepting that as we approach the (impossible) point of 'full democracy', we enter a grey area. If a full range of demanding social and economic (and perhaps ecological) rights were to be constitutionalized, little would be left for 'ordinary' democratic decision. We can hypothesize that even if a full democracy were possible, it would not be desirable, since in a sense it would undermine itself.[19]

Democracy and competing values

A democracy – or a partial democracy – always exists *somewhere*, within some unique set of background conditions. In a huge variety of ways, those background conditions can and will constrain the extent and the character of the democratic regime achieved.

In this context we need to consider a range of values, or political principles, that we can expect in theory (and which, in some cases, we know in practice) to operate at variance with the democratic principle. Arguably, the key ones to consider in a full analysis are: (a) political stability, (b) justice, (c) nationalism, (d) the environmental imperative and (e) efficiency.

Is there a satisfactory trade-off principle to guide us when we are faced with conflicting principled demands? There is no such obvious principle. Consistency is one possibility (Barry, 1965), but it is quite conceivable that to be consistent may be to be consistently wrong. Another alternative is to derive trade-off rules according to the canons of a higher principle to which the two competing, and subordinate, principles bear some logical or moral relation (Goodin and Wilenski, 1984). In the case of democracy, however – at least as I have presented it – it is not at all clear that this approach might help us. Democracy is here conceived as a value in itself. Perhaps insofar as other values, linked perhaps to justice, may derive directly from the equality assumption, then equality could be the higher principle upon which trade-offs can be conducted.

It might be argued, of course, that the key notions contained within the theory of democracy itself – such as the best-judge principle, suitably interpreted – could be used to suggest procedures by which trade-offs ought to be conducted. This approach is attractive for those who feel that democracy – or at least a democratic procedure – represents a higher principle than all others. That claim is not a part of the argument I am presenting. Ultimately, I do not think that any secure conclusions about value trade-offs can be reached within democratic theory. If they can be reached at all, it will be between the democratic principle and other, competing, principles.

Just as full constitutionalization of an extensive range of social and other rights – beyond what I have suggested above – may not always be desirable, so between democracy and other competing values there is no necessary prescription that democracy must 'win' when principles conflict.[20] Ever more democracy is not necessarily a good thing. We will want some stability as well at times, for example (assuming for the moment that the two might clash). Rarely, however, is this said explicitly. Ought we really to be frightened to suggest that we would ever want to be anything other than wholly democratic in our political logic and our political actions? If we are to gain a clear view of democracy – if we are to isolate its character and its value for us, separately from other considerations – then we must view in a clearheaded way how it will often be diluted in the desire to see realized certain other key political principles.[21]

Conclusion

This chapter has covered a great deal of ground in a limited space, leaving many key assumptions undefended. I hope at least to have said enough to convince readers that the principles upon which the indices of democracy are based require careful justification and elucidation. Quite specific indices of democracy can follow deductively from abstract arguments about definition and justification.

None of us deserves privilege in the realm of politics. Responsiveness and equality are – or at least, should be – the keys to political legitimacy. Once we have teased out what democracy is, and what it demands of citizens and governors, we can begin to understand clearly the magnitude of the task facing democratizers around the globe. Perhaps, in a small way, we will even be contributing to their efforts.

Notes

In addition to participants in the ECPR workshop on 'Indices of Democratization', the author would like to thank the members of the University College London Political Philosophy Group and those attending the London School of Economics Graduate Seminar in Political Philosophy for their many helpful comments and criticisms.

1 For variants on this approach, see, e.g., Lijphart (1984: 2) and Schumpeter (1952: 269).

2 See Holden (1974: 6) for a discussion of this idea.

3 For a discussion of essential contestability in this context, see Arblaster (1987: 5–8).

4 A broadly sceptical justification does not mean a 'postmodern' justification (see Saward, 1994).

5 See Levin (1992) for the ways in which these and other comparable claims have proved powerful in the development of the American, British, French and German political systems.

6 This fits closely with Walzer's view: 'All arguments for exclusive rule, all anti-democratic arguments, if they are serious, are arguments from special knowledge' (1983: 285).

7 Fallibilism is now standard in the philosophy of science – Laudan comments that 'we are all fallibilists now' (1990: 133). Popper expresses it thus:

> The status of truth in the objective sense, as correspondence to the facts, and its role as a regulative principle, may be compared to that of a mountain peak which is permanently, or almost permanently, wrapped in clouds. The climber may not merely have difficulties in getting there – he may not know when he gets there,

because he may be unable to distinguish, in the clouds, between the summit and some subsidiary peak. (1983: 185–6)

Friendly critics of Popper are if anything more fully fallibilist than Popper himself. Lakatos, for example, writes: 'The demarcation line between the soft, unproven "theories" and the hard, proven "empirical basis" is non-existent: all propositions of science are theoretical and, incurably, fallible' (1980: 16).

8 I borrow the use of the term 'spheres' from Walzer, who uses it to distinguish processes of interaction which take place around different social goods within a community.

9 This involves adopting a broad definition of politics. If politics is about power, and power is a ubiquitous phenomenon (see Foucault, 1980), then medicine, health and education, for example, are political. Feminist writers have done the most in recent years to foster broader definitions of politics (see Pateman, 1987).

10 It might be objected that the very complexity considered here makes the need for contingent, specialized knowledge in politics so much the greater. But as Dryzek (1990) argues, the process of 'mapping' this complexity is a task that is thoroughly subjective, and ultimately is not amenable to any specialized form of systems planning alone. The only type of political system which could conceivably allow for contingent, superior knowledge in the broader realm of political decision-making would be a highly decentralized system of functional representation and autonomy. I do not know of such a system historically, and cannot see how it could be reconciled with the territorial basis of political authority.

11 For a full discussion of the 'best-judge principle', see Goodin (1990).

12 This may seem an unduly 'negative' route to take in the search for a justification of democracy. Citizens, it seems, are being stripped of the glossy dignity that universal assertions of autonomy or capacities for rationality normally grant to them. This objection, however, does not hold. For one thing, the equality assumption does not lack prescriptive strength because of the style of its derivation; weaknesses must be sought in the argument, not in the presumed character of the argument. Further, as Barber (1984) has elegantly shown, sceptical arguments for democracy can take on a highly positive tone by stressing the liberating nature of overturning rarely questioned theoretical myths.

13 Some writers reach a similar point but proceed to assert a foundational equality, or assume that it is enough that many people believe that we are equal in some important respect. See, e.g., the arguments of Botwinick (1985) and Dahl (1989).

14 This more rigorous definition should help to add value to the concept of democracy as a tool for comparative analysis.

15 See the accounts of majority rule in Dahl (1989), Lively (1975), McLean (1987) and Spitz (1984).

16 Mechanisms of direct democracy – most obviously the referendum – do not necessarily require smaller political units (Saward, 1993). A key task of democratic theory is to ascertain whether a given political unit is democratically governed, and not to question the 'givenness' of the unit itself.

17 See the discussion of self-binding in Elster (1988).

18 Cf. Rawls' arguments on the 'fair value of liberty' (1972: 204, 225–6).

19 Compare with Williams' comment that consistently applying the principle of equality of opportunity might lead to 'a quite inhuman society' (1962: 130–1).

20 This approach to democratic theory forms a compromise between broadly universalist and particularist views (see Parekh, 1993, for an extended discussion). Democracy does, as I have argued, involve certain unavoidable commitments for

those who espouse it. However the values that might be used to modify or dilute the degree of democracy realized in a given political unit (e.g. a nation-state) might vary widely from one place to another, and the democrat must grant to such values a sceptical but healthy respect.

21 It is worth noting that, in general terms, considerable dilution of the democratic ideal, as presented here, would still leave us with a political system infinitely more democratic than, for example, the contemporary British state.

References

Arblaster, A. (1987) *Democracy*. Milton Keynes: Open University Press.

Barber, B. (1984) *Strong Democracy: Participatory Politics for a New Age*. Berkeley: University of California Press.

Barry, B. (1965) *Political Argument*. London: Routledge and Kegan Paul.

Beetham, D. (1993) *Auditing Democracy in Britain*. Democratic Audit Paper No. 1. Human Rights Centre, University of Essex, Colchester/Charter 88 Trust, London.

Botwinick, A. (1985) *Wittgenstein, Skepticism and Political Participation*. New York: University Press of America.

Brennan, G. and Lomasky, L. E. (1989) 'Introduction', in G. Brennan and L. E. Lomasky (eds), *Politics and Process*. Cambridge: Cambridge University Press. pp. 1–10.

Dahl, R. A. (1989) *Democracy and Its Critics*. New Haven, CT and London: Yale University Press.

Dryzek, J. (1990) *Discursive Democracy*. Cambridge: Cambridge University Press.

Dworkin, R. (1987) 'What is equality? Part 4: political equality', *University of San Francisco Law Review*, 22(1): 1–30.

Elster, J. (1988) 'Introduction', in J. Elster and R. Slagstad (eds), *Constitutionalism and Democracy*. Cambridge: Cambridge University Press. pp. 1–17.

Foucault, M. (1980) *Power/Knowledge* (ed. C. Gordon). New York: Pantheon.

Goodin, R. E. (1990) 'Liberalism and the best-judge principle', *Political Studies*, 38(2): 181–95.

Goodin, R. E. and Wilenski, P. (1984) 'Beyond efficiency', *Public Administration Review*, 44: 512–7.

Hadenius, A. (1992) *Democracy and Development*. Cambridge: Cambridge University Press.

Held, D. (1987) *Models of Democracy*. Cambridge: Polity.

Holden, B. (1974) *The Nature of Democracy*. London: Thomas Nelson.

Holden, B. (1988) *Understanding Liberal Democracy*. London: Philip Allan.

Holmes, S. (1988) 'Precommitment and the paradox of democracy', in J. Elster and R. Slagstad (eds), *Constitutionalism and Democracy*. Cambridge: Cambridge University Press. pp. 195–240.

Kymlicka, W. and Norman, W. J. (1992) 'The Social Charter debate', in *Network Analysis no. 2*. Ottowa: University of Ottowa.

Lakatos, I. (1980) *The Methodology of Scientific Research Programmes* (eds, J. Worrall and G. Currie). Cambridge: Cambridge University Press.

Laudan, L. (1990) *Science and Relativism*. Chicago, IL: University of Chicago Press.

Levin, M. (1992) *The Spectre of Democracy*. London: Macmillan.

Lijphart, A. (1984) *Democracies: Patterns of Majoritarian and Consensus Government in Twenty-One Countries*. New Haven, CT and London: Yale University Press.

Lively, J. (1975) *Democracy*. Oxford: Blackwell.

McLean, I. (1987) *Democracy and New Technology*. Cambridge: Polity.

May, J. D. (1978) 'Defining democracy: a bid for coherence and consensus', *Political Studies*, 26: 1–14.

Mill, J. S. (1912) *Three Essays*. Oxford: Oxford University Press.

Parekh, B. (1993) 'The cultural particularity of liberal democracy', in D. Held (ed.), *Prospects for Democracy*. Cambridge: Polity. pp. 156–75.

Pateman, C. (1987) 'Feminist critiques of the public/private dichotomy', in A. Phillips (ed.), *Feminism and Equality*. Oxford: Blackwell. pp. 103–26.

Peirce, C. S. (1940) *The Philosophy of Peirce: Selected Writings* (ed. J. Buchler). London: Routledge and Kegan Paul.

Pennock, J. R. (1989) 'The justification of democracy', in G. Brennan and L. E. Lomasky (eds), *Politics and Process*. Cambridge: Cambridge University Press. pp. 11–41.

Popper, K. (1983) *A Pocket Popper* (ed. D. Miller). London: Fontana.

Rawls, J. (1972) *A Theory of Justice*. Oxford: Oxford University Press.

Ryan, A. (1970) *The Philosophy of the Social Sciences*. London: Macmillan.

Sartori, G. (1987) *The Theory of Democracy Revisited* (2 vols). Chatham, NJ: Chatham House.

Saward, M. (1993) 'Direct democracy revisited', *Politics*, 13(2): 18–24.

Saward, M. (1994) 'Postmodernists, pragmatists and the justification of democracy', *Economy and Society*, 23(2): 201–16.

Schumpeter, J. A. (1952) *Capitalism, Socialism and Democracy* (5th edn). London: Allen and Unwin.

Spitz, E. (1984) *Majority Rule*. Chatham, NJ: Chatham House.

Sunstein, C. R. (1988) 'Constitutions and democracies', in J. Elster and R. Slagstad (eds), *Constitutionalism and Democracy*. Cambridge: Cambridge University Press. pp. 327–53.

Thorson, T. L. (1962) *The Logic of Democracy*. New York: Holt, Rinehart and Winston.

Walzer, M. (1983) *Spheres of Justice*. Oxford: Blackwell.

Williams, B. (1962) 'The idea of equality', in P. Laslett and W. G. Runciman (eds), *Philosophy, Politics and Society* (2nd series). Oxford: Blackwell. pp. 110–31.

2

Key Principles and Indices for a Democratic Audit

David Beetham

The purpose of this chapter is to report on a novel use of democratic indices, as a self-critical tool for the assessment or 'audit' of the quality of democracy in one's own country; to explain and defend the conception of democracy used, and the method whereby specific indicators have been derived from it; and to explore how far such indices are usable both beyond the UK and outside the context of the established Western democracies.

First, it is necessary to explain the idea of a 'democratic audit' itself. This is the simple but ambitious project of assessing the state of democracy in a single country. Like other Western countries, the UK calls itself a democracy, and claims to provide a model for others to follow. Yet how democratic is it actually? And how does it measure up to the standards that it uses to assess others, including the countries of the Third World? Such questions are not accidental, but are provoked by a widespread sense of disquiet within the UK at the state of its political institutions – a disquiet which runs deeper than the mere fact that a single party has been in power for so long.[1]

Auditing standards is currently in vogue in all areas of public life. Auditing the condition of democracy, however, raises novel problems which go beyond the parameters of a conventional audit. First is the sheer complexity of the enterprise. Most audits relate to a single institution or service. But what is a democratic audit precisely an audit of? Any political system involves a complex interrelationship of different institutions, arrangements and practices, whose connection and even whose boundaries may be far from clear. Providing a specification of what exactly is to be audited must constitute an important preliminary undertaking of such a project.

Secondly, there exist few clearly established or universally agreed criteria to serve as benchmarks for audit, in comparison with those used in accountancy, say, or management. One way round this might be to adopt the practice employed in some audits, that is, of assessing an institution or service, not against external or independent criteria, but against its own internally generated goals or standards. Could we not then assess the state of democracy in the UK against the standards its practitioners claim to be guided by, or by the values implicit in the political system, or even by what citizens themselves understand democracy to mean?

We rejected such an approach for a number of reasons.[2] First, it is by no means evident that the standards employed by political practitioners, or the values inherent in the UK's political system, are altogether democratic ones. Such a procedure would be to assume precisely what has to be investigated. On the other hand, to ask people what they understand democracy to mean, although an interesting exercise in itself, would be unlikely to provide any clear or consistent criteria for an audit. Through frequent misuse the term 'democracy' in popular parlance has come to mean whatever political arrangements the speaker personally approves of, and has become emptied of any objective referent.[3] A final reason for not basing an audit on internally derived criteria is that the UK belongs to a family group of countries which call themselves 'liberal democracies'. We should therefore expect to be able to define certain common criteria or standards of democracy which are applicable to them all, rather than being unique to the UK alone. This does not exclude discussing the criteria used with those whose work or activity forms the subject of audit; indeed, a public discussion about what democracy involves is itself an important aspect of such a project. But it should not form the starting point for the criteria to be used.

The project of a democratic audit, then, not only requires a clear specification of what exactly is to be audited. It also requires a robust and defensible conception of democracy, from which can be derived specific criteria and standards of assessment. An account of this conception and these criteria is provided in the following section.

Principles and indices of democracy

Our starting point in defining democracy was to reject the dichotomy made by Schumpeter (1952: ch. 22) and many others since, between an ideal conception of democracy and one based upon the existing institutions and procedures of Western political systems.[4] To base a definition of democracy on the latter alone has a number of obvious disadvantages. First, no reason can then be advanced as to why we should call these institutions 'democratic', rather than, say, 'liberal', 'pluralist', 'polyarchic', or whatever other term we choose. Secondly, we would be particularly vulnerable to the charge that our conception of democracy was Eurocentric, because it provided no way of discriminating between those non-Western institutions and procedures which offered genuinely alternative ways of realizing democracy, and those which could not properly be called democratic at all. Thirdly, and most importantly from the standpoint of a 'democratic audit', to base our conception of democracy entirely on a set of existing institutions and practices offers no means of addressing the crucial critical question: how might they be made more democratic? We would simply have no criteria against which they themselves might be assessed. This might not prove too troublesome if our purpose were a purely explanatory one: of investigating, say, what socio-economic circumstances had historically facilitated the emergence or the consolidation of given political institutions, such as multi-party elections and universal suffrage. But it becomes a fatal inadequacy if our purpose is to assess how democratic these institutions are in practice, or what makes them so.

On the other hand, a purely abstract conception of democracy, or a simple statement of democratic ideals and principles, is of limited value on its own unless we can show how these principles could be practically realized at the level of a whole society, and how they have become historically embodied in the institutions through which successive generations have sought to 'democratize' the enormous power of the modern state. The institutions developed from these struggles have an exemplary significance for contemporary democracy, to be sure; but this is so only insofar as we can show what makes them democratic, and how they might become more so. In this sense, to divorce a consideration of democratic principles from the institutions and practices through which they can be realized is simply misconceived.

One reason why many writers on comparative politics have shied away from a general definition of democracy is the enormous variety of such definitions in the literature of recent political theory, and the disagreement which has surrounded them. Some would even put democracy into the category of 'essentially contested concepts', whose definition depends irreducibly upon the theorist's ideological presuppositions.[5] In my judgement, the extent and significance of such disagreements has been greatly exaggerated. Most of the disagreements turn out on closer inspection to be not about the meaning of democracy, but about its desirability or practicability: about how far democracy is desirable, or about how it can be most effectively or sustainably realized in practice. Such disputes are entirely proper, but it is misleading to present them as disputes about the meaning of democracy itself.

If we examine the main currents of theorizing about democracy from the ancient Greeks onwards; if we pay attention to what those claiming to struggle for democracy have been struggling for; in particular, if we notice what the opponents of democracy throughout the ages have objected about it: then a relatively clear and consistent set of ideas emerges. Democracy is a *political* concept, concerning the collectively binding decisions about the rules and policies of a group, association or society. It claims that such decision-making should be, and it is realized to the extent that such decision-making actually is, subject to the control of all members of the collectivity considered as equals. That is to say, democracy embraces the related principles of *popular control* and *political equality*. In small-scale and simple associations, people can control collective decision-making directly, through equal rights to vote on law and policy in person. In large and complex associations, they typically do so indirectly, for example through appointing representatives to act for them. Here popular control usually takes the form of control over decision-*makers*, rather than over decision-making itself; and typically it requires a complex set of institutions and practices to make the principle effective.[6] Similarly political equality, rather than being realized in an equal say in decision-making directly, is realized to the extent that there exists an equality of votes between electors, an equal right to stand for public office, an equality in the conditions for making one's voice heard and in treatment at the hands of legislators, and so on.

These two principles, of popular control and political equality, form the guiding thread of a democratic audit. They are the principles which inform those institutions and practices of Western countries that are characteristically democratic; and they also provide a standard against which their level of democracy can be assessed. As they stand, however, they are too general. Like the indices developed by other political scientists, they need to be broken down into specific, and, where possible, measurable, criteria for the purpose of assessment or audit.[7]

To do this we have separated the process of popular control over government into four distinct, albeit overlapping, dimensions. First and most basic is the popular election of the parliament or legislature and the head of government. The degree or extent of popular control is here to be assessed by such criteria as: the *reach* of the electoral process (that is, which public offices are open to election, and what powers they have over non-elected officials); its *inclusiveness* (what exclusions apply, both formally and informally, to parties, candidates and voters, whether in respect of registration or voting itself); its *fairness* as between parties, candidates and voters, and the range of effective choice it offers the latter; its *independence* from the government of the day; and so on. These criteria can be summed up in the familiar phrase 'free and fair elections', though this phrase does not fully capture all the aspects needed for effective popular control.

The second dimension for analysis concerns what is known as

'open and accountable government'. Popular control requires, besides elections, the continuous accountability of government: directly, to the electorate, through the public justification for its policies; indirectly, to agents acting on the people's behalf.[8] In respect of the latter, we can distinguish between the *political* accountability of government to the legislature or parliament for the content and execution of its policies; its *legal* accountability to the courts for ensuring that all state personnel, elected and non-elected, act within the laws and powers approved by the legislature; its *financial* accountability to both the legislature and the courts. Accountability in turn depends upon public knowledge of what government is up to, from sources that are independent of its own public relations machine. In all these aspects, a democratic audit will need to assess the respective powers and independence, both legal and actual, of different bodies: of the legislature and judiciary in relation to the executive; of the investigative capacity of the media; of an independent public statistical service; of the powers of individual citizens to seek redress in the event of maladministration or injustice.

Underpinning both the first two dimensions of popular control over government is a third: guaranteed civil and political rights or liberties. The freedoms of speech, association, assembly and movement, the right to due legal process, and so on, are not something specific to a particular *form* of democracy called 'liberal democracy'; they are essential to democracy as such, since without them no effective popular control over government is possible (see Beetham, 1993b). These rights or liberties are necessary if citizens are to communicate and associate with one another independently of government; if they are to express dissent from government or to influence it on an ongoing basis; if electoral choice and accountability is to be at all meaningful. A democratic audit will need to assess not only the legally prescribed content of these citizens' rights, but also the effectiveness of the institutions and procedures whereby they are guaranteed in practice.

A fourth dimension of popular control concerns the arena of what is called 'civil society': the nexus of associations through which people organize independently to manage their own affairs, and which can also act as a channel of influence upon government and a check on its powers.[9] This is a more contestable dimension of democracy, not only because the criteria for its assessment are much less well formed than for the other three areas, but also because there is room for disagreement as to whether it should be seen as a necessary *condition for* democracy, or as an essential *part of* it. Our view is that a democratic society is a part of democracy, and goes beyond the concept of 'civil society', with its stress on the *independence* of

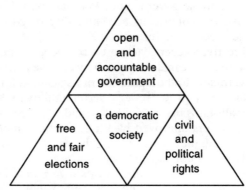

Figure 2.1   *The democratic pyramid*

societal self-organization, to include such features as: the representativeness of the media and their accessibility to different social groups and points of view; the public accountability and internal democracy of powerful private corporations; the degree of political awareness of the citizen body and the extent of its public participation; the democratic character of the political culture and of the education system.

The criteria or indices of popular control can thus be divided into four interrelated segments, which go to make up the major dimensions of democracy for contemporary societies. They can be represented diagrammatically as a pyramid, in which each element is necessary to the whole (see Figure 2.1). A complete democratic audit should examine each segment in turn, to assess not only the effectiveness of popular control in practice, but also the degree of political equality in each area: under free and fair elections, how far each vote is of equal value, and how far there is equality of opportunity to stand for public office, regardless of which section of society a person comes from; under open and accountable government, whether any individuals or groups are systematically excluded from access to, or influence upon, government, or redress from it; under civil and political rights or liberties, whether these are effectively guaranteed to all sections of society; under democratic society, the degree of equal opportunity for self-organization, access to the media, redress from powerful corporations, and so on.

These different criteria for what makes a country or political system democratic have been consolidated into thirty separate questions to guide the audit process in the different areas specified (see pp. 36–9). Answering all these questions is a very considerable undertaking, which requires a team of 'auditors' with the expertise to bring together a wide range of data, not only about the formal rules of the political system but also about its actual practice, and to assess it against the criteria agreed. Before examining these questions in detail, however, it is necessary to answer some basic objections which can be levelled at the audit project itself (and which have already been levelled in exploratory discussions and seminars): can an approach based upon individually and independently specifiable criteria really capture the character of a political system as a whole and 'in the round'? To what extent are these criteria really measurable, and on what sort of scale? How do these indicators relate to those developed by other political scientists? Is a democratic audit a proper subject for academic inquiry?

Some objections answered

The first objection to be answered is that the character and quality of a country's democracy cannot be assessed by 'ticking off' a set of specific criteria considered independently of one another. Since a political system operates through a complex interrelationship between its various institutions and practices, it can be argued that it is only by situating these in the context of the whole that they can be properly evaluated. So, for example, the UK Parliament may look inadequate in terms of its powers of scrutiny of the executive when compared with the US Congress, until we recognize that the main agent of parliamentary accountability is an opposition party acting as an alternative 'government in waiting'; and that the main source of weakness of the Parliament over the past decade has been, not so much the absence of specific scrutinizing powers, as the opposition's lack of credibility as such an alternative. From here it is a short step to arguing for the 'exceptionalism' of the UK political system, which makes any assessment of it against generalizable democratic criteria inappropriate.

Now it cannot be denied that political institutions have to be evaluated in their context, and that this will often make a qualitative rather than a purely quantitative assessment appropriate. However, it does not follow that we should therefore abandon generalizable criteria against which to assess the differing practices of different countries or political systems. Of course parliamentary systems differ from presidential ones, as do federal from unitary ones. What matters is not that all should conform to a single model, but how far the distinctive arrangements of each can meet the democratic criteria, which have been specified in intentionally generalizable terms. From the standpoint of a democratic audit, the question is not whether, say, the UK should or should not have a bill of rights, but how effective its chosen legal and constitutional arrangements are for protecting the civil and political rights and liberties of its citizens. To answer such a question we do need criteria that are generalizable beyond the UK itself.

In this context it is particularly important to distinguish differences between countries which can be seen as comparable means to attain a broadly similar goal (such as government accountability or individual rights), from differences which are more clearly differences in respective degrees of democracy. Many of the claims for the UK's 'exceptionalism' are simply a cover for undemocratic arrangements: a non-elected second chamber of parliament; a monarchy that not only has a legitimate constitutional role, but also serves as the apex of an aristocratic landed and financial interest; a habit of obsessively secretive government; an unparalleled concentration of power in the hands of the central executive. Much of this is not only 'exceptional', but exceptionally undemocratic, when compared with other established Western democracies. These and other distinctive elements of the UK's political system may possess a certain historical legitimacy, though that is now wearing progressively thinner; but that is not the same as saying that they count as 'democratic'.

This brings me to a second issue, about the measurability of the indices used in a democratic audit, and along what kind of scale. It should be evident from everything said so far that we see democracy not as an all-or-nothing affair but as a comparative concept, with each of the indices representing a continuum rather than the simple alternative of democratic/non-democratic. Of course, both in common parlance and in the language of comparative politics we talk of Western 'democracies', in contrast to a variety of non-democratic political systems; and by this we indicate a clustering of historically sustainable institutions and practices which embody recognizably democratic principles. Yet this language also obscures significant differences of kind and degree, and the extent to which democratic institutions can coexist with undemocratic, or, in the case of the UK, with pre-democratic, ones. And the fact that, at the margin, we have considerable difficulty in deciding whether certain countries should really count as 'democratic' at all suggests that such characterizations are far from a simple all-or-nothing affair.

Consistent with the conception of democracy as a continuum, therefore, all the questions for audit are phrased in comparative terms: to what extent . . . ? how far . . . ?, etc. But the idea of a continuum does not in itself determine what a 'good' democratic standard or benchmark should be, nor where the beginning and end-point of that continuum should be situated. Should our frame of reference and standard of comparison be a country's own past, or the level attained by comparable countries of a given type, or some ideal standard beyond either? The first of these – comparison with a country's own past – presupposes that the appropriate data are available in comparative form for a given point in the past, which is unlikely for more than a few indices; and in any case, on its own it may not represent a particularly impressive level of attainment.[10] The third – the ideal standard – avoids this latter drawback, though at the expense of ignoring questions of practicability or attainability altogether. Most appropriate, therefore, would seem to be a set of benchmarks based upon reference to other comparable countries, particularly where the comparison can be used to establish a benchmark of 'best practice'. Such a benchmark already exists for some areas of the democratic audit, for example in internationally accepted standards for the conduct of elections or the defence of civil and political rights.[11] In other areas levels of best practice are in the process of formulation or consolidation, for example US or Swedish legislation on freedom of information sets an attainable standard for open government (see Michael, 1982: chs 8–10). In yet others, comparative analysis can help to establish such standards where these are not yet recognized.

However, it would be mistaken to imagine that benchmarks established by comparative analysis will be wholly uncontestable. Should the reference point for the proportion of women Members of Parliament be the high 30s percentage achieved by the Nordic countries, or the 50 per cent suggested by the strict principle of equality? Should the standard for the degree of electoral proportionality be set at 100 per cent, regardless of other democratic requirements for the electoral system? From one point of view it may not matter, provided the scale is sufficient to show where a given country stands in a comparative group of countries. Yet how the scale is itself constructed may contain assumptions which are contestable, and which require justification at the very least.

Here it becomes necessary to say something about the measurability of the indices used. Some of the phenomena being assessed, particularly those involving elections, can be readily measured, and the measurement can be used directly to construct a democratic scale of assessment. Thus the proportions of the adult population who are registered as electors, who actually vote, and who vote for the winning party or coalition, can readily form part of an index of electoral democracy.[12] Most political phenomena, however, can only be judged qualitatively; and the conversion of these judgements into quantitative indices to facilitate comparison and assessment involves subjective elements that are obscured by the apparently objective numerical indicators. This is true, for example, of the numerical indices of freedom published yearly by Freedom House, and of various published scales of democracy, in which countries are scored out of 10 or 100 as the case may be.[13] In a democratic audit of a single country, the disadvantages of such numerical conversions outweigh the advantages. It is preferable to leave such assessments in the form of qualitative judgements, in which the different points of strength and weakness can be identified. Any comparative assessments in these areas will therefore inevitably be 'broad brush' in character, and will lack the (spurious) precision of quantitative tables.

This point already touches on our third question, about the difference between the indices developed for the purpose of democratic audit and those used by other writers. Naturally there are significant areas of overlap with the democratic indicators to be found in the existing literature of political science, especially in the areas of electoral democracy and civil and political rights. It would be both remarkable and disturbing if there were no convergence over the criteria for 'free and fair elections' or 'civil and political rights', where there exist the most clearly established international standards. Even here, however, our insistence on the democratic principle of political equality takes us beyond the very minimal acknowledgement of universal suffrage typical of most other indices, to which we add such criteria as: equal value for each vote, equal opportunity to stand for public office, fair access for all social groups and parties to the means of communication with the electorate, and so on. And our extension of the democratic indices into the areas of open and accountable government and a democratic society constitute a considerable extension of focus beyond these other indices.[14]

A second point of difference is that we have not sought to aggregate the different criteria into a single scale of freedom or democracy, whereby countries are rated according to their overall 'score'. Our expectation is that the UK, like any other established democracy, will prove to be much better in some areas than others. A democratic audit should be able to show citizens of a country where its institutions and practices are satisfactory, from a democratic point of view, and where there is particular cause for concern or room for improvement. Any overall judgement, therefore, is likely to be a nuanced one; and the different indices will have to be kept separate to enable it to be so.

The above differences inevitably reflect a significant difference of purpose between a democratic audit and other indices of democracy.[15] Whether the latter have set out to explore the conditions for the sustainability of developing democracies, or to assess the differing levels of freedom of non-Western countries, they have taken the minimal or threshold level of the established democracies as their standard point of reference, and as representing the summit of attainment. There is an unintentionally self-congratulatory effect, as a consequence, of learning from one such scale that the UK rates 99.3 out of 100, compared with, say, Burkina Faso at 13.5 (Inkeles, 1991: 16–18). Our purpose has been to extend this range so that it can be used as a self-critical tool with regard to the established democracies; and to deploy a conception of democracy which can both explain why their institutions (and which institutions) are justifiably termed 'democratic', and be used to indicate how and where they might become more so.

This difference suggests a final objection to such a project: whether it is appropriate for academics to be engaged in such an explicitly evaluative and judgemental exercise. My own impression is that those who work within the field of normative political theory have less difficulty with this objection than those whose main work lies in analytical or explanatory political science. Much of what political philosophers are engaged in lies in trying to establish defensible criteria for, say, justice (what would count as a just distribution of social benefits and burdens), or freedom, or democracy.[16] From this it is only a short step to ask: how does a particular situation, or institution, or social practice, measure up to these criteria? The distinction between pure and applied, or the theoretical and its application, serves here quite well. If the 'pure' or theoretical task lies in determining what are the criteria for a just distribution, the application would lie in collecting evidence about a given distribution and assessing it against the criteria so established. And the same with democracy.

Of course the prescriptive conclusion – you must do *x* to make the arrangements more just or more democratic – does not follow straightforwardly. The particular value at issue may conflict with others, or with certain practical imperatives. Nevertheless, insofar as people claim their society to be just, or democratic, or whatever, then these are appropriate criteria of assessment to be used; and any significant short fall should thereby be a legitimate matter for public concern.

In any case, democratic indices of any kind are necessarily evaluative and judgemental, even if their primary purpose is an explanatory one, such as exploring the socio-economic conditions for a given level of democracy. Assigning measures on a scale is a judgemental exercise, and especially so where they become evidence to be used in the foreign policy of one country towards others. It is not unreasonable for those at the receiving end of such judgements to ask whether the countries making them are prepared to be judged by similar criteria. Academics who are involved in assessing their own countries may appear more 'political' in doing so, but the activity is not essentially different in this regard from assessing the level of democracy elsewhere; and it remains an important part of the democratic audit idea that it should be primarily a self-assessment by those who live and work in the country in question, even if they may call on external auditors for assistance.

Thirty indices of democracy

The indices developed for the democratic audit of the UK have been expressed in the form of questions, which the auditing process will seek to answer. The questions are grouped according to the four areas or dimensions of democracy already outlined. The boundaries between the areas are not watertight, and some questions relate to more than one area. Some of the questions are also much 'bigger' than others. Thus single questions on the powers of parliament in relation to the executive, or on the civil liberties of citizens, could well be broken down into a sub-set of further questions. The exact balance between them must be a matter of judgement and emphasis.

The first set of questions (1–5) concerns the electoral process, its reach, inclusiveness, independence, integrity and impartiality, as well as how equally it treats its citizens, how much effective choice it offers them, and how far governmental outcomes actually reflect the choices made.

1 How far is appointment to legislative and governmental office determined by popular election, on the basis of open competition, universal suffrage and secret ballot?

2 How independent of government and party control are the election and procedures of voter registration, and how free from intimidation and bribery is the process of election itself?

3 How effective a range of choice and information does the electoral and party system allow the voters, and is there fair and equal access for all parties and candidates to the media and other means of communication with them, and an overall balance in the treatment of the various parties and candidates by the media?

4 To what extent do the votes of all electors carry equal weight, and how far is there equal effective opportunity to stand for public office, regardless of which social group a person belongs to?

5 What proportion of the electorate actually votes, and how closely does the composition of parliament and the programme of government reflect the choices actually made by the electorate?

The second set of questions (6–18), involving the area of 'open and accountable government', embraces a wide range of different issues.

Questions 6 and 7 concern the responsiveness of government to public opinion, and of representatives to their constituents. Questions 8–11 concern different aspects of accountability: of non-elected officials to those elected, of the executive to parliament, and of Members of Parliament to the public, as well as the issue of government openness and freedom of information. Questions 12–14 concern the rule of law, the legal accountability of public officials, the independence of the judiciary and the effectiveness of avenues for individual redress. Question 15 examines the issue of equal opportunity in appointment to public office. Questions 16–18 examine the territorial dimensions of democracy, on the assumption that a vigorous and responsive sub-central or local tier of elected government, and effective public accountability at the supra-national level, are important aspects of a country's democratic arrangements.

6 How systematic and open to public scrutiny are the procedures for government consultation of public opinion and of relevant interests in the formation and implementation of policy and legislation?

7 How accessible are elected politicians to approach by their electors, and how effectively do they represent constituents' interests?

8 How effective and open to scrutiny is the control exercised by elected politicians over the non-elected personnel and organs of the state?

9 How extensive are the powers of parliament to oversee legislation and public expenditure, and to scrutinize the executive; and how effectively are they exercised in practice?

10 How accessible to the public is information about what the government does, and about the effects of its policies, and how independent is it of the government's own information machine?

11 How publicly accountable are elected representatives for their private interests and sources of income that are relevant to the performance of their public office, and the process of election to it?

12 How far are the courts able to ensure that the executive obeys the rule of law; and how effective are their procedures for ensuring that all public institutions and officials are subject to the rule of law in the performance of their functions?

13 How independent is the judiciary from the executive, and from all forms of interference; and how far is the administration of law subject to effective public scrutiny?

14 How readily can a citizen gain access to the courts, ombudsman or tribunals for redress in the event of maladministration or the

failure of government or public bodies to meet their legal responsibilities; and how effective are the means of redress available?

15 How far are appointments and promotions within public institutions subject to equal opportunities procedures, and do conditions of service infringe employees' civil rights?

16 How far do the arrangements for government below the level of the central state satisfy popular requirements of accessibility and responsiveness?

17 To what extent does sub-central government have the powers to carry out its responsibilities in accordance with the wishes of its own electorate, and without interference from the centre?

18 How far does any supra-national level of government meet the criteria of popular control and political equality, whether through national parliaments or through representative institutions of its own?

Questions in the third section address issues of civil and political rights. With regard to the longstanding debate about whether social and economic rights should be included as an integral component of democracy, we incline to the more limited definition of democratic rights (question 19), though question 20 asks how far the equal enjoyment of them is constrained or frustrated by socio-economic inequalities. Questions 21 and 22 assume that the development of civil rights NGOs and of rights education are significant indicators of how seriously a society takes the defence of basic rights, alongside its other procedures for their safeguard. Question 23 addresses the contentious issue of the rights of aliens; it acknowledges the right of a democratic country to determine who should gain admittance to live in the country, though only on non-arbitrary criteria, and on the assumption that residence over time itself generates legitimate claims to citizenship.

19 How clearly does the law define the civil and political rights and liberties of the citizen, and how effectively are they defended?

20 How secure are citizens in the exercise of their civil and political rights and liberties; and how far is their equal enjoyment of them constrained by social, economic or other factors?

21 How well developed are voluntary associations for the advancement and monitoring of citizens' rights, and how free from harassment are they?

22 How effective are procedures for informing citizens of their rights, and for educating future citizens in the exercise of them?

23 How free from arbitrary discrimination are the criteria for

admission of refugees or immigrants to live within the country, and how readily can those so admitted obtain equal rights of citizenship?

The final group of questions is premised on the assumption that the quality and vitality of a country's democracy will be revealed in the character of its civil society as well as in its formal institutions: in the accountability and internal democracy of its civil associations and corporations; in the range and representativeness of public participation and of the organs of public opinion; and in the broader political culture and the degree of popular confidence in the political system.

24 How effectively are the major institutions of civil society subject to external regulation in the public interest?
25 How easy is it for the citizen to gain redress if his or her vital interests are damaged by the activities of such institutions?
26 To what extent are the major institutions of civil society subject to control internally by their own members, employees or beneficiaries?
27 How widespread is political participation in all its forms; how representative of different sections of society is it; and how far is it limited by social, economic or other factors?
28 How open are the media to access from all sections of opinion and social groups, and how effectively do they operate as a balanced forum for informed political debate?
29 How far do the traditions and culture of the society support the basic democratic principles of popular control and political equality?
30 To what extent do people have confidence in the ability of the political system to solve the main problems confronting society, and in their own ability to influence it?

Conclusion

It is worth considering, in conclusion, how far the indices and questions developed for the democratic audit of the UK can be used elsewhere. If the derivation of the criteria from the two basic principles of democracy is sound, and if our conception of good or best practice drawn from a comparative analysis of Western democracies is valid, then the criteria should be applicable to other comparable countries and political systems. Naturally, the precise wording of the questions and the balance between them will vary from place to place, as will also the respective local priorities for analysis and investigation. What causes most concern about a country's democratic life will necessarily vary according to time and place. Yet it is important to have an overall map of the relevant issues, such as the thirty questions provide, within which more specific concerns about a country's democratic condition can be located. Insofar as this map was designed to be non-UK-specific, it will have corresponding relevance elsewhere.

Whether the same criteria are appropriate to developing countries and developing democracies raises more complex questions, about their possible Eurocentrism among others. The definition of democracy in terms of the two general principles of popular control and political equality does in theory allow for their institutionalization in different ways; and enables us to recognize democracy as an aspiration in many different societies and in various historical forms. However, the Western experience of lengthy struggle to subject the enormous power of the modern state to popular control, and the institutions developed from that struggle, do in my view have a more universal significance, simply because the modern state form, with its monopoly of law-making and -enforcing power, is itself now effectively universal. For this reason, the proclaimed alternatives to Western or liberal democracy, whether populist, collectivist, single-party or whatever, have usually turned out to be not different variants of democracy but simply much less democratic forms. This can be said, while also recognizing that the species 'liberal democracy' has itself shown considerable variation, for example between presidential and prime ministerial, unitary and federal, majoritarian and consensual forms, and so on;[17] and the development of further variants cannot be ruled out in advance.

A different argument questions whether a full range of democratic standards or criteria constitutes an appropriate frame of reference for countries involved in a 'transition to democracy'. Even supposing that such a transition is indeed in process (rather than a transition to something else), the history of democracy's development in Europe suggests that the process is a lengthy one, embracing not only periodic reverses, but also the consolidation of incomplete stages or levels as a precondition for later ones (see Hall, 1993). So a lengthy process of state- and nation-building preceded democratization; the limitation of the powers of elected officials and of the scope of electoral politics ensured the acceptability of open political competitions prior to universal suffrage; and so on. Although these stages cannot be precisely replicated in the late twentieth century, any democratic assessment which ignores the gradated character of democracy's development, so it could be argued, may prove to be simply ahistorical.

In my view it is those involved in the democratic struggles in such countries who are best placed to judge the appropriate criteria against which their political systems should be assessed. It is not for those who enjoy the advantages of longstanding democratic arrangements to deny to others as desirable or attainable standards those they take for granted themselves, even if their own countries do not fully measure up to them. The justification for democracy remains today, at the lowest, that all known alternatives are worse; and that it avoids the lunacies and barbarisms that have characterized unaccountable and secretive regimes throughout the twentieth century. At the best, if offers a system of decision-making that treats its citizens equally; that is sensitive to their opinions and interests; that prefers open persuasion and compromise to the assertion of will and arbitrary fiat; that guarantees basic liberties; and that allows for societal and political renewal without massive upheaval and cataclysm. Such values have everywhere to be struggled for, rather than merely taken for granted. To this end, the evidence and argument of a democratic audit can play a useful part.

Notes

The Democratic Audit of the UK is financed by the Joseph Rowntree Charitable Trust, and its first two volumes will be published by Routledge in 1995 under the editorship of Kevin Boyle, Stuart Weir, David Beetham and Francesca Klug. I am grateful to the other editors and to the participants in the ECPR workshop on 'Indices of Democratization' for their comments on this chapter. An earlier version of the indices appeared in Beetham (1993a).

1 A succession of books appeared throughout the 1980s which were critical of the political condition of the UK. See, e.g., Ewing and Gearty (1990), Graham and Prosser (1988), Harden and Lewis (1986), Hewitt (1982), Michael (1982).

2 The 'we' here is the collective, not the royal or the literary, 'we'.

3 The nadir of such usage was the self-designation of the Communist regimes of East and Central Europe as 'people's democracies'.

4 For a recent assertion of the dichotomy, see Huntington (1991: 6–7): 'After Schumpeter . . . theorists increasingly drew distinctions between rationalistic, utopian, idealistic definitions of democracy, on the one hand, and empirical, descriptive, institutional, and procedural definitions, on the other, and concluded that only the latter type of definition provided the analytical precision and empirical referents that make the concept a useful one.'

5 From Macpherson (1966) to Held (1987), the idea of there being different concepts or models of democracy has become well-established. For concepts as 'essentially contestable', see Gallie (1965).

6 I prefer 'popular control' to Dahl's 'responsiveness to citizens' preferences' because it embraces direct and indirect democracy in a single principle, although there is no space to give a fuller justification for it here, or for the conclusion that such control has normally to be a mediated control in complex associations (see Dahl, 1971: 1–2).

7 For the development of such indices, see Dahl (1971: ch. 1), Bollen (1980), Hadenius (1992: ch. 3) and Inkeles (1991: chs 1–3).

8 Without this continuous accountability, electoral democracy becomes highly vulnerable to Rousseau's objection, to the effect that the people of England are only free once every five years when choosing whom to be subservient to (Rousseau, 1967: 78).

9 The concept 'civil society' re-emerged in the 1970s and 1980s in debates about democracy in the context of both developing countries and Communist systems (see, e.g., Keane, 1988).

10 These issues are discussed more fully in the chapters by Weir and by Dunleavy and Margetts in this volume. It is expected that the audit of the UK will in fact be repeated in the future, against the base-line established by the first audit.

11 Election monitoring by international panels of experts under the auspices of the UN, EU, Commonwealth, etc. is now well-established, as are standards and procedures of human rights attainment under a range of international treaties.

12 For the last of these, see the chapter by Dunleavy and Margetts in this volume.

13 For a review of the Freedom House surveys by their author, see Gastil (1991).

14 See the literature cited in note 7 above.

15 This point is developed more fully in the Introduction to this volume.

16 I take the example of justice, because it has been so exhaustively debated in recent political philosophy.

17 The classic discussion of different variants is Lijphart (1984); see also Lijphart (1992).

References

Beetham, D. (1993a) *Auditing Democracy in Britain*. Democratic Audit Paper No. 1. Human Rights Centre, University of Essex, Colchester/Charter 88 Trust, London.

Beetham, D. (1993b) 'Liberal democracy and the limits of democratization', in D. Held (ed.), *Prospects for Democracy*. Cambridge: Polity. pp. 55–73.

Bollen, K. A. (1980) 'Issues in the comparative measurement of political democracy', *American Sociological Review*, 45: 370–90.

Dahl, R. A. (1971) *Polyarchy: Participation and Opposition*. New Haven, CT and London: Yale University Press.

Ewing, K. D. and Gearty, C. A. (1990) *Freedom under Thatcher*. Oxford: Clarendon Press.

Gallie, W. B. (1965) 'Essentially contested concepts', *Proceedings of the Aristotelian Society*, 56: 167–98.

Gastil, R. D. (1991) 'The comparative survey of freedom: experiences and suggestions', in A. Inkeles (ed.), *On Measuring Democracy: Its Consequences and Concomitants*. New Brunswick, NJ and London: Transaction Publishers. pp. 21–46.

Graham, C. and Prosser, T. (eds) (1988) *Waiving the Rules*. Milton Keynes: Open University Press.

Hadenius, A. (1992) *Democracy and Development*. Cambridge: Cambridge University Press.

Hall, J. A. (1993) 'Consolidations of democracy', in D. Held (ed.), *Prospects for Democracy*. Cambridge: Polity. pp. 271–90.

Harden, I. and Lewis, N. (1986) *The Noble Lie*. London: Hutchinson Education.

Held, D. (1987) *Models of Democracy*. Cambridge: Polity.

Hewitt, P. (1982) *The Abuse of Power*. Oxford: Martin Robertson.

Huntington, S. P. (1991) *The Third Wave: Democratization in the Late Twentieth Century*. Norman: University of Oklahoma Press.

Inkeles, A. (ed.) (1991) *On Measuring Democracy: Its Consequences and Concomitants*. New Brunswick, NJ and London: Transaction Publishers.

Keane, J. (ed.) (1988) *Civil Society and the State*. London: Verso.

Lijphart, A. (1984) *Democracies: Patterns of Majoritarian and Consensus Government in Twenty-One Countries*. New Haven, CT and London: Yale University Press.

Lijphart, A. (ed.) (1992) *Parliamentary versus Presidential Government*. Oxford: Clarendon Press.

Macpherson, C. B. (1966) *The Real World of Democracy*. Oxford: Clarendon Press.

Michael, J. (1982) *The Politics of Secrecy*. Harmondsworth: Penguin.

Rousseau, J. -J. (1967) *The Social Contract* (ed. G. D. H. Cole). London: J. M. Dent. (Original work published 1762.)

Schumpeter, J. A. (1952) *Capitalism, Socialism and Democracy* (5th edn.). London: Allen and Unwin.

3

More Participation, More Democracy?

Geraint Parry and George Moyser

In any attempt to measure the extent of democracy, the degree of popular political participation must constitute one of the indices. Democracy meant originally the 'rule', or 'power', of 'the people'. To put it at its most simplistic, a regime in which the people exercised no part in rule could not qualify as 'democratic' (although some may have claimed that it did). But, conversely, should one conclude that the more the people participate in politics, the more democratic the system of government? Unfortunately, things are not so simple.

The definition of democracy as the power of the people is derived from its Greek original. This fact, however obvious, may still alert one to the difficulties in taking popular participation as a measure of democratization, not least because of the discontinuities between the ancient and modern experiences of 'democracy' (see Farrar, 1988; Finley, 1973; Held, 1987). The prime political discontinuity is that in Athens the term 'power' of the people meant something that it cannot mean in the modern world. The 'people', meaning the citizens, exercised control over policy by *direct* acts of will in the assembly. In addition, the citizens had the opportunity to be chosen, by lot, to carry out the executive tasks of government. Clearly citizen participation in the modern world is very far removed from this. As John Dunn puts it: 'in no modern state do its members, male or female, decide what is in fact done, or hold their destiny in their own hands. They do not, because they cannot' (1992: vi).

Thus democracy as the 'power' of the people has to be attenuated to 'rule' of the people or to some rather weaker term which captures the elements we associate with modernity – institutionalized popular influence, procedures of accountability. In the era when something to be called democracy was reinvented (even if termed 'republic'), the claim advanced in its favour was its superiority to the direct popular forms of the ancient world rather than any element of continuity (Wokler, 1994). This is seen in Federalist Paper 63, where one element in the 'most advantageous superiority' of the American system lay in 'the total exclusion of the people in their collective capacity' from any share in government. It is not, in fact, that popular participation is being totally excluded – in republican terminology it is one of the elements in mixed government. But this participation is to be mediated through political leaders who, with relative rapidity, became professionalized (Pizzorno, 1970).

Citizen participation thus ceased to be the *paramount* indicator of democracy. It has been joined by several others – the competitiveness of élites, the representativeness of representation, the control of bureaucracy, the independence of the judiciary, freedoms of various kinds. Thus when Dahl opened his treatment of democratization in *Polyarchy* (1971) he employed two broad indicators. One was, indeed, participation – measured by the right to take part in elections and office. The other was 'public contestation' (competition for office and political support). This is taken to be a measure of 'liberalization' (Dahl, 1971: 1–9). Each element, Dahl suggests, is possible in the absence of the other. Political contestation may increase without a corresponding increase in participation, thereby creating competitive oligarchies such as existed in nineteenth-century Europe. Equally, participation in elections may be provided without increasing political choice. It is only when liberalization occurs in tandem with participation that one can speak of democratization (or of the emergence of polyarchies, since Dahl would add a range of other indicators for full democratization to be identified). Thus, in isolating participation as an indicator of democracy, no claim is being advanced that it is *the* indicator. Indeed, the significance to be attached to participation, or to various forms of participation, turns very much on the conception of democracy which is held.

A broad distinction can be drawn between a 'participatory' or 'radical' conception and a 'realist' conception which places its stress on political leadership, accountability and representation (see Nordlinger, 1981: 207; Sartori, 1987: 39–55). In distinguishing these two dispositions, one is doing some disservice to the nuances of various theorists by putting into a single camp writers who do differ in various ways. To place Pateman, Gould and Barber into the 'participatory' school is not to deny significant differences in emphasis. The same is true for such 'realists' as Schumpeter, Sartori and Nordlinger. Nevertheless, the distinction between the approaches will serve the purpose of suggesting how conceptions of democracy can result in contrasting evaluations of participation.

The participatory democrats may trace a genealogy from ancient models of citizenship or, within modern thought, from Rousseau or from J. S. Mill and G. D. H. Cole. None believes that existing democracies live up to their ideals of participatory citizenship. Indeed, contemporary institutions serve, rather, to discourage such ideals and so participationists look for changes in the structures of politics to widen citizen involvement. People would not only go to the polls but would also attend party meetings, take part in referendums and even 'participate' in the executive arm of government and the workplace. The process of taking part becomes integral to democracy. Deliberation, the search for consensus, the desire to encourage the reticent or the less privileged to have their say, the educative effects of involvement – all are valued in different ways (see Barber, 1984; Pateman, 1970: 42). For all, the decisive test of a democracy is its capacity to encourage its population to play an active role in its government.

This is not the case for the realists. Sartori, for example, contends that democracy is 'the by-product of a competitive method of leadership recruitment' (1987: 152). The search for indicators of democracy will start with the competition between political leaders. It will not end there because competition is not itself democracy but produces democracy. It does so because the leaders can only win the competition by appealing to the people. Hence democracy 'still results from the sheer fact that the *power* of deciding between the competitors is in the hands of the demos' (Sartori, 1987: 151; original emphasis). Thus the index of democratization would also be sought for in some, probably qualitative, account of the '*responsiveness* of the leaders to the led' (Sartori, 1987: 156; original emphasis; but see also below).

The popular input required is at once all important yet minimal. It is all important in that elections constitute the decisive point in democracy. It is minimal in that the ordinary citizen is asked to do little more than turn out on election day. Indeed, Schumpeter (1952) would go so far as positively to discourage citizens from intervening between elections.They are urged to respect a division of labour between themselves and the professional politicians. In short, for Sartori and Schumpeter, participation, apart from voting, is not taken to be a key indicator of democracy. Representation or élite responsiveness would be more relevant.

Participation as a multiple indicator

That one theory should pay special attention to one mode of participation – voting – and virtually none to others is a reminder of the multidimensionality of 'participation'. This has been stressed by most studies of participation since the work of the Verba and Nie team (Parry et al., 1992; Verba and Nie, 1972; Verba et al., 1978). The various modes of taking part in politics – voting, party campaigning, group activity, contacting representatives and officials, protesting – have a number of different characteristics, not least their effects on

Table 3.1 *Five modes of political participation and associated
levels of activity (N = c. 1,570)*

Activity	% Yes/At least once	% Often/Now and then
(A) Contacting:		
Member of parliament	9.7	3.4
Civil servant	7.3	3.1
Councillor	20.7	10.3
Town hall	17.4	8.9
Media	3.8	1.6
(B) Groups:		
Organized group	11.2	6.7
Informal group	13.8	6.4
Issue in group	4.7	2.3
(C) Protest:		
Attend protest meeting	14.6	6.1
Organize petition	8.0	2.1
Sign petition	63.3	39.9
Block traffic	1.1	0.3
Protest march	5.2	2.1
Political strike	6.5	2.3
Political boycott	4.3	2.3
(D) Party campaigning:		
Fund-raising	5.2	4.3
Canvasing	3.5	2.6
Clerical work	3.5	2.4
Attend party rally	8.6	4.9
(E) Voting:		
Local	86.2[1]	68.8[2]
National (% voted 1983)	82.5	
European (% voted 1984)	47.3	

[1] % some or more

[2] % most or all

political outcomes. Hence there is a strong argument for treating
each mode of participation as a distinct indicator of democratization.
For Britain, which will serve as an illustration, some idea of the broad
participatory modes and their specific activity levels is given in Table
3.1.

The table indicates fairly clearly the modest levels of activity to be
found over a five-year period. The first column of figures shows the
percentages of those who have performed the activities at least once
in the period. Contacting at local level scores respectably but few
activities even make double figures. The second column sets a slightly

Table 3.2   *Overall political activity scale (N = 1,434)*

Score	%	Cumulative %
0	3.2	3.2
1	3.9	7.1
2	5.2	12.3
3	8.6	20.9
4	9.6	30.5
5	14.1	44.6
6	8.8	53.4
7	7.8	61.2
8	6.4	67.6
9	5.8	73.4
10	3.8	77.2
11–20	17.1	94.3
21–30	3.5	97.8
31–40	0.7	98.5
41–50	1.0	99.5
51–60	0.4	99.9
61–100	0.1	100.0

Note: Min. = 0; Max. = 86.0; Mean = 8.2; Median = 6.0; Mode = 5.0.

higher standard and includes only those who declared that they had performed the acts either 'often' or 'now and then'. By this criterion, activism drops to very low levels indeed (see Parry et al., 1992). The core of people sustaining participation in Britain is proportionately small although in absolute numbers they may appear to have a greater presence (assuming that 1 per cent represents something over 400,000).

Table 3.2 presents the levels of participation in an alternative form – this time merging the five modes into one general scale running from 0 to 100 (see the note at the end of this chapter for the scale construction). Hence the average citizen (median) scores only 6 and the most frequent score (mode) is 5. Because of the near universality of voting at least once in a five-year period, only 3.2 per cent score zero. But equally only 2.2 per cent score above 20. Where one would draw the line between activism and quiescence or between 'gladiators' and 'spectators', to use Milbrath's terminology (1977), is somewhat arbitrary, but, wherever it is drawn, the activist category will contain a small minority of the population.

Voting

For very obvious reasons, voting has been traditionally taken as the prime indicator of democratic participation. As has been pointed out, it plays the crucial role in the realist theory and its significance would not in general be denied by participatory democrats. Yet, even assuming that the other characteristics of an election are in existence (genuine choice, lack of fraud, etc., etc.), there are a number of problems in taking voting turnout as the prime democratic test.

Voting is the one political activity which is performed by the vast majority of the population. This gives it an exceptional importance but also means that it is a highly atypical measure of activism. Furthermore, voting turnout is often manipulated by the political class as well as being affected by electoral laws such as on registration (Steed, 1972). Hence, it is not necessarily the case that 98 per cent turnouts represent a deeper mass commitment to democracy than figures around 70 per cent, or, as in the USA, around the 50 per cent mark.

Indeed, despite the importance of elections in the realist school, it is not clear how important voting *turnout* is to the argument. It is the mere fact of the election – the opportunity to throw the rascals out, the chance of exercising a veto – which matters (Riker, 1982). It is not necessary to attribute to all members of the school the 'defence of apathy' which was found in some writers of the 1960s. Nevertheless, it is understandable that Schumpeter's strictures on the political rationality and competence of citizens should find echoes in such works as McCloskey's much cited, even notorious, article on consensus and ideology. For him, the potentiality for authoritarianism and ideological inconsistency amongst the wider population meant that it was a blessing in disguise that they did not participate more actively (McCloskey, 1964: 376–9).

There is little sign of this in Sartori. Although he is much exercised about the lack of understanding, the crisis of under-comprehension, the poor quality of political information (Sartori, 1987: 115–30, 428–39; 1989), his concern is rather for the lack of understanding of the politician than of the ordinary citizen. Certainly questions of competence offer further reasons for his rejection of participatory or 'referendum democracy'. But, revealingly, and in some contrast here to Schumpeter, the incompetence of the mass is less crucial: 'If, in fact, elections decide about who will decide, the implication is that the burden of rationality does not rest – in the electoral theory of democracy – on electorates: It is shifted on to their representatives' (Sartori, 1987: 110).

For the participatory democrat, the problem with employing voting as a measure of democratization is that, as it operates in liberal democracies, it carries an excessive burden. An average of twelve crosses on a ballot paper in a lifetime is an insufficient test of democratic citizenship. Moreover, as Verba and Nie have argued

(1972: 322–7), voting is something of a blunt instrument. Whilst it is egalitarian, it also conveys relatively little information to élites as to policy preferences. One answer may be to increase the opportunities to vote and to do so in ways which allow the voter to discriminate more finely between policies both as to their benefits and their costs (see, for example, Barber, 1984: 284–90).

At a more obvious level,the multiplicity of offices open for election in the USA provides a very different perspective on the usual picture of voting turnout in that country. As Ivor Crewe has noted: 'The average American is entitled to do far more electing – probably by a factor of three or four – than the citizen of any other democracy' (1981: 232). Thus turnout in general elections is less important as an index than the quality of the vote. Russell Dalton's question remains pertinent: 'Why have the electoral opportunities of European citizens not kept pace with the general expansion of democratic politics?' (1988: 57).

Other modes of participation

To remedy the thin quality of voting, participatory democrats seek for supplementary modes of citizen activism. Compared with voting, a greater intensity and specificity of participation is possible, but, under present conditions, the experience is generally shared only by small minorities. Even in the USA, which 'out-performs' most other countries, in no mode does anywhere near a majority get involved. In Britain, for example, the vast bulk of the population engage in none of the activities of contacting, party campaigning, group work or direct action (see Table 3.1), and the intense activists can appear almost eccentric in the extent of their deviation from the norm.

Are these levels any indication of the extent or health of democracy? There are various ways of interpreting them. One would be to argue that it is dissatisfaction rather than satisfaction which is likely to lead people to contact their local councillor or go on a protest demonstration. In Britain, dissatisfaction with the poll tax introduced by the Conservative government in 1989–90 stimulated widespread protests, sometimes in unlikely localities. Hence, activism may indicate widely felt concern not only about policy but also about the capacity of the political system to respond to felt needs. Some kinds of protest, including extreme forms of direct action, are attempts to draw the attention of élites to issues which have been ignored. In all these ways, activism may indicate a failure of democracy as much as its success. The interpretation of quiescence (the dominant motif of Table 3.1) is equally problematical. Quiescence may for some reflect satisfaction, but this certainly cannot be assumed for all. Some may feel so estranged as to 'exit'; others may feel the costs of action outweigh the benefits; yet others that the problem is insoluble. Hence no facile inferences can be made about the mood of the people and the health of democracy.

The political

Underlying this discussion is an assumption that the activities delineated above do indeed constitute the realm of meaning for 'political participation'. Yet this, too, raises problems that affect how measures are to be constructed – problems revolving around the question: what is 'political' participation (Parry, 1972)?

Difficulties are, for example, often raised about the political character of much contacting of representatives and officials by individuals. How far should these activities count as participation within a democracy? If one were to confine one's attention to what ordinary citizens regarded as 'political' actions or issues, the sphere of political science would be considerably reduced. In Britain, fewer than 20 per cent of local respondents regarded their action as 'political'. More regarded local issues as political, but even here fewer than half perceived housing, transport matters, law and order or environment and planning problems in this light (Parry and Moyser, 1988: 38–51). The reasons are a matter of speculation but 'politics' has a common association with party involvement, whilst 'political' has long carried pejorative connotations.

Politics is a constructed term and one need not be restricted by ordinary language. Nevertheless, there is another reason why some contacting activity might be construed as non-political and, hence, irrelevant as a democratic indicator. It can be argued that what Verba and Nie (1972) labelled 'particularized contacting' – getting in touch with representatives and officials about a personal or family matter –lacks the generality which is conceptually part of the political. This is a persuasive argument in principle. In practice it is more questionable. First, the sharp distinction between the private and the public can be difficult to draw. It is a shrewd tactic to dress private advantage in the clothes of the public interest – many environmental matters are of this kind. In other cases there is a genuine mixture of the personal and the public. Parents raise issues over the availability of a school place for their child and may themselves, or as a consequence of the accumulation of such queries, thereby elevate this into a problem for the local authority. Equally, private 'consumer' complaints about public housing and other services can, when concentrated, become major issues of local politics, precipitating further collective 'political' activity. Secondly, it is a mistake to dismiss the consumerist element in contacting as irrelevant to any measure of democracy. Responsiveness to complaints about service implementation may not be the most noble aspect of democracy but it is not to be disregarded as an element in generating the respect and support of citizens. There is that much truth in notions of a citizens' charter – better a combination of voice and loyalty than to encourage alienation and exit!

Participation and political opportunity structures

For participatory democrats, the reorientation of civic life they seek would entail an expansion of the opportunities to participate. The realists, by contrast, would be largely content with the opportunities that have evolved in the liberal democracies. The range of these opportunities is perhaps more open to unambiguous cross-national comparisons. Mention has already been made of the frequent opportunities to American citizens to vote. Similarly, the countries in which the referendum or the initiative is available can be readily enumerated. But the opportunity structures can go much further than this. Mill (1991) suggested the incorporation of as many persons as possible in jury service or in parish offices, forming part of his school of public spirit. To them he famously added his advocacy of worker co-operatives. This 'would realize, at least in the industrial department, the best aspirations of the democratic spirit' (Mill, 1965: 793).

The widening of participatory opportunities may encompass the bureaucracy, education, social services, the family (Held and Pollitt, 1986, offers a useful survey). Nearly all involve some form of decentralization or devolution and many require fundamental challenges to the domination of organized knowledge systems. From a participatory standpoint, such structures of opportunity should be included within an index of democratization, although in many cases there will be argument about their unalloyed democratic nature. Examples might include elected parental government of schools, lay involvement in the operation of some social services such as day-care centres, running housing co-operatives, participation in local environmental protection agencies, and citizen input into allocation of medical resources (for various possibilities, see, for example, Boaden et al., 1982; Gyford, 1991). Similarly, the expansion of 'third force' organizations between the market and the state in Britain and America has led to a new arena of participation (Ware, 1989a, 1989b). But distinctions have to be drawn between the consumerist and the citizenship orientations of these developments. Some, perhaps the majority, constitute efforts to decentralize services to the local government or welfare consumer. Others are more bottom-up and part of an attempt at increasing citizen participation (Gyford, 1991; Hoggett and Hambleton, 1987).

There are almost certainly considerable opportunities in these arenas to increase participation in matters about which the ordinary person, as consumer or citizen, has the capacity to be well-informed (Parry, 1989). In the same way, a participatory democrat would wish to enhance the representative process. Although pluralist democracies place such stress on representation, it is arguable that they are insufficiently representative in at least two ways. First, the interests are represented in an unequal and somewhat haphazard manner. Secondly, the interests are not themselves organized internally in a sufficiently democratic manner.

The conventional pluralist response to the first problem is to leave things to the operation of the pressure group market. The biases, under-participation and obstacles to entry in this market are sufficiently well-known at least to call into question its bland acceptance, and most pluralists now accept this (Dahl, 1982). Another response in recent years has been the revival of interest in earlier forms of pluralism based on functional representation (Hirst, 1989). Alongside, and distinct from this, there has been a new interest in group rights (Kymlicka, 1989). In general, if representation is one measure of democracy, then the extent to which the density and complexity of modern civil society is registered may need to be incorporated into the scale. Generally the objective is a denser system of representation (see also Bobbio, 1987; Leca, 1992).

The second dimension of any group representation, whether or not formalized, is the internal democracy of the groups. The propensity of all groups towards oligarchy means that they are not necessarily representative of those whom they purport to represent. This has, from a radical standpoint, long been a powerful argument against the democratic claims of orthodox pluralism (McConnell, 1966). It is, however, as significant in the case of the representative quality of local community activists as in the case of national corporate representation. Thus, in *Dilemmas of Pluralist Democracy*, Dahl (1982: 80) made the point that systems of corporate pluralism raised fundamental issues of the alienation of final control over the public agenda from citizens and elected representatives. Decentralizing will not therefore be democratic if it means devolving to unaccountable oligarchies (Smith, 1985). For the realist democrat, by contrast, all this is irrelevant. It is one of the errors of the anti-élitists, Sartori assets, that they 'seek democracy in structures, not in *interactions*' (Sartori, 1987: 151; original emphasis).

Equality and participation

As potentially significant to a democracy as the amount of participation is the equality of that participation – a major concern of the
Verba and Nie team. Indeed, the dilemma that Verba and Nie raise is
that simply to increase the level of citizen participation, without any
other concomitant changes, could be to reinforce inequality. Moreover, the more effective the participation, the more the advantaged
in society might be able to get themselves heard (see also Pizzorno,
1970).

One person, one vote is, supposedly, encapsulated in electoral
systems. This makes voting a relatively egalitarian mode of participation. But one person, one voice is certainly not true of any other
mode of citizen activity. The multidimensionality of participation
means that the various modes are not skewed in precisely the same
way (Parry et al., 1992; Verba and Nie, 1972; Verba et al., 1978). In
the UK, for example, it seems that greater individual resources in
terms of wealth or education do not translate into higher participation across every dimension of activity. However, perhaps more
significant is that those who are disadvantaged under-participate
(Parry et al., 1992: 63–84). They have not succeeded in compensating
for their weak economic position by raising their political voices
(Parry and Moyser, 1991).

If all modes of participation are reduced to a single overall scale
(which can be misleading in the way it irons out important variations), the skew in participation appears more consistent. This can
be seen in Table 3.3, which provides illustrations of the ways in which
participation levels (using the 0–100 scale, see the note at the end of
this chapter) can vary according to social or personal background.
Thus the usual association between participation and education is
upheld. That combination of personal resources which is summarized
by the concept of class also shows the advantage that the salariat
possesses, although other class differences are relatively small.
Gender differences in citizen participation are slight, which perhaps
only highlights more the unequal position of women at élite levels. If
one brings into the account 'collective resources' such as membership
of voluntary groups, it is seen that this is strongly associated with
higher levels of activism. The more one is a joiner, the more one
participates. Clearly there are many interacting forces involved, but
for present purposes the interest lies in the generally positive
association between personal resources and group membership. The
group world, on the whole, is also the world of the advantaged. The
voluntary groups to which the less advantaged belong tend to be the
least politically active and thus do not give a boost to participation

Table 3.3 *Overall political activity scores by various social and
personal characteristics*

(A) Education

	No qual.	Below 'O' level	'O' level	'A' level	College & FE	Degree
Score	6.6	7.8	8.5	10.3	10.8	13.9
(N)	(686)	(169)	(247)	(89)	(146)	(98)

(B) Class

	Working class	Manual & forepersons	Petit bourgeois	Routine non-manual	Salariat
Score	7.2	7.9	7.2	7.6	11.2
(N)	(445)	(76)	(127)	(231)	(301)

(C) Gender

	Male	Female
Score	8.7	8.1
(N)	(621)	(806)

(D) Member of parties, trade unions and formal groups

	None	1	2	3	4	5
Score	5.2	6.8	7.3	9.9	11.5	18.3
(N)	(366)	(350)	(267)	(230)	(111)	(106)

Note: Each set of scores represents the bivariate relationship, i.e. not controlling for the other factors. For a multivariate analysis, see Parry et al. (1992).

(Parry et al., 1992: 85–111). Of course, there are very many individual exceptions. And it does not exclude the possibility that some of the advantaged may be active in groups which campaign for the disadvantaged. Nevertheless, the capacity of the better-off to organize collectively in their own defence should no more be neglected in examining political participation than it is in studies of pressure politics in general.

A final summary way of seeing the way in which, even in a country often regard as an exemplar of democracy, unequal resources can relate to participation is presented in Table 3.4. Here the overall political activity scale is set alongside a scale of 'resources' comprising educational qualifications, wealth and number of organizational memberships (see the note at the end of this chapter for scale construction). This emphasizes quite dramatically that the more

Table 3.4 *Political activity score by resource level (N = 1,210)*

Resource score	Activity score	% in category
0	3.94	1.5
1	4.45	6.6
2	6.11	8.6
3	5.90	10.3
4	6.53	11.6
5	7.58	11.9
6	7.59	11.2
7	9.43	8.2
8	8.07	8.2
9	9.84	5.5
10	9.87	5.4
11	13.93	4.1
12	13.90	3.3
13	16.64	1.7
14	20.13	0.9
15	24.81	0.5
16	41.29	0.3
17	51.71	0.2
	Mean: 8.39*	Total: 100.0

* Missing data on the resource variable affect the mean score slightly compared with Table 3.2.

resources one possesses, the more likely it is that one will participate in politics. Those at the bottom have only a faint voice; those at the top speak up more. These considerations have clear implications for the expansion of the opportunity structure. It could well be the case that devolved centres of decision-making would increase the opportunities for the advantaged to participate – and to do so with greater effectiveness – in policies which are of material concern to themselves. Decentralization can protect autonomous spheres of action for well-entrenched, well-resourced groups. Many examples could no doubt be cited where protection of the local environment was the public screen behind which better-off residents campaigned to resist developments which might have benefited the unemployed or the poorly paid. The common accusation of 'NIMBYism' directed against local participants can itself be a weapon employed by major interests, but its very currency is some recognition that the public interest may suffer at the hands of participating groups.

Thus decentralization which may appear to enhance one measure of democratization – the opportunity to share in decision-making – does not necessarily ensure the achievement of equality in terms of either input or output. Indeed, it may create inequality and unfairness. To the degree that fairness requires uniformity of consideration and treatment, this can point in the direction of a significant measure of centralization. At the very least, the autonomy of devolved centres of decision-making must be constrained by some minimal constitutional rules.

The effectiveness of participation and democratic responsiveness

There are at least two dimensions to the 'effectiveness' of participation. One would be the extent to which the most active participants are representative of the concerns of the mass of the inactive population. The second is the degree to which the élite appear to respond to citizen participation. Neither dimension proves easy to measure.

The representative nature of the activists is, of course, closely related to the equality of participation. Even if activism is skewed in the favour of the advantaged, this does not *necessarily* mean that their priorities differ entirely from those of the worse-off. In the UK comparison, the *agendas* of activists and inactive showed some divergences but they were not very strong. There was some tendency for the less active to give higher priority to material issues of wages and unemployment, whereas the active put more emphasis on 'quality of life' matters or on education (Parry and Moyser, 1991: 89–92). Moreover, when one turned the emphasis around to look at who expressed concern about what issues, there was some evidence that such 'issue-publics' contain an over-representation of those who might be expected to have a material benefit. Thus the salariat and the wealthy were more evident in environment and planning matters, the highest educated were more highly represented amongst those expressing concern about education. Even so, the university-educated were also highly interested in matters of un-employment which did not necessarily affect them personally and directly (Parry et al., 1992: 254–66).

There are, however, limits to evidence of this sort. First, it refers to agendas – to the priorities given to issues – not to solutions. This problem will be taken up again below. Secondly, the political opportunity structure is again relevant. Many of the material concerns of the disadvantaged, such as wages or unemployment, are less amenable to effective citizen political participation. By comparison, local problems of planning or traffic control or school closure may permit more opportunities and access for effective intervention.

The degree of responsiveness of élites to citizen participation would appear to be a central index of the rule of the people. Yet it is notoriously difficult to examine. Studies of party manifesto commitments and governmental legislation have offered some comfort to notions of electoral accountability (Hofferbert and Budge, 1992). However, the extent to which citizens make an input into the manifesto, other than through the rule of anticipated reactions, is questionable. Within participation studies, use has been made of concurrence measures (Parry et al., 1992; Verba and Nie, 1972). It has to be admitted, however, that there are significant limits to their use. They correlate the priorities of the active and less active members of the public. Although they seem to suggest that élite priorities correspond more closely to those of the activists, even controlling for background factors, the agreement is over agendas not solutions. It is not necessarily informative to know that there is a concurrence as to what *needs* a solution if we do not know whether there is a similar agreement as to the *best* solution. This is not to dismiss concurrence. Rather, it may need to be refined and developed.

For some in the realist school, a vague indication of agreement on agendas may be all that can reasonably be expected. The public may have a notion of the issues which affect them but only the political class has a clear conception of the alternative solutions in any detail (Nordlinger, 1981). That is what the political class is elected to do. Elections have decided who is to govern and provide only weak indications of what is to be done (Sartori, 1987: 109). Such theories also put a different gloss on the idea of leadership responsiveness as a measure of democracy. The argument is familiar from traditional discussions of representation but is one with abiding relevance. To cite Sartori again:

> . . . responsiveness is but one of the elements of representative government. A government that simply yields to demands, that simply gives in, turns out to be a highly irresponsible government, a government that does not live up to its responsibilities. A representative is not only responsible to, but also responsible *for*. (Sartori, 1987: 170; original emphasis)

The distinction between responsiveness and responsibility implies that quite sharp divergences between the views of citizens, whether participants or inactive, and political representatives should cause no misgivings to a liberal democrat. Yet again the argument is that, in the last analysis, only one mode of participation needs to be taken into account in the indices of democracy – the free vote at election time between alternative sets of professional politicians (but see Beetham, 1993: 64).

Problems of indices

There seem to be no entirely uncontestable indices of participation such that we can say, without further explanation or qualification, that more of the activity in question presents solid evidence that democracy is more extensive in the collectivity. Rival theories of democracy point to very different evaluations of participation in general and of its sundry components.

Lurking behind this is a larger question about the validity of indices in the political or social sciences in general, and it may be worthwhile alluding briefly to some examples of the way this great debate has impinged on studies of participation. Political scientists often wish to draw comparisons between participation levels in different countries. Raw figures are sometimes cited. Yet contextual qualification usually speedily follows. Earlier, mention was made of voting levels in the UK and the USA. These had then to be placed in the context of the differing political opportunity structures for voting. But this would only be the beginning of the problem in sorting out the factors explaining, for example, American exceptionalism as it manifests itself in the different modes of participation. First, a high level of political participation in country A and a low level in country B may not indicate a more participatory culture in A but may be a compositional effect. The differences may be simply due to the higher average level of education in A than in B. Controlling for compositional effects may transform the relative standings of countries on the participation index (see Przeworski and Teune, 1970; see also Verba et al., 1978: 32–45). A second difficulty faced by these comparative approaches lies in discerning whether there exists a deep structure common to the participatory patterns in each country (see Verba et al., 1971)). The first stage of removing compositional effects presumes both that the basic relationship between resources and participation, and the differentiation between the various modes of participation, are similar in each country compared. If these relationships differ, then comparison becomes virtually meaningless, because, in a sense, the phenomena being investigated are fundamentally incomparable. It was, of course, the claim of Verba et al. (1978: 24–7) that not only did such a deep structure exist, but that also it was evident even when faced with the toughest test of its presence by the employment of a 'maximum difference' research design in which highly contrasting cultures are deliberately chosen for study.

A more thoroughgoing attack on the employment of transnational, transcultural indices comes from the 'interpretivist' school. For such commentators, the meaning of 'participation' is specific to a culture, sub-culture or even individual. Thus Schwartz (1984) argues that participation is a subjective phenomenon which is contingent on the 'conceptual lens' through which the world of action is observed. For him, an Iranian and a Westerner would attach quite different meanings to participation, making comparison impossible except by a form of cultural imperialism which imposes one set of concepts and meanings on everybody (Schwartz, 1984: 1128–32; see also Parekh, 1993: 171–2).

There must be something in such claims. There are problems in, for example, comparing participation in the 'foundation elections' of Central and Eastern Europe with the 'normal' elections of established democracies (see articles in *Electoral Studies*, 9(4), 1990). In general, they remind us of the need to scrutinize the 'functional equivalence' of indicators closely, and not to rely on just one or two alone. Beyond that, an answer may also be provided by the very cultural imperialism to which Schwartz refers – the dissemination of Western liberal democracy (for Sartori, the only democracy) and of its conceptual frameworks. For it is only within a context of agreed political vocabularies that we can make sense of producing indices of democratization. But, as we have seen, even where there is some consensus on the concept of democracy, different conceptions give rise to alternative proposals as to what should enter into the index and with what weighting.

Note

The overall political participation score (0–100) in Tables 3.2–3.4 is calculated as follows. Nineteen items had responses scored: 'Never' = 0; 'Once' = 1; 'Now and then' = 3; 'Often' = 5. The two national and European voting items were scored: 'Yes, voted' = 1; 'Did not vote' = 0. The local voting items were scored: 'Never' = 0; 'Some elections' = 1; 'Most elections' = 2; 'Every election' = 3. This gives a maximum of 19 $\times$ 5 + 2 $\times$ 1 + 3 = 100. Note that this maximum score is over a five year period. The survey was carried out in 1984–5 and was funded by the ESRC, whose support is gratefully acknowledged. The co-directors were Geraint Parry and George Moyser. The overall resources scale (0–19) is calculated by adding educational qualifications (0 for none up to 5 for degree), wealth (0 for lowest 5 per cent in wealth to 5 for richest 5 per cent), and number of organizational memberships (0–9). This gives a scale of 0 to 19 but the highest resource score attained was 17.

References

Barber, B. (1984) *Strong Democracy: Participatory Politics for a New Age*. Berkeley: University of California Press.

Beetham, D. (1993) 'Liberal democracy and the limits of democratization', in D. Held (ed.), *Prospects for Democracy*. Cambridge: Polity. pp. 55–73.

Boaden, N., Goldsmith, M., Hampton, W. and Stringer, P. (1982) *Public Participation in Local Services*. London: Longman.

Bobbio, N. (1987) *The Future of Democracy*. Cambridge: Polity.

Crewe, I. (1981) 'Electoral participation', in D. Butler, H. R. Penniman and A. Ranney (eds), *Democracy at the Polls: A Comparative Study of Competitive National Elections*. Washington, DC: American Enterprise Institute. pp. 216–63.

Dahl, R. A. (1971) *Polyarchy: Participation and Opposition*. New Haven, CT and London: Yale University Press.

Dahl, R. A. (1982) *Dilemmas of Pluralist Democracy: Autonomy vs Control*. New Haven, CT and London: Yale University Press.

Dalton, R. (1988) *Citizen Politics in Western Democracies*. Chatham, NJ: Chatham House.

Dunn, J. (ed.) (1992) *Democracy: The Unfinished Journey 508 BC to AD 1993*. Oxford: Oxford University Press.

Farrar, C. (1988) *The Origins of Democratic Thinking*. Cambridge: Cambridge University Press.

Finley, M. (1973) *Democracy Ancient and Modern*. London: Chatto and Windus.

Gyford, J. (1991) *Citizens, Consumers and Councils: Local Government and the Public*. Basingstoke: Macmillan.

Held, D. (1987) *Models of Democracy*.Cambridge: Polity.

Held, D. and Pollitt, C. (1986) *New Forms of Democracy*. London: Sage.

Hirst, P. (ed.) (1989) *The Pluralist Theory of the State*.London: Routledge.

Hofferbert, R. and Budge, I. (1992) 'The party mandate and the Westminster model: election programmes and government spending in Britain, 1948–85', *British Journal of Political Science*, 22: 151–82.

Hoggett, P. and Hambleton, R. (eds) (1987) *Decentralization and Democracy: Localizing Public Services*, Occasional Paper 28, Bristol: School for Advanced Urban Studies.

Kymlicka, W. (1989) *Liberalism, Community and Culture*. Oxford: Oxford University Press.

Leca, J. (1992) 'Questions on citizenship', in C. Mouffe (ed.), *Dimensions of Radical Democracy*. London: Verso. pp. 17–32.

McCloskey, H. (1964) 'Consensus and ideology in American politics', *American Political Science Review*, 58: 366–81.

McConnell, G. (1966) *Private Power and American Democracy*.New York: Knopf.

Milbrath, L. (1977) *Political Participation: How and Why Do People Get Involved in Politics* (2nd edn). Chicago, IL: Rand McNally.

Mill, J. S. (1965) *Principles of Political Economy: Collected Works of John Stuart Mill Vol. III* (ed. F. E. L. Priestley). Toronto: Toronto University Press. (Original work published 1848.)

Mill, J. S. (1991) *Considerations on Representative Government* (World's Classics edn). Oxford: Oxford University Press. (Original work published 1861.)

Nordlinger, E. (1981) *On the Autonomy of the Democratic State*. Cambridge, MA: Harvard University Press.

Parekh, B. (1993) 'The cultural particularity of liberal democracy', in D. Held (ed.), *Prospects for Democracy*. Cambridge: Polity. pp. 156–75.

Parry, G. (1972) 'The idea of political participation', in G. Parry (ed.), *Participation in Politics*. Manchester: Manchester University Press. pp. 3–38.

Parry, G. (1989) 'Democracy and amateurism – the informed citizen', *Government and Opposition*, 24: 489–502.

Parry, G. and Moyser, G. (1988) 'What is "politics"? A comparative study of local citizens and leaders', in D. Sainsbury (ed.), *Democracy, State and Justice: Critical Perspectives, and New Interpretations. Essays in Honour of Elias Berg.* Stockholm: Almqvist and Wiksell International. pp. 33–54.

Parry, G. and Moyser, G. (1991) 'Voices and signals – active citizens and the market-place', in M. Moran and M. Wright (eds), *The Market and the State: Studies in Interdependence.* Basingstoke: Macmillan. pp. 81–99.

Parry, G., Moyser, G. and Day, N. (1992) *Political Participation and Democracy in Britain.* Cambridge: Cambridge University Press.

Pateman, C. (1970) *Participation and Democratic Theory.* Cambridge: Cambridge University Press.

Pizzorno, A. (1970) 'An introduction to the theory of political participation', *Social Science Information*, 9: 29–61.

Przeworski, A. and Teune, H. (1970) *The Logic of Comparative Social Inquiry.* New York: Wiley.

Riker, W. (1982) *Liberalism vs Populism: A Confrontation between the Theory of Democracy and the Theory of Social Choice.* San Francisco, CA: Freeman.

Sartori, G. (1987) *The Theory of Democracy Revisited.* 2 vols. Chatham, NJ: Chatham House.

Sartori, G. (1989) 'Under-comprehension', *Government and Opposition*, 24: 391–400.

Schumpeter, J. A. (1952) *Capitalism, Socialism and Democracy* (5th edn). London: Allen and Unwin.

Schwartz, J. (1984) 'Participation and multisubjective understanding: an interpretivist approach to the study of political participation', *Journal of Politics*, 46: 1117–41.

Smith, B. (1985) *Decentralization: The Territorial Dimension of the State.* London: Allen and Unwin.

Steed, M. (1972) 'Participation through western democratic institutions', in G. Parry (ed.), *Participation in Politics.* Manchester: Manchester University Press. pp. 80–101.

Verba, S. and Nie, N. (1972) *Participation in America: Political Democracy and Social Equality.* New York: Harper and Row.

Verba, S., Nie, N. and Kim, J.-O. (1971) *The Modes of Democratic Participation: A Cross-National Comparison.* Beverly Hills, CA: Sage.

Verba, S., Nie, N. and Kim, J.-O. (1978) *Participation and Political Equality.* Cambridge: Cambridge University Press.

Ware, A. (1989a) *Between Profit and the State.* Cambridge: Polity.

Ware, A. (1989b) *Charities and Government.* Manchester: Manchester University Press.

Wokler, R. (1994) 'Democracy's mythical ideals: the Procrustean and Promethean paths to popular self-rule', in G. Parry and M. Moran (eds), *Democracy and Democratization.* London: Routledge. pp. 21–46.

4

The Duration of Democracy: Institutional vs Socio-economic Factors

Axel Hadenius

In an article on the lessons to be learnt, especially in Latin America, from the political changes that have taken place in Southern Europe, Arend Lijphart points out the importance of institutional arrangements for the maintenance of democratic rule. The message is, for example, that a proportional electoral system is more conductive than the plurality formula, that the parliamentary mode of executive selection is better than the presidential, and that a decentralized, federal form of government is preferable to a centralized, unitary one (Lijphart, 1990: 71–81). These proposals link up with a main tenet in Lijphart's work, namely the establishment of such political institutions as can further cooperation between different groups in society and hence could contribute to the reduction of political conflicts. The argument is thoroughly elaborated in his seminal study, *Democracy in Plural Studies* (1977: 25–44), where he advocates a so-called consociational democracy, a democracy of compromise and accommodation, which beside proportionalism and decentralization is marked also by grand coalitions and decisions made by mutual veto.

Lijphart may serve as the pivotal figure of the 'school' which emphasizes the significance of political institutions for the upholding of democracy. Notwithstanding that certain social and economic circumstances might have a detrimental effect in the context, these obstacles, it is held, can be circumvented by means of skilful political engineering; it is foremost a matter of finding the appropriate institutional solutions to the problems.

An opposite view has been maintained by scholars of a politico-cum-sociological bent, amongst whom Seymour M. Lipset stands out as the most prominent representative. Lipset has not ignored the institutional side of the matter however. In his classic study on the prerequisites of democracy, he recommends, for instance, the application of federalism and parliamentarism, and an electoral system in accordance with the plurality method. Yet he makes clear that 'such variations in system of government, while significant, are much less important than those derived from basic differences in social structure' (Lipset, 1959: 98).

The question as to what kind of circumstances are the most crucial for the survival of democracy is naturally an issue of great scholarly concern, but it may also have considerable practical consequences. If the view which Lijphart represents is correct, this would imply that those who are engaged in the safeguarding of democracy – which is currently a most topical theme on the international scene – ought to devote their energy to the design and adjustment of political institutions. One should, as it were, set to work the way the Founding Fathers of the American Constitution once did; but not necessarily, of course, with the same outcome. If, on the contrary, the Lipset camp has good reasons for its claims, one should instead address and try to change the material and social conditions which basically set the terms of the forms of government. Economic and social engineering, of one sort or another, then become the priority in the interest of supporting the maintenance of popular rule. To strain the argument, in this perspective, an industrialist like Henry Ford or an innovator in the area of social policy like Lord Beveridge could be expected to make far greater contributions for the benefit of democracy than persons centring on the problems of constitution-making, such as James Madison and Hans Kelsen.

However, reviewing the comparative research which has been made on the topic at issue, it is difficult to judge which side is right, or whether both might in part have a point. In his study, Lipset dwelt on many factors which he assumed to have a bearing on the maintenance of democracy, but the investigation that he presented in a more systematic form was centred on variables pertaining to the level of socio-economic development (wealth, industrialization, education and urbanization). Similar explanatory factors were heeded in the follow-up of Lipset's inquiry which was carried out by Phillip Cutright some years later (Lipset, 1959: 75–100; Cutright, 1963: 256–9). Socio-economic conditions of another nature are observed in a more recent study of democratic stability by Edward N. Muller. In this case, differences in the distribution of income among citizens is the main interest, but as a control variable the degree of economic development is considered too (Muller, 1988: 61–5).

The empirical scrutiny provided in Lijphart's study, by means of broad historical illustrations, is focused only on the institutional arrangements championed by the author (Lijphart, 1977: 119–222). A more systematic investigation has lately been presented by André Blais and Stephane Dion. These authors probe the impact of electoral systems on the survival of democracy. Besides this, the colonial background is also taken into consideration. As in Lijphart, however, the significance of socio-economic circumstances is not interrogated in their inquiry (Blais and Dion, 1990: 255–62).

We can thus conclude, first, that overall only a few comparatively geared, empirical studies on the duration of democracy are available, and, secondly, that the ones that are carried out have been centred on conditions of either a socio-economic or an institutional nature. Hence, the investigation which is to be reported in this chapter is the first of its kind insofar as it includes explanatory variables of both categories.

More exactly, the following explanatory conditions will be addressed. On the institutional side, I will account for (a) the kind of electoral system that is applied, (b) the existence, or not, of a federal mode of government, and (c) executive selection through presidentialism vs parliamentarism. Furthermore, I will probe the significance of (d) colonial background. The other set factors include, first of all, a number of indicators of social and economic development. In addition to this, the distribution of income in society will be taken into consideration.

Below I shall explore more thoroughly how these circumstances are considered to affect the well-being of democracy. First, however, it is time to specify the characteristics to be explained and to detail the way the inquiry is to be accomplished.

Democratic durability and the cases under study

It almost goes without saying that the question regarding the duration of democracy should not be confused with the one pertaining to the level of democracy, from the lowest to the highest degree at a certain point of time (Hadenius, 1992: 2; Muller, 1988: 52).Targeting the former question, we are interested only in those states which within a certain period of time have upheld a relatively high degree of democracy; we want to find out why some of these states have managed to maintain this form of government longer than others. Yet, in addressing this problem, the researcher must start by clarifying the kind of borderline criteria to be applied, that is, what requirements should be met to classify a state as in the main democratic (or not).

In Lipset's study, two sorts of criteria were used. For Europe and English-speaking countries (that is, British dominions) the author made a distinction between (a) stable democracies and (b) unstable democracies and dictatorships. The requisite for placement in the first category was 'the uninterrupted continuation of political democracy since World War I, and the absence over the past 25 years of a major political movement opposed to the democratic "rules of the game"'. For Latin America, Lipset (1959: 73–4) employed a more moderate condition as he distinguished here between, on the one hand, democracies and unstable democracies and, on the other hand, stable dictatorships. Beside the fact that we are given no elucidation of the state of affairs political democracy represents, and that the criterion regarding movements opposed to democracy could hardly be seen as relevant,[1] the approach involves methodological problems too. Since it includes a number of states which have never over the period practised democratic modes of government (stable dictatorships), it is not solely an inquiry into democratic durability, but, simultaneously, also a study of the maintenance of non-democracy. Furthermore, the use of different standards for various parts of the world must be seen as a shortcoming; not only does it hamper comparability, it also seems hard to justify from the point of view of democratic theory (Hadenius, 1992: 35).

Cutright wanted to work out a more elaborated, unitary measurement. Whereas Lipset had applied a dichotomy (or in fact two), Cutright aimed at establishing a dependent variable in the form of a scale. He thus presented an index where the states were given points for each year during the period from 1940 up to 1960 with regard to how the legislative and executive branches of government were elected (Cutright, 1963: 255–6). Accordingly, the index is focused only on the electoral side of democracy (disregarding political freedoms). Furthermore, it suffers from methodological flaws, since it is a summary measure of yearly gradings of democracy, from a low to a high degree, and thus conflates the problems concerning the level and the duration of democracy (Bollen, 1980: 382–4; Muller, 1988: 52).

Like Lipset, Muller uses a dichotomy but applies universal and more appropriate criteria. Examining a period of twenty years, starting at 1960, he makes a distinction between stable and unstable democracies. The latter are states which have turned to authoritarian rule 'because of military or executive coup, fraudulent elections or the imposition of long-term restrictions on political liberty, or the outbreak of a civil war' (Muller, 1988: 52).

Blais and Dion cover a period from 1900 up to 1985, and their interest is concentrated on some basic aspects regarding electoral proceedings: 'the designation of political decision-makers through regular and competitive elections with secret universal suffrage' (Blais and Dion, 1990: 253). When these standards are upheld over a time-span of ten years (1975–85), a country is classified as a stable democracy. As an additional measure, these authors also consider how long democracy survived before it fell – which is referred to as a coup. In view of a common understanding of the concept of political democracy (Dahl, 1989: 220–4; Hadenius, 1992: 28–32; Sartori, 1987: 21–33), it must be seen as a drawback that Blais and Dion (as Cutright) are not accounting for violations of political freedoms, for example by means of extensive state-of-emergency regulations. Accordingly India, Malaysia and Sri Lanka are considered democratic throughout the ten-year period, which seems dubious (cf. Muller, 1988: 55; Powell, 1982: 5–6). The authors assert that interferences such as a state of emergency are not undemocratic as long as the decisions are made by organs which have been elected in a satisfactory manner (Blais and Dion, 1990: 352). This stands out as a curious argument indeed. Holding that view, Hitler's *Machtüber-nahme* in 1933 (after having been elected) or the measures taken by Fujimori in Peru in 1992 could be adjudged democratically fully acceptable.[2]

The criteria to be applied in my inquiry include a number of requisites pertaining to the electoral process as well as to the upholding of essential political freedoms. In the former event, universal suffrage is, first of all, prescribed. Furthermore, the elections should be open (competitive) and honest, and the organs which are elected should not have their competence curtailed by other, non-elected powers (for example, the military). Besides this, the following political freedoms are accounted for: organizational freedoms (the right to establish parties and other associations, to hold meetings, rallies, etc.), freedoms of opinion (freedom of expression and of the media), and the absence of political violence and repression (such as political murder, disappearances, torture and the holding of political prisoners).[3]

In testing the impact of institutional factors in particular, it seems appropriate to concentrate on such states where political life has been more or less fragile, for it is there that the significance of, for instance, the electoral system could be expected to be the greatest. In countries which long ago established a stable democratic order, there is far less reason to assume that a change of the institutional arrangements considered here should in any important sense infringe on the maintenance of the mode of government; instead, in these countries, other consequences concerned primarily with the fine-tuning of democracy (not its very existence) become the subject of scrutiny (Blais and Dion, 1990: 250; Taagepera and Shugart, 1989: 235).

The selection of states has therefore been limited to the so-called Third World. Since we are addressing the duration of democracy, the countries of interest, of course, are only those which for some time during the period under study have exhibited relatively high democratic performances. In addition, the following requirements should be met. First, the period should be uniform for all states – having

Table 4.1   *Three measurements of democratic durability*

	Political democracy (years)*	Electoral democracy (years)*	Coup
Argentina	6.1	7.9	X
Bolivia	7.2	7.2	X
Brazil	4.8	4.8	X
Chile	3.7	3.7	X
Colombia	19.8	20.0	
Equador	5.4	5.4	X
Peru	9.3	9.5	X
Uruguay	7.2	8.0	X
Venezuela	20.0	20.0	
Costa Rica	20.0	20.0	
Honduras	5.6	8.1	X
Barbados	20.0	20.0	
Dominica	11.5	11.5	X
Jamaica	19.1	20.0	
Trinidad & To.	18.8	20.0	
Botswana	20.0	20.0	
Gambia	16.5	20.0	
Ghana	3.9	4.2	X
Mauritius	3.1	20.0	
Nigeria	3.9	3.9	X
Senegal	6.8	6.8	X
Cyprus	19.7	20.0	
Israel	20.0	20.0	
Lebanon	5.4	6.4	X
Turkey	6.1	8.1	X
India	18.2	20.0	
Pakistan	1.1	3.1	X
Philippines	6.6	6.6	X
Sri Lanka	1.3	20.0	
Fiji	17.3	17.3	X
Nauru	20.0	20.0	

* Periods of political democracy (PD) and electoral democracy (ED): *Argentina* PD: May 1973–May 1974, Dec. 1984–; ED: May 1973–Mar. 1976, Dec. 1984–. *Bolivia* Aug. 1979–Nov. 1979, Oct. 1982–. *Brazil* Mar. 1985–. *Chile* –Sept. 1973. *Colombia* PD: –Sept. 1989. *Equador* Aug. 1984–. *Peru* PD: July 1980–Oct. 1989; ED: July 1980–. *Uruguay* PD: –Feb. 1973, Nov. 1985–; ED: –Feb. 1973, Mar. 1985–. *Honduras* PD: Apr. 1971–Dec. 1972, Jan. 1986–; ED: Apr. 1971–Dec. 1972, Dec. 1981–. *Dominica* July 1978–. *Jamaica* PD: –July 1976, June 1977–. *Trinidad & Tobago* PD: –Apr. 1970, Nov. 1970–Oct. 1971, June 1972–. *Gambia* PD: –Aug. 1981, Feb. 1982–. *Ghana* PD: –Aug. 1971, Sept. 1979–Dec. 1981; ED: –Jan. 1972, Sept. 1979–Dec. 1981. *Mauritius* PD: Nov. 1976–. *Nigeria* Oct. 1979–Sept. 1983. *Senegal* Apr. 1983–. *Cyprus* PD: July 1974–Dec. 1974. *Lebanon* PD: –May 1975; ED: –May 1976. *Turkey* PD: –Mar. 1971, Jan. 1974–Dec. 1978; ED: –Mar. 1971, Oct. 1973–Sept. 1980. *India* PD: –June 1975, Mar. 1977–. *Pakistan* PD: Dec. 1988–; ED: –Dec. 1971, Dec. 1988–. *Philippines*–Sept. 1972, Feb. 1986–. *Sri Lanka* PD: –Apr. 1971. *Fiji* –May 1987.

different periods for different countries, which is in fact the case in Blais and Dion, is not conducive for comparability. Secondly, all states should be independent throughout the period – this is to assure that the form of government is not enforced by some superior power. Given these restrictions, two objectives come to the fore. In order to safeguard a solid empirical basis, we want to have a large number of cases, on the one hand, and a time period which is as long as possible, on the other. Unfortunately, these desires are in practice contradictory. The more we extend the period, the more we reduce the number of states that could be included (owing to the provision that all states be independent through the time of inquiry). Therefore, the most reasonable balance is to cover a period of twenty years, from 1970 up to 1989, which makes possible the inclusion of thirty-one states.

The main measurement of democratic durability is a scale denoting the total number of years political democracy has been maintained.[4] In the interest of linking up with previous research, I have also worked out two additional measures, namely electoral democracy and coup. These pertain to the criteria used by Blais and Dion. The former, like political democracy, is a time-scale, but differs to the extent that it disregards political freedoms. The latter, by contrast, is a dichotomy, indicating whether or not a coup has taken place during the period or if a state has entered the period having a regime that has been brought to power by such means.[5] The values in each respect for the countries under study are rendered in Table 4.1.[6] As is evident, the figures for political democracy and electoral democracy are fairly equal overall, but with two exceptions: Mauritius and Sri Lanka. This is due to an extensive use of emergency regulations: in the case of Sri Lanka, from the early 1970s throughout the period; and in Mauritius, up to the mid-1970s.

Looking at the statistical association between the measurements – which is documented in Table 4.2 – we find a very close connection between the occurrence of coups and the duration of electoral democracy, which is certainly understandable. A coup is by definition an assumption of power by illegal, unconstitutional means which normally implies, in a democratic setting, a dismissal of elected officials and the abolition of the electoral process as such. For understandable reasons (which have been dwelt upon above), the correlation between political democracy and the two other measures is less perfect, but is nevertheless considerably strong. The result is that our main indicator of democracy does fairly well in terms of homogeneity; whether we take into account its two components, election and political freedoms, or just one of these does not make a major difference (cf. Hadenius, 1992: 70). Hence it is reasonable to

Table 4.2   *The association between the three measurements of democratic durability: correlation coefficients*

	Coup	Electoral democracy
Political democracy	−0.79	0.87
Electoral democracy	−0.93	

assume that in explanatory testing the three variables would, by and large, yield the same outcome. That is indeed true when it comes to socio-economic variables – here it really does not matter which of the measurements we are applying. However, this does not hold overall for the institutional factors. Therefore, in the case of the latter, it will in some instances be worthwhile to take note of the other measurements beside political democracy.

Explanatory variables

As for electoral systems, we shall observe only the difference between plurality elections and proportional representation. The major virtue of the first system (the 'first-past-the-post' formula) is that it normally produces clear-cut majorities in parliament and, by this, strong and stable governments. That in turn is believed to promote general political stability. Owing to its inherent tendency to favour larger parties in the distribution of parliamentary seats, it reduces the effective number of parties. The plurality formula stimulates the formation of a few socially broad-based and in ideological respects fairly homogeneous parties. Due to their fragmented character – they could be seen as institutionalized political coalitions – these parties may serve as organs for assimilation of great parts of the population, and as instruments for merging different political interests in society. This is assumed to further national integration and to breed political tolerance and moderation. Extremist groups, whose actions might be a threat to the democratic proceedings, are (in consequence of the systematic under-representation of smaller parties) kept away from the centres of decision-making, with many of their followers being eventually absorbed by the 'regular' parties. Moreover, stemming from the fact that the plurality vote tends to give a distinct outcome in terms of winners and losers, elections normally have a direct impact on the formation of government and what policies are to be pursued. Accordingly, in the case of widespread disappointment among the citizens with the incumbent government's performances, they can easily vote the party in charge out of office. This way, the plurality formula strengthens political responsibility and accountability (Blais, 1991: 240–3; Blais and Dion, 1990: 253–4; Powell, 1982: 120–32; Taagepera and Shugart, 1989: 67–9).

The basic premise of proportional representation (PR) is that the diversity of opinions in society should be reflected in the key political bodies. All political interests and corresponding parties, small and large alike, are given the same chance of being represented in relation to the votes they have yielded. This greater fairness (in terms of equal opportunity) is presumed to contribute to the legitimacy of the democratic process. Notwithstanding, compared to the plurality system, PR certainly exhibits some obvious drawbacks. Proportional elections are usually less decisive with respect to the making of government. With many relatively small parties represented, the formation of a cabinet often becomes a hazardous business, where the game of inter-party bargaining may be more crucial than the 'message' from the voters. For the same reason, governments are overall weaker and far less long-lived under the proportional formula. The advocates of PR can, on the other hand, point to a number of merits of this system. Providing good prospects of representation even for minority groups and new political tendencies, the system is more inclusive and responsive in a broader sense than the plurality method; it guarantees all segments of society a voice at the halls of political decision-making. Thus, it is believed to reduce potential conflicts and turmoil in society and to enhance political order. Furthermore, electoral turnout is generally higher under PR. The reason is that this formula makes possible a broader range of real alternatives before the voters, which increases the incentive to take part. With the more fragmented party system that tends to come with PR, there are also in general closer ties between parties and various groups in society, which makes people feel greater identity with some of the parties that are standing. Due to the lack of a clear-cut political majority in parliament, but instead a number of minorities that must cooperate in order to form a government platform, the proportional system is said to further a willingness among political leaders to make compromises and to apply a consensual political style, which might increase political tolerance and eventually reduce hostility between opposed political groups – accordingly here, this is believed to be an effect of the inter-party game, whereas under the plurality system, the logic of intra-party relationships is assumed to serve the equivalent purpose (Blais, 1991: 243–6; Blais and Carty, 1990: 175–9; Crewe, 1981: 251–2; Lijphart, 1990: 74–5; Powell, 1982: 111–32).

The dispute over electoral systems pertains to the question

regarding the merits of grand government coalitions. As mentioned above, this form of cabinet is part of the consociational 'package' emphasized by Lijphart; the idea was originally proposed by Arthur Lewis (who in several respects has been a source of inspiration to Lijphart). The advantage of grand, oversized governments, the argument goes, is that they enable a wide array of parties (and connected supporting groups) to take part in the key organ of national decision-making. Thus no segment of importance in society will be excluded from the power and the access to patronage which come with ministerial portfolios. This is believed to be a matter of significance particularly in less-developed countries, where political positions are often in great demand, due to the fact that they represent well-nigh the only track to economic and social elevation. Under such conditions, where the stakes in the political contest become very high, political life may take the shape of an implacable zero-sum game – a tendency which can, however, be matched through the establishment of institutions of extensive power-sharing. By such arrangements, the political actors involved will collaborate with their political foes and formulate policies based on mutual agreement. This in its turn may pave the way for the development of a culture of accommodation, trust and understanding among initially strongly divided political groups (Lewis, 1965: 64–6; Lijphart, 1977: 25–30).

Being closely linked to the notion of PR – it can be seen as an application of that view to the executive branch of government – the grand coalition concept has been charged with drawbacks of a similar nature. Its major weakness, it has been maintained, lays in the area of lacking responsiveness and accountability. Since the general shape of government is not to be contested in elections, the balloting process certainly loses one of its more exciting ingredients. From the citizens' point of view, the casting of votes (as well as other kinds of involvement) might appear a politically fairly empty undertaking, for whatever will be the verdict, the formation of government is essentially a foregone conclusion. Cementing, as it were, the political agenda, the grand coalition formula tends to strengthen the impact of political élites, at the risk of eroding the popular trust and engagements in the political institutions. In addition, broad coalition cabinets have been criticized for scoring low in terms of effective governance. Since they are compromised of several, sometimes strongly opposed, political camps, whose vital interests may not be threatened, decision-making becomes a time-consuming process, the outcome of which often takes the shape of watered-down, harmless compromises. Also on this account, coalition governments are accused of undermining the general legitimacy of the democratic system (Horowitz, 1985: 569–75; Lijphart, 1977: 47–52).

In the case of federalism vs unitary government, scholars of democracy have in general been in favour of the former system. Especially with respect to developing countries, many of which have been torn by ethnic and regional divisions, federalism has often been pointed to as a way of laying the ground for the maintenance of democratic rule. One argument is that federalism provides more political positions to distribute: beside the national scene there exist a large number of political arenas of importance. Political groups which cannot vindicate their position in the national competition may thus be compensated by the prospects of success at the regional (state) level. In societies where positions in the public apparatus are regarded as crucial by key political actors, a federal structure may therefore serve to counteract the winner-takes-all tendency, and a resultant strong polarization, which otherwise is prone to emerge. Also in other regards, federalism is held to contribute to a moderation of political conflicts. Since it entails a decentralized mode of decision-making, it provides scope for discretion in various matters. The different segments of society can thus be given autonomy in certain salient issues (for example, in the areas of education, culture and revenue). This way, the national political process might be relieved of a number of potentially highly controversial topics. As a rationale for federalism, it has also been maintained that it offers greater opportunity for political schooling. Under this system, even minority groups have the possibility of controlling offices of significance and of exerting political power, which is believed to further their socialization into a democratic political culture. Providing an arena of influence relatively close at hand geographically, federalism can also be expected to facilitate the organization of parties and interest groups at the local level. Moreover, by its very nature, the system denotes a diffusion of political power, which for the Fathers of the American Constitution, the archetype of a federalist order, was a most central concern. In their understanding, as for their successors, federalism contributed to an order of checks and balances which served to restrain the abuse of power and to safeguard the maintenance of popular rule (Dahl, 1971: 226; Horowitz, 1990a: 217–26; Lijphart, 1977: 41–3; Lipset and Rokkan, 1967: 53).

Accordingly, federalism is assumed to have several advantages: it creates a divided power structure and makes possible the incorporation of many segments of society into the legislative and executive process. Simultaneously, it may in several ways help to cool down the tensions between rival political groups. Hence, the system has been characterized as a token of a polity of accommodation and compromise: 'federalism, the middle way' (Rothchild, 1970: 220; see also Powell, 1982: 270). Despite its widely alleged merits, however, the notion of federalism has been looked upon with distrust by political leaders in many countries. The system has been denounced as costly and inefficient, as it entails a small-scale administrative structure, duplication of tasks, and often slow and complicated decision-making processes. In addition, the devolution of power is believed to feed centrifugal political forces. Establishing (or maintaining an already existing) federal order has been feared to lay the basis of separatist tendencies; decentralization of authority is seen as the first step towards secession. The application of a centralized, unitary form of government is thus held to be a requisite of the preservation of national peace and concord (Horowitz, 1990a: 224; 1985: 222–4; Rothchild, 1970: 207, 218; Zolberg, 1966: 62–3, 70).

As compared to the institutional factors which have so far been addressed, relatively little attention has been paid to the question of whether differences as to how the executive is selected – through parliamentarism or presidentialism – might be of importance in the context of democratic durability. However, this matter has recently been brought to the fore through the writing of Juan Linz. This author strongly maintains that presidentialism in several respects has proved to be to the detriment of democracy. One of the main disadvantages, in his mind, is that in presidential elections too much is at stake for the parties involved: the winning candidate gains all the power and glory, the loser gets nothing. Under such conditions, the political struggle becomes a zero-sum game, marked by hard polarization. Under parliamentarism, the outcome of elections is many times less clear-cut as far as the yield is concerned. Coalition governments and other sorts of power-sharing are here fairly common, breeding an atmosphere of cooperation and unity among the parties. The President's fixed term in office further adds to the problem. Since there are no hopes for shifts over the period of the mandate, losers must wait many years for the possible access to the (often outstanding) power resources of the executive. This state of affairs might cause alienation among the political opposition and eventually undermine its democratic loyalty. The rigidity which comes with the fixed term also makes it extremely difficult to remove a government which has proved incapable of handling upcoming problems or whose front figure has been embroiled in scandals or lost the confidence of his or her following. In similar circumstances, in a parliamentary system, the changes that are needed can be more smoothly carried through. A further problem, partly pertaining to the former, is the case when the majority of the legislature represents a political tendency opposed to the President, giving rise to an institutional rivalry that may erupt into political and social strife. At times, such conflicts have tempted the military to intervene in order to break the stalemate. Furthermore, the two-dimensional function of the President, being both the head of state and the chief executive, combined with the personalization of power embedded in the popular mandate, may imbue the holder with an assumption of a supreme political standing, leading him or her to refuse to acknowledge the constitutional limits of the office. By contrast, under parliamentarism, the Prime Minister operates more like a politician among others, acting as the spokesman of the majority in parliament rather than appearing as the voice of the nation or the tribune of the people (Lijphart, 1990: 75–9; Linz, 1990: 52–68; Linz and Stepan, 1989: 56–7; Przeworski, 1991: 34; for a somewhat divergent view, see Horowitz, 1990b: 73–6).

Coming finally amongst institutional factors to the colonial background, the conventional wisdom holds that a British heritage is an advantage from a democratic viewpoint. The main arguments run as follows. Earlier and to a greater degree than other colonial powers (France, Portugal, Spain, etc.), Britain established organs of representation in its territories. However limited in competence, these institutions made the native population (or at least the élite strata) familiar with the pluralistic form of government, and set a tradition of representation through free and fair elections which could in several places be maintained after independence. Furthermore, the British have been hailed for developing a well-functioning administrative system, particularly a judiciary, in the colonies. At the same time, the local population was – through the policy of so-called indirect rule – to a significant degree incorporated in the administrative process. Thus, it has been claimed, the people in the former British colonies became socialized into an administrative culture which has served to counterbalance tendencies to arbitrary and despotic use of power (Emerson, 1960: 230–6; Killingray, 1986: 416–18; Smith, 1978: 71–2; Weiner, 1987: 19–20).

Turning to the socio-economic side of the puzzle, we will first of all inquire into the impact of social and economic development, which will be measured in terms of literacy rate, energy consumption and the percentage employed in agriculture. According to the theory of modernization, which is here at issue, development in these areas will bring about a general change of society that will promote democratic rule. A higher educational level among the population is believed to lead to further openness and tolerance, and to give the man and woman in the street greater opportunity of being informed and gaining a deeper insight into political issues. This in turn can be expected to increase political participation, manifested in higher electoral turnout as well as in greater involvement in party and associational activities. Through enhanced popular education and a concomitant industrialization, and with that an increased overall prosperity, groups which have formally been excluded from influence will obtain improved political resources and thus better chances of having a say in public life. Economic progress will also create a greater national asset to be used for distributional purposes. Hence it will be less difficult to meet various demands on the public sector, which may reduce the level of tension between competing groups. This can lay the ground for an amelioration of antagonism in society and for the establishment of the peaceful mode of conflict-solving that democracy implies (Apter, 1987: 25; Deutsch, 1961: 474–8; Pennock, 1979: 223–32; Randall and Teobald, 1985: 18–21).

From antiquity up to current times, it has been widely presumed that the distribution of income and wealth among citizens is critical to the functioning of the democratic form of government. A sharp division between rich and poor in a society is considered to be detrimental to the upholding of democracy. The heart of the matter, it has been maintained, is that economic resources are prone to be transferred into political resources. An unequal economic distribution not only determines people's social standing and way of living, it also affects the potential to take effective political actions in protecting one's interests. What is more, economic and political influence in conjunction may give rise to a process of accelerated resource concentration, which increases the inequalities and strengthens the tension and mistrust in society even further. On the other hand, trying thoroughly to cope with these problems by political reforms is not an easy endeavour. One option is to attack the roots of inequality and launch a property redistribution programme, for example a land reform. However, such efforts tend either, if the agenda is seriously enacted, to meet obstinate resistance from the group that is hit, motivating it eventually to take undemocratic actions, or turn out (for the aforesaid reasons) to be mere rhetoric – thus alienating many of those who were to benefit from the programme. The other option is to attempt to improve the circumstances of the have-nots through extensive public spending (on employment, housing, education, etc.). In the short run, such inputs might work highly satisfactorily, but in the longer perspective this kind of policy – usually referred to as economic populism – has in many instances resulted in severe problems of economic imbalance (drained fiscal assets, huge foreign debts and rampant inflation), undermining widely in society thereby the support of the democratic system. In other words, deep economic cleavages are considered to give rise to profound social and political conflicts, which by the same token makes it hard, in a democratic setting, forcefully to address the basic predicaments (Dahl, 1971: 54–5, 88–9; Pennock, 1979: 232–3; Sachs, 1989: 2–10, 23–5).

Previous research

As was indicated above, two of the institutional factors considered here – namely the electoral system and the colonial background – have been investigated in an earlier study. In their empirical testing, Blais and Dion found that democracy was more likely to fall in countries having proportional elections. The authors therefore conclude that 'the plurality system is more conductive to the survival of democracy than proportional representation' (Blais and Dion, 1990: 256). This tendency was modified, however, by the observation that among less developed countries, those having a heritage of British influence exhibited a far better record regarding democratic stability than others. Yet, since these circumstances were closely interrelated – almost all former British territories applying the plurality formula – the authors confine themselves to remark that both the electoral system and the colonial background presumably are of importance (Blais and Dion, 1990: 258, 262).

The significance of coalition governments and presidentialism contra parliamentarism have not been examined in prior research on the duration of democracy. However, differences among countries with regard to the level of socio-economic development and the distribution of income have been traced before. Lipset (1959: 75–9) demonstrated a strong positive association between all his socio-economic indicators and the upholding of democracy. This connection was documented with even greater distinctiveness in Cutright's (1963: 256–60) technically more advanced investigation. In both studies, that evidence is read as a substantiation of the authors' theoretical premise, namely that it is the one thing – socio-economic conditions – that impacts the other – the forms of government. Notwithstanding, what has been revealed is only a statistical relationship, which might also be interpreted the other way around, implying that the maintenance of high standards of democratic performance lays the ground for improvements in the area of socio-economic development. In other words, what we can see, given the measurements applied, is the existence of a connection, but we are provided with no means of checking the matter of causality, that is, what determines what (Rustow, 1970: 342).

Muller addressed the effect of income inequality on democratic stability. As could be expected in view of the theoretical reasoning on this topic, the author finds a close negative association between the upper-quintile income share in the countries under study and the

Table 4.3   *Institutional factors and political democracy: differences in year average and correlation coefficients*

	Average	(N)	
Federal	11.8	(9)	
Non-federal	11.5	(22)	r = 0.02
Coalition	13.0	(7)	
No coalition	11.1	(24)	r = 0.11
Plurality	12.2	(19)	
PR	11.2	(12)	r = 0.08
Parliamentarism	15.0	(13)	
Presidentialism	9.0	(18)	r = 0.43

ability to preserve democratic institutions. Controlling even for differences in economic growth, the general picture remains the same. Muller thus argues that 'if a democratic regime is inaugurated in a country with an extremely inegalitarian distribution of income, high inequality is likely to undermine the regime and cause democratic institutions to be replaced by authoritarian rule' (1988: 66). However, even in this case, the causal nature of the relationship constitutes a problem, since a reciprocal effect between these matters could very well be assumed.[7]

So much for the prior inquiries into these matters. Let us now see how the explanatory proposals of an institutional and a socio-economic vein respectively stand the test on the basis of the evidence at hand in this study.

Findings

Probing first the significance of institutional factors, we find a correspondence between four of these and the duration of political democracy reported in Table 4.3. As we know, it has been widely assumed that the employment of federal structures will invigorate democracy. However, using here a fairly broad definition of federalism – implying that all states having some constitutionally regulated regional autonomy with locally elected officials are referred to this category – we get no support for that presumption, as federal and non-federal states exhibit on average almost identical records of democratic durability.[8]

We can see from the N in the table that federal structures are not very common in the countries under inquiry, and that is even more true for coalition governments. Accounting for the practice of oversized cabinet coalitions within the period as well as a decade

Table 4.4   *Institutional factors and political democracy: three multiple regressions*

	Standardized regression coefficient	T value	Explained variance (%)
Parliamentarism	0.44	2.518	
Federalism	0.06	0.351	18.5
Parliamentarism	0.42	2.501	
Coalition	0.11	0.564	19.3
Parliamentarism	0.47	2.522	
Plurality	0.11	0.564	19.1

before (since in this event it seems reasonable to consider also the recent historical legacy), we ascertain that less than a quarter of our sample of states, only 7 out of 31, had had such experiences. Do these then diverge from the rest in terms of democratic performances? In fact, that is the case: states having applied coalition governments tend to have higher duration scores than the others. This observation certainly accords with the arguments put forward by Lijphart. Nevertheless, we must conclude that it is hardly a pronounced substantiation of his claims.[9]

When it comes to the electoral system, we notice a better outcome for the category of states that have applied the plurality formula.[10] This result is in tune with the findings by Blais and Dion, although the effect displayed in their study is more distinct. To some extent this divergence seems to be contingent on the difference in measurements employed. For if instead of political democracy we use electoral democracy (which is closer to the criteria utilized by Blais and Dion), a more marked result can be observed: the average for states having plurality elections being 14.5 years as compared to 12.0 years for those under PR ($r = 0.19$). Notwithstanding, even that should be judged as a quite modest tendency.

Turning to the difference among the states with regard to how the executive is selected – the theme stressed particularly by Linz – a far more manifest effect appears.[11] It signifies that political democracy has generally been maintained considerably longer under parliamentarism than under presidentialism, a finding that indisputably lends support to Linz's critical assessment of the latter system. Moving one step further in our examination, from bivariate to multivariate testing, the Linzian point becomes underscored even more. In pair-wise probing against the other institutional conditions treated so far, as documented in Table 4.4, the distinction between

Table 4.5   *Colonial background and political democracy:*
difference in year average and correlation coefficient

	Average	(N)	
British background	14.2	(15)	
No British background	9.2	(16)	$r = 0.37$

Table 4.6   *Colonial background and electoral democracy:*
difference in year average and correlation coefficient

	Average	(N)	
British background	16.6	(15)	
No British background	9.7	(16)	$r = 0.50$

parliamentarism and presidentialism stands out clearly as the dominant explanatory factor.

As we recall, Blais and Dion's scrutiny indicated that democratic
procedures are more likely to be upheld in countries that have been
under British influence than in others. The findings in this study point
in the same direction. However, as can be seen in Tables 4.5 and 4.6,
the effect varies quite considerably depending on what measurement
of democratic durability we are considering. The matching of the
variables provides evidence of an obvious connection between the
duration of political democracy and the factor at issue: a British
colonial background makes on average a difference of five years of
democratic rule. Yet in the event of electoral democracy, the effect is
even more pronounced. Here it is a matter of an almost seven-year
gap to the advantage of the former British countries, and we notice
too that correlation coefficient reaches as high as the 0.5 level.
Looking at the occurrence of coups – which as a measurement relates
to the breakdown (or not) of the electoral democratic institutions –
we find an equally marked tendency: while coups are fairly rare
phenomena among the British ex-territories, such undertakings have
been the common pattern among states with a different colonial
connection.

Since it is a well-known fact that certain democratic characteristics
tend to accompany British heritage – not only the plurality vote but
also the parliamentary form of cabinet selection – it is of course
interesting to ascertain whether the impact of parliamentarism vs
presidentialism stands the test on control for differences in colonial
background (or if it is just a spurious reflection of the latter factor).

Table 4.7 *Executive selection, colonial background and political democracy: multiple regression*

	Standardized regression coefficient	T value	Explained variance (%)
Parliamentarism	0.32	1.505	
British background	0.16	0.766	19.7

Note: The correlation coefficient (r) for the two explanatory variables is 0.62. Accordingly, there should be no risk of colinearity.

Table 4.8 *Executive selection, colonial background and electoral democracy: multiple regression*

	Standardized regression coefficient	T value	Explained variance (%)
Parliamentarism	0.20	1.505	
British background	0.38	1.872	28.4

This is illustrated in Tables 4.7 and 4.8. Once again we get disparate results for the measurements reported. As regards political democracy, our main object of scrutiny, we can safely establish that it is not the colonial factor that is the answer to our query (a T value on the 0.77 level can by no standards be adjudged as statistically significant[12]). Here it is the distinction between states with respect to how the executive is selected that makes the important difference. Accordingly, the positive effect of parliamentarism – and vice versa when presidentialism is applied – emerges as the key institutional precondition for the upholding of political democracy.

As for electoral democracy, it is the other way around. In this event, the British factor proves to have great consequence, whereas the impact of the cabinet selection factor is of minor importance (and statisically not confirmed). In other words, in the interest of maintaining the electoral democratic proceedings, the former British countries find themselves in an advantageous position. This finding in turn sheds light on the question as to how, more precisely, the British influence played a role in patterning the political circumstances in the countries concerned. As was outlined before, two aspects have been emphasized in this context. The one points to the long tradition of regular and fair elections set by the British, whereas the other takes notice of the establishment of administrative and judicial institutions to protect civil rights and the rule of law. Since the latter pertains to the upholding of political freedoms (included in the political democracy index, which is less closely tied to the British factor), it is reasonable to believe the former aspect to be the more essential one. This, in addition, suggests more generally that certain democratic procedures can be strengthened through reiterated practice. An early introduction of some basic requirements of democratic government, therefore, seems to make their application at some later point in time more likely (cf. Huntington, 1991: 40–6).

As regards the institutional condition which emerged as most crucial concerning political democracy – the form of government selection employed – it is hardly reasonable to believe that for its part it could be a consequence of the upholding of democratic rule (implying that democracies in the course of time tend to go from the one form to the other – a pattern which certainly does not appear to be substantiated by evidence). Thus in this event, we need not doubt that the causality runs in the direction that has been conjectured.[13] However, the possibility of an inverse relationship must generally be seen as a problem with respect to socio-economic factors (Muller, 1988: 52). To cope with this dilemma, one could try to gather information on these matters dating from an early point in time, so that the assumed causal circumstances antedate the changes in mode of government that eventually occur. That kind of information (from 1970) has been possible to obtain for the measurements of social and economic development. However, as regards income inequality, the data available are scattered quite extensively over the period under study. Hence, in this instance, our causal inferences (insofar as any relationships of importance appear) must be based on the assumption that the income distribution patterns are fairly stable over time, and by the same token, not easily changed through political action. On top of this, we also face a problem here to the extent that for more than a third of the sample of states we could not find any useful data on the distribution of income. For these reasons, the outcome in this area should be expounded with special caution.

The results in bivariate testing of the socio-economic variables are presented in Table 4.9. Starting with the characteristics that pertain to the theory of modernization, as is commonly the case, the per capita energy consumption is used as an indicator of the general standard of living (per capita GNP being the equivalent measurement, giving an almost identical outcome[14]), while the percentage employed in agriculture is aimed at denoting more specifically the degree of advancement in production life. Besides this, the literacy rate in the population illustrates the level of development in the realm of popular education.[15] As is evident, all these variables

Table 4.9   *Socio-economic factors and political democracy: correlation coefficients*

Energy consumption	0.43
Employed in agriculture	−0.46
Literacy	0.30
Income share, lowest 20%	−0.36

exhibit connections of a predicted nature, thus indicating that development in these respects promotes the duration of democratic government – an outcome that certainly conforms with the conclusions made in Lipset's and Cutright's prior examination of these matters.[16]

In the theoretical discourse on the prerequisites of the forms of government, it has for a long time been held that grave economic gaps in the population have an injurious effect on popular rule. In his empirical inquiry into the issue, Muller (1988) presented evidence attesting to the accuracy of this presumption. Glancing at the finding documented in Table 4.9, we can conclude that the present study points in the same direction. Reported there is the correspondence between the political democracy index and the share of the personal income received by the 10 per cent of the population who earn the most in different countries, resulting in a quite distinct negative connection – which suggests (given the assumed direction of causality) that democracy is generally more fragile in those states where the richest part of the population appropriates the largest share of the 'cake'.

Thus in bivariate testing all socio-economic factors considered have demonstrated essential associations with the duration of democracy. Now, to what extent does this pattern change on mutual control between the variables? Since the three measurements of level of development are internally fairly strongly connected,[17] it is reasonable to reckon upon the existence of spuriousness. Furthermore, it is interesting to see whether this study attests to Muller's finding that the connection in the case of income equality is maintained even on control for differences in socio-economic development between the countries.

Taking a look at Table 4.10, we can establish that the importance of literacy, the indicator of the degree of popular education, fades considerably in the context of the two other socio-economic variables. As for these two, both do fairly well in mutual control; however, insofar as energy consumption is concerned, it is a matter of a very low degree of statistical significance (only at the 0.10 level in

Table 4.10   *Socio-economic factors and political democracy: five multiple regressions*

	Standardized regression coefficient	T value	Explained variance (%)
Energy consumption	0.37	1.865	
Literacy	0.10	0.505	18.9
Employed in agriculture	−0.41	−2.162	
Literacy	0.11	0.578	21.9
Energy consumption	0.26	1.380	
Employed in agriculture	−0.36	−2.162	26.0
Energy consumption	0.33	1.745	
Income share, lowest 20%	−0.21	−1.112	21.6
Employed in agriculture	−0.37	−2.015	
Income share, lowest 20%	−0.20	−1.081	24.1

one-tailed testing).[18] Coming to the second query, the one regarding the effect of income inequality, we find – by contrast to Muller – that this variable does not hold its own in pair-wise confrontation – not even if the most modest requirement of statistical significance is applied. In other words, this investigation points to the fact that in the area of socio-economic prerequisites of democratic durability, it is the level of economic development that stands out as the decisive condition.

What remains to be addressed, however, is the most central question of this study, namely if it is the circumstances of an institutional or a socio-economic nature – or both – that basically set the terms for the well-being of the democratic mode of government. On the institutional side, it is natural to concentrate on what emerged as the prime explanatory variable – the form of executive selection. Will the impact of this factor remain when the leading economic variables are also accounted for – and vice versa? We find the outcome of such probings in Table 4.11. As can be seen, even in these testings the key institutional variable, parliamentarism vs presidentialism, demonstrates an essential impact. Equally interesting, our two measures of economic advancement hold their own as explanatory factors as well. With reservation for the fact that the total level of explained variance is not particularly high (circa 30 per cent), indicating that other circumstances might be of importance too, the findings that have been documented certainly lead us to the conclusion that conditions of both sorts are of significance for the upholding of democratic rule.[19]

Table 4.11 *Institutional and socio-economic factors and political democracy: two multiple regressions*

	Standardized regression coefficient	T value	Explained variance (%)
Parliamentarism	0.40	2.561	
Energy consumption	0.35	2.211	30.4
Parliamentarism	0.30	1.781	
Employed in agriculture	−0.35	2.076	29.0

Final remarks

While acknowledging the uncertainty which comes with the restricted number of cases under study – and particularly so with regard to the income distribution variable – this investigation conveys a fairly distinctive message. In the area of institutional prerequisites of democratic durability, one characteristic has turned out to be more important than others, that is, the way the executive side of government is selected. More precisely, democracy seems to thrive in parliamentary systems but has difficulties in surviving in a presidential environment. Furthermore, we can establish that there is also a socio-economic condition of importance, namely the degree of economic development. Briefly put, countries which have reached a higher standard of living and have moved above the agricultural stage of production are more likely than others to maintain political democracy. Accordingly, in supporting democratic rule, there would be room for engineering – by both economic and constitutional innovators.

Notes

1 Of concern to Lipset here is whether Communist or Fascist parties received more than 20 per cent of the votes. However, the essential point as far as democracy is concerned is not the distribution of votes in the elections but the actual effects on the mode of government.

2 Historically, such a conception could be traced back to a Jacobin notion of popular government (Holden, 1974: 41–2).

3 For a more detailed account of these criteria, see Hadenius (1992: ch. 3). To be classified as democratic, a state should have a total score of 75 or higher on the 0–10 point index of level of democracy presented there. Moreover, regarding each criterion considered, the state should be placed in the highest quartile on the individual scale applied.

4 It should be noted that to be accounted for, democratic institutions must be in

place for more than one month. In practice, this limitation affected only one country, namely Chile in 1991.

5 This refers to successful interferences, where the new regime remains in office for more than a month. Therefore, the coup in Gambia in 1981 is not taken into account (it was not successful), nor the transition of power in Cyprus in 1974 (it lasted only a week). By far the most common type of coup is military intervention, but it can also be the party in government (as in the case of Senegal) or the President himself (as in the Philippines) who usurps power.

6 The main sources that have been utilized are *Amnesty International Yearbook* (various years), *Encyclopaedia Britannica, Freedom in the World, Political Rights and Civil Liberties* and *Keeting's Record of World Events.*

7 As Muller points out, his conclusions are validated on the conditions that the observations regarding inequality precede or are simultaneous with the date of breakdown of democracy – a requirement which, given the nature of the data at hand, can only be roughly fulfilled (Muller, 1988: 52, 54–5).

8 If instead of a dichotomy we employ a scale, divided with regard to different degrees of federalism – (1) strong federalism (e.g. Argentina and India), (2) weak federalism (e.g. Pakistan and Venezuela), (3) partial regional autonomy (e.g. Mauritius and Trinidad and Tobago), and (4) no federalism – we get almost the same outcome ($r = 0.04$). It should be noted that in this case, as for the electoral system and the executive selection, if the forms have been changed within the period of inquiry, which occurred in a few instances (such as Sri Lanka, which turned from PR and parliamentarism to plurality vote and presidentialism in 1978), the classification is based on the system that was applied for the longest time.

9 Using more confined measures, distinguishing between coalition experiences of shorter and longer continuation, does not in any considerable regard change the result ($r = 0.10$–0.15).

10 In the case of more than one body of representation, what is referred to are the elections to the lower chamber.

11 To be classified as a presidential system two criteria should be met: (a) direct popular elections, and (b) fixed term in office. It is worth mentioning, furthermore, that the tendency reported is of a corresponding magnitude against electoral democracy and coup ($r = 0.44$ and 0.41, respectively).

12 The following significance levels are applicable:

Two-tailed testing		One-tailed testing	
	T value		T value
0.01 level	2.58	0.01 level	2.33
0.05 level	1.96	0.05 level	1.65
0.10 level	1.65	0.10 level	1.28

13 This should indeed also hold true for the British influence in the case of electoral democracy.

14 $r = 0.42$.

15 Information on socio-economic circumstances is taken from the *Handbook of International Trade and Development Statistics*, UNCTAD, 1988; *ILO Yearbook of Labour Statistics: Retrospective Edition of Population Censuses 1945–89*, 1990; and *UNESCO – Statistical Yearbook*, 1988.

16 Having instead utilized information from the late 1980s, we would have yielded the following results: energy consumption: 0.43; agriculture: 0.24; literacy: 0.33 – which attest to the fact that in large measure the relationships are persistent over the period.

17 $r = 0.46$–0.53. See also Hadenius (1992: 84).

18 See above, note 12.

19 In the case of electoral democracy we get the following results:

	Standardized regression coefficient	T value	Explained variance (%)
British background	0.44	2.783	
Energy consumption	0.24	1.498	31.1
British background	0.44	2.812	
Employed in agriculture	−0.31	2.010	34.9

References

Apter, D. E. (1987) *Rethinking Development: Modernization, Dependency, and Postmodern Politics*. Newbury Park, CA: Sage.

Blais, A. (1991) 'The debate over electoral systems', *International Political Science Review*, 12 (3): 239–60.

Blais, A. and Carty, R. C. (1990) 'Does proportional representation foster voter turnout?', *European Journal of Political Research*, 18: 167–81.

Blais, A. and Dion, S. (1990) 'Electoral systems and the consolidation of new democracies', in D. Ethier (ed.), *Democratic Transition and Consolidation in Southern Europe, Latin America and Southeast Asia*. London: Macmillan. pp. 250–65.

Bollen, K. A. (1980) 'Issues in the comparative measurement of political democracy', *American Sociological Review*, 45: 370–90.

Crewe, I. (1981) 'Electoral participation', in D. Butler, H. R. Penniman and A. Ranney (eds), *Democracy at the Polls: A Comparative Study of Competitive National Elections*. Washington, DC: American Enterprise Institute. pp. 216–63.

Cutright, P. (1963) 'National political development: measurement and analysis', *American Political Science Review*, 28: 253–64.

Dahl, R. A. (1971) *Polyarchy: Participation and Opposition*. New Haven, CT and London: Yale University Press.

Dahl, R. A. (1989) *Democracy and Its Critics*. New Haven, CT and London: Yale University Press.

Deutsch, K. W. (1961) 'Social mobilization and political development', *American Political Science Review*, 55: 403–14.

Emerson, R. (1960) *From Empire to Nation: The Rise of Self-Assertion of Asian and African Peoples*. Cambridge, MA: Harvard University Press.

Hadenius, A. (1992) *Democracy and Development*. Cambridge: Cambridge University Press.

Holden, B. (1974) *The Nature of Democracy*. London: Thomas Nelson.

Horowitz, D. L. (1985) *Ethnic Groups in Conflict*. Berkeley: University of California Press.

Horowitz, D. L. (1990a) *A Democratic South Africa? Constitutional Engineering in a Divided Society*. Berkeley: University of California Press.

Horowitz, D. L. (1990b) 'Comparing democratic systems', *Journal of Democracy*, 1 (4): 73–9.

Huntington, S. P. (1991) *The Third Wave: Democratization in the Late Twentieth Century*. Norman: University of Oklahoma Press.

Killingray, D. (1986) 'The maintenance of law and order in British colonial Africa', *African Affairs*, 85: 4411–37.

Lewis, W. A. (1965) *Politics in West Africa*. London: Allen and Unwin.

Lijphart, A. (1977) *Democracy in Plural Societies: A Comparative Exploration*. New Haven, CT: Yale University Press.

Lijphart, A. (1990) 'The southern european examples of democratization: six lessons for Latin America', *Government and Opposition*, 25: 68–84.

Linz, J. J. (1990) 'The Perils of Presidentialism', *Journal of Democracy*, 1 (1): 51–70.

Linz, J. and Stepan, A. (1989) 'Political crafting of democratic consolidation or destruction: European and South American Comparisons', in R. A. Pastor (ed.), *Democracy in the Americas: Stopping the Pendulum*. New York: Holmes and Meir. pp. 41–61.

Lipset, S. M. (1959) 'Some social requisites of democracy: economic development and political legitimacy', *American Political Science Review*, 53: 69–105.

Lipset, S. M. and Rokkan, S. (1967) 'Cleavage structures, party systems and voter alignments: an introduction', in S. M. Lipset and S. Rookan (eds), *Party Systems and Voter Alignments: Cross-National Perspectives*. New York: Free Press. pp. 1–64.

Muller, E. N. (1988) 'Democracy, economic development, and income inequality', *American Sociological Review*, 53: 50–68.

Pennock, J. R. (1979) *Democratic Political Theory*. Princeton, NJ: Princeton University Press.

Powell, G. B., Jr (1982) *Contemporary Democracies: Participation, Stability, and Voice*. Cambridge, MA: Harvard University Press.

Przeworski, A. (1991) *Democracy and the Market: Political and Economic Reforms in Eastern Europe and Latin America*. Cambridge: Cambridge University Press.

Randall, V, and Teobald, R. (1985) *Political Change and Underdevelopment: A Critical Introduction to Third World Politics*. London: Macmillan.

Rothchild, D. (1970) 'The limits of federalism: an examination of political institutional transfer in Africa', in M. E. Doro and M. S. Newell (eds), *Governing Black Africa: Perspectives on the New States*. London: Macmillan.

Rustow, D. A. (1970) 'Transitions to democracy: toward a dynamic model', *Comparative Politics*, 2: 337–63.

Sachs, J. D. (1989) *Social Conflict and Populist Politics in Latin America*. Cambridge, MA: National Bureau of Economic Research, Working Paper No. 2897.

Sartori, G. (1987) *The Theory of Democracy Revisited*. 2 vols Chatham, NJ: Chatham House.

Smith, T. (1978) 'A comparative study of French and British decolonization', *Comparative Studies in Society and History*, 20: 70–102.

Taagepera, R. and Shugart, M. S. (1989) *Seats and Votes: The Effects and Determinants of Electoral Systems*. New Haven, CT and London: Yale University Press.

Weiner, M. (1987) 'Empirical democratic theory', in M. Weiner and E. Ozbudun (eds), *Competitive Elections in Developing Countries*. Durham, NC: Duke University Press. pp. 3–36.

Zolberg, A. R. (1966) *Creating Political Order: The Party-States of West Africa*. Chicago, IL: Rand McNally.

5

Is the Degree of Electoral Democracy Measurable? Experiences from Bulgaria, Kenya, Latvia, Mongolia and Nepal

Jørgen Elklit

Following Robert A. Dahl (1971: 1), this chapter builds on the understanding that democracy is a system of government characterized by its continuing responsiveness to the preferences of its citizens, considered as political equals.

Dahl assumes that for a government to be continuously responsive to the preferences of its citizens, it is required that these all have opportunities (a) to formulate preferences, (b) to signify preferences to the government by individual as well as collective action, and (c) to have preferences weighed equally in the conduct of the government, that is, with no discrimination because of the content or the source of the preference (Dahl, 1971: 2).

When these democratic ideals are applied to the real world, it becomes evident (a) that no countries satisfy the requirements perfectly, and (b) that countries differ in the degree to which they fulfil them. In order to be able to distinguish between ideal democracy and actual approaches to that ideal, Dahl uses the term *polyarchy* to refer to the latter (1971, 1986a, 1986b, 1989).[1]

In *Democracy and Its Critics*, Dahl defines polyarchy as 'a political order distinguished by the presence of seven institutions, all of which must exist for a government to be classified as a polyarchy'. These institutions – which refer to actual, not only to nominal rights and institutions – are elected officials, free and fair elections, inclusive suffrage, the right to run for office, freedom of expression, alternative information and associational autonomy (Dahl, 1989: 221).

These seven requirements can be seen as constituting two different dimensions of democratization – liberalization (or public contestation) and inclusiveness (or participation) – and democratization is then to be understood as a development on both dimensions (Dahl, 1971: 4–8; see also Svensson, 1991). Among recent empirical works in the same tradition are Hadenius (1992), Bollen (1991), and Coppedge and Reinicke (1991).

Diamond et al. (1988: xvi; also Sørensen, 1993: 12–13) have defined political democracy in basically the same way as a system of government meeting the conditions of competition, political participation and civil and political liberties. Obviously, these characteristics are not variables which always come in full scale. Consequently, systems of government are *more or less* democratic.

It has further been maintained that democratization is a broader process than just changing the system of government on these dimensions. It has been argued that one also has to pay attention to the development of key societal institutions with a potential for furthering democracy, that one has to secure the fulfilment of basic human needs, and that the training in and learning of democracy should also be promoted (Kusterer, 1992).

A more narrow definition of democracy is provided by Reeve and Ware (1992: 26), who claim that three conditions should be met for an elected body to be fully democratic: the electorate shall consist of all those directly affected by the decisions of the body, all members of the body shall be fully accountable, and all voters must have an equal vote.

This chapter concentrates on the electoral elements in the democratization process. This element is conceptually close to what is often called political democracy, which also focuses on political rights and liberties. I, however, prefer to talk of electoral democracy – with the parallel concept of the process of electoral democratization – since this concept focuses directly on those elements of leadership selection and public participation – and the conditions therefore, that is, effective political liberties and an efficient electoral administration – which in particular pertain to competitive elections as a key instrument in the promotion of democracy. As in Kusterer (1992), the degree to which electoral democratization is embedded in relevant prerequisites of democracy (sustainment of political and civil liberties, a non-partisan administration, media and NGO capacity for information and civic education, effectiveness of the education system and the administration of justice, etc.) should also be taken into account.

Harrop and Miller stress that the wider political environment must meet certain conditions in order to sustain free and democratic elections. Following Mackenzie, they list four conditions of which one is particularly important, even though it is not always explicitly referred to, that is, the 'acceptance throughout the political community of certain rules of the game which structure and limit the struggle for power' (Harrop and Miller, 1987: 6–7).

Comparative studies of political development and democratization are often primarily quantitative. One reason is that the measures of democratization and political institutionalization used – participation, electoral turnout, per cent enfranchised, degree of politicization – as well as the indicators of explanatory factors – for example, indices of societal modernization – easily lend themselves to measurement and quantitative analysis. Valuable as such studies are, they may be blamed for relying too much on variables subjectable to quantitative analysis, at the expense of studying more thoroughly the impact of the political institutions themselves on democratization, or for including variables only distantly connected to the core concept.

This chapter follows another avenue, arguing that the study of democratization will benefit from a renewed concern for the significance of political institutions. Such assessment of political institutions and their contributions to democratization requires an in-depth preoccupation with individual cases of democratization. This point is also inherent in Sørensen's claim that 'detailed analysis of specific cases is necessary in order to ascertain in a more profound manner their democratic qualities' (1993: 19) and in Gladdish's discussion of Lijphart (Gladdish, 1993; Lijphart, 1991).

The democratic character of an election and the contributions of individual institutions to electoral democratization should preferably be studied by looking at all components of individual electoral systems. This means that the degree of democracy of an election (and an electoral system) – if at all measurable – should be rated on the basis of a detailed scrutiny of all relevant administrative procedures and regulations, the behaviour of relevant institutions, the possibilities for a fair election campaign as provided for by the government – and not only by correlating indices of modernization with turnout, etc.

The approach of this chapter to the comparative study of electoral democratization is thus one of comparing individual cases. Since the assessments will often be of an intuitive and qualitative character, the question of how to measure degrees of electoral democracy becomes a key issue.

One problem which immediately comes to mind is that of level of measurement. Most of the variables included can be measured on a nominal or ordinal scale level only. Any aggregate expression on the basis of such variables will be at the same level of measurement, namely nominal or ordinal scale level. One also has to consider the incomparability as well as the multi-dimensionality of some of the individual indicators of electoral democratization.

Thus, the chapter also contributes to ongoing debates about (a)

qualitative vs quantitative approaches to the study of democratization, and (b) the true character of the apparent interval or
ratio-level indices of democratization provided by Freedom House
(McColm et al., 1991) , UNDP (1991, 1992), and Hadenius (1992), or
advocated by Bollen (1991). (See also Kusterer, 1992: 19ff.; Sørensen, 1993: 17–20.)

The post-1989 wave of democratization comprises a bewildering
diversity of elements: constitutions have been changed to provide for
more democracy; judiciaries have been reformed; civil liberties have
been introduced (or taken seriously); electronic and printed media
have become more open and critical; opposition media have been
given financial support; referendums and multi-party, competitive
elections have been held; parliaments have been allowed to debate;
and politicians have been held accountable for their doings.

Thus, this chapter, which mainly concentrates on qualitative
comparisons of individual electoral systems and electoral democratization processes, accounts only in part for the entire democratization process. Furthermore, the processes do not have the same
chronological starting point; nor are the actors, number of elections
conducted, or sequence of events identical. All five are nevertheless
in the *decision phase* of transition to democracy (Rustow, 1970;
Sørensen, 1993: 40ff.), which reduces the problems in comparing
them.

How should electoral democracy – a multidimensional concept –
be operationalized? This chapter will utilize as many as fourteen[2]
elements, taking as its point of departure the seven institutional
guarantees which Dahl over the years has argued are necessary for a
polyarchy (1971: 3; 1986b: 230; 1989: 233).

The seven institutions are operationalized by looking at one or
more specific indicators. A close connection between the basic
concepts and the operational definitions is evident, as also noticed by
Coppedge and Reinicke (1991: 49). The operational definitions cover
the democratic ideal at one end of a democratic/non-democratic
continuum. Since each electoral system will have a specific value on
each dimension/variable, we should be able to measure if an electoral
system is *more or less* democratic than another electoral system on
that particular dimension. It remains to be seen if we will also be able
to claim that one electoral system is more democratic than another
(Reeve and Ware, 1992: 3).

Evidence from five countries

Our empirical evidence comes from five countries: Bulgaria, Kenya,
Latvia, Mongolia and Nepal. The selection of countries has in part

Dahl's seven institutions of polyarchy:	The fourteen operational elements:
1 Elected officials	All Members of Parliament and the President (if any) must be politically accountable to the voters within time limits fixed in advance.
2 Free and fair elections	The weight of the votes of various voters should be identical.
	The electoral system – as well as its administration – should not be manipulated to the benefit of any political party or candidate. Electoral fraud and rigging – or malpractice during counting – should be avoided.
	Equal access to public-owned electronic media, newspapers and magazines must be provided for, at least for national political parties.
	Election-related violence or coercion must not occur.
3 Inclusive suffrage	The electorate should consist of all adults directly affected by the decisions of the body to be elected (Dahl, 1986a; May, 1978; Reeve and Ware, 1992: 26, 52).
	Registration procedures should include in the election register all individuals enfranchised (Harrop and Miller, 1987: 44–5).
4 The right to run for public office	All voters have the right to run for public office.
5 Freedom of expression	Freedom of speech must not be impeded.
	Freedom of assembly must not be impeded.
	All political parties and groupings should be allowed to contest elections, that is, to register.
6 Existence and availability of alternative information	The right to seek alternative information must not be impeded.
7 Associational autonomy	Freedom of organization must not be impeded.
	All kinds of political organizations should be allowed; there should be no discrimination against ethnic, racial, religious or other parties.

been determined by the author's experiences as an election law consultant and election observer. The main quality of the sample in a comparative perspective is, however, that it covers both former communist and non-communist countries, both Second and Third World countries, and both former one-party and 'non-party' states. Furthermore, the five countries have reached different levels of democracy during the last couple of years, even though they are all in the decision phase of transition to democracy. The kind of data collection used here allows a more updated discussion and categorization of recent developments than is often the case. (For relevant background on the countries see Ashley, 1990; Barkan, 1993; Batbayar, 1993; Bell et al., 1990; Borre et al., 1991; NEMU, 1993.)

Table 5.1 gives basic information about the five electoral systems. Factual information has been collected from a number of sources, including the author's in situ observations, but some of the information includes judgements open for discussion. Therefore, this table should be seen as only a first attempt to construct a comparative overview. It might be used for comparisons within individual countries as well as for comparisons between countries.

Nepal might function as an example of the first approach. After a popular uprising in the spring of 1990, political parties were legalized and an interim coalition government appointed. The main objective of this government was to ensure that a new constitution was implemented and multi-party elections held not later than May 1991. Following the promulgation of the constitution in November 1990 and the enactment of the electoral legislation in December/ January 1990/1991 (by the government, which had been given legislative power), elections were called for 12 May 1991 (Borre et al., 1991). Civil liberties, separation of powers, etc. are well provided for in the constitution, which also divides the legislature into two houses. The lower house is elected by plurality in 205 single-member constituencies by an electorate which is registered automatically. The upper house is partly elected indirectly, partly appointed by the King. Voting age is theoretically 18; in practice, however, somewhere between 18 and 19.

The main problem as regards the degree of electoral democracy was that the registration apparatus was unable to ensure (a) that all eligible voters were entered into the electoral register and (b) that those entered only appeared on the register in one constituency. The Chief Electoral Commissioner has estimated that between 5 and 10 per cent of the target electorate was not included, while he did not want to estimate the number of double registrations (Tiwari, 1992: 215–16; United States Election Observer Report, 1991: 20, 28). There is, however, no reason to suspect that the condition of the

Table 5.1   *Performance on fourteen indicators of electoral democracy in five countries, 1990–1993*

	Bulgaria	Kenya	Latvia	Mongolia	Nepal
Elected officials	Yes; 4-year terms	Yes; 5-year terms; **the President appoints 12 (of 200) MPs**	Yes; 3-year terms	Yes; 4-year terms	Yes; 5-year terms
Weight of votes	1990: ½ first past the post (FPTP); ½ PR (d'Hondt with 4% threshold). 1991: PR (d'Hondt with 4% threshold)	FPTP	PR (pure Sainte-Laguë with 4% threshold)	**Block vote; 26 multi-member districts (with 2, 3 or 4 seats); voters have 2, 3 or 4 votes respectively**	FPTP; **3% threshold (at the previous election)**
Electoral fraud	1990; some. 1991: Not to my knowledge	**Yes, some (but less than the losers claimed)**	No	Not to my knowledge	Not very significant
Equal access to mass media	Yes; to a reasonable degree	No	Yes; to a reasonable degree	Yes; guaranteed in electoral law	No
Election-related violence or coercion	**1990; Yes, but difficult to ascertain how much. 1991: Not to my knowledge**	**Yes, some**	No	No	Not a major problem

Table 5.1   *Continued*

	Bulgaria	Kenya	Latvia	Mongolia	Nepal
Electorate	M + F: 18+	M + F: 18+	M + F: 18+; non-Latvian residents (more than 30%) excluded	M + F: 18+	M + F: 18+; Indian residents in the Terai excluded
Registration	Voluntary; voters' list contained many errors	Voluntary; administration unsatisfactory; 15% or more not included for 'technical' reasons	Voting was based on the possession of passports	Automatic	Automatic; 5–10% not included; double registration
Right to run for office	Age: 21+; not holders of state posts	Age: 21+; must speak both English and Swahili; police, army and other state personnel cannot run; independent candidates not allowed	Age 21+; former or present KGB and security service personnel, etc. cannot run	Age 25+; all eligible Mongolian citizens	Age: 25+; a number of public employees are not allowed to run
Freedom of speech	Yes; constitutionally guaranteed	Yes, in principle	Yes	Yes; constitutionally guaranteed and emphasized in electoral law	Yes

Table 5.1 *Continued*

	Bulgaria	Kenya	Latvia	Mongolia	Nepal
Freedom of assembly	Yes; constitutionally guaranteed	**Not equal access to rally permits**	Yes	Yes; constitutionally guaranteed and emphasized in electoral law	Yes; constitutionally guaranteed
All political parties should be allowed to contest elections	**1991: Movement for Rights and Freedom had difficulties in registering**	**Islamic Party of Kenya (and several small parties) denied registration**	Yes; social organizations are also allowed to put up candidates	Yes	**Nepal Sadvabana Party was only hesitantly registered; four parties denied registration**
Right to and availability of alternative information	Yes; constitutionally guaranteed	Yes	Yes	Yes; constitutionally guaranteed	Yes; constitutionally guaranteed
Freedom of organization	Yes; constitutionally guaranteed	Registration still required	Yes	Yes	Registration still required
Formation of political parties should not be impeded	**Ethnic, racial and religious parties are not allowed**	**Religious parties cannot register**	No restrictions	No restrictions	**Communal- and sectarian-oriented parties cannot register**

Note: Bold type indicates elements of particular concern.

voters' register per se has jeopardized an unbiased outcome of the elections. Nevertheless, it has deprived a substantial proportion of the Nepalese voters of their voting rights, thereby denying them participation in appointing the parliamentary representatives, which cannot but reduce the legitimacy of parliament and government, however slightly. Other deviations from democratic norms and procedures in Nepal were:

1 obvious differences between political parties as regards media access and exposure during the election campaign;
2 that some political parties were denied registration;[3]
3 that young voters and some public employees were not allowed to run for public office;
4 that the weight of votes differed considerably, since the largest constituency had seventeen times as many voters as the smallest. However, the small constituencies are located in the Himalayas, where transport is both difficult and time-consuming.
5 The Nepalese Constitution requires that a party in order to register must have bagged at least 3 per cent of the national vote in the previous election.[4] This makes it virtually impossible for a small party to present itself to the electorate a second time. Therefore, it restricts the range of choice for the voters.
6 Only Nepalese citizens can register. Since the Terai region has many residents of Indian background, who depend primarily on decisions in the Nepalese Parliament, one can argue that in a true democracy they should be given the vote.

Compared to the pre-1990 situation, Nepal has come a long way towards electoral democratization. Apart from the problem of ensuring a higher quality in the registration process – which should be praised for being automatic – six areas, which in varying degrees can be seen as detrimental to reaching a full-scale electoral democracy, can be identified. Together, these areas of concern are almost coextensive with three of Dahl's institutions necessary for polyarchy, namely free and fair elections, inclusive suffrage, and the right to run for office. These institutions fall – more or less – within Dahl's dimension of inclusiveness (or participation). The dismissal of the dimension of inclusiveness by Coppedge and Reinicke (1991: 51) therefore seems somewhat precipitate (see also Hadenius, 1992: 39ff.).

How much do these various areas of concern detract from the overall democratic character of the 1991 general elections in Nepal? No definite answer will be provided here – and certainly not in quantitative terms – but there is still some way to go as regards institutional arrangements before the situation is fully acceptable from an ideal democratic point of view.[5] The situation as regards the remaining four institutional arrangements – to be summarized under the heading of liberalization – is obviously much better.

The various concerns are difficult to compare or to enter into an evaluation scheme. However, I shall argue that the two most important are the de facto denial of voting rights to a considerable number of otherwise eligible voters and the unequal access to mass media. The latter factor gave the major party an undue advantage. The electoral system chosen had a similar effect. But how important were these factors compared to others?

Some comparison problems

A comparison between Nepal and Bulgaria demonstrates that Bulgaria is closer than Nepal to the democratic ideal as represented by three of Dahl's institutional arrangements (free and fair elections, inclusive suffrage, and the right to run for office). The relative order of the two systems in this particular respect is thus evident.

A comparison between Latvia and Nepal (or Latvia and any of the countries) reveals that Latvia differs from the other countries in its denial (or postponement) of voting rights to a large proportion of its residents, that is, the Russians. The reasons for this policy are not difficult to understand, but Latvia nevertheless scores low on this indicator of electoral democracy.[6]

Exact evaluations are difficult, since they presuppose a clear position vis-á-vis the denial of voting rights to resident non-citizens. The position taken here is that the situations in Nepal and Latvia place these countries in a second and third position, respectively, after the other countries (Kenya is possibly in an intermediate position, because of the situation in North Eastern Province). Hadenius (1992: 39–42) has shown how one can pay attention to both suffrage requirements and the proportion of seats filled on some other basis than election. It is, however, problematic that neither Hadenius, nor Coppedge and Reinicke (1991) include a concern for the effectiveness of the registration procedures.

The de facto allocation of voting rights also depends on whether the systems rely on voluntary or automatic registration and the administrative capabilities of the registration systems (Harrop and Miller, 1987: 44f.). The relative order in this respect is Mongolia, Latvia and Bulgaria together, Nepal fourth, and Kenya fifth. In the Kenyan case, one has the impression that the registration system – including the issuance of national identification cards which is a prerequisite for being registered as a voter – was deliberately administered in such a way that some voters were effectively denied voting rights (*Kenya: Pre-election Assessment Report*, 1992; Macrory et al., 1992).

These two indicators of the degree to which Dahl's suffrage requirements are met, might be combined to allow us – at least in theory – to tell relatively precisely which percentage of the adult resident population is on the voters' list and which therefore might exercise voting rights. Even though it is difficult to establish reliable population figures, one can provide an estimate of relative scores in this respect: Mongolia: 1.00; Bulgaria: 0.97; Nepal: 0.87; Kenya: 0.86; and Latvia: 0.70.

If one multiplies this estimate with Hadenius' measure of the proportion of parliamentary seats filled in elections, a rather efficient measure of the franchise is arrived at, even when it remains an estimate. Since this factor only deviates from 1.0 in Kenya (where it is 0.93) the only change is Kenya, where the value drops to 0.80, while the other four remain as above. Thus, the rank order is stable.

The next concern is the degree to which the right to run for office is provided for. All five countries require that prospective candidates for parliament do not belong to the youngest age group: three have established an age limit of 21 years, while two require candidates to be 25 years old. Furthermore, a number of state employees are not allowed to run for office in Bulgaria, Kenya and Nepal, while Latvia has excluded people who are or have been linked to security services. Kenya also requires proficiency in two languages. This requirement is not a major obstacle for would-be candidates; it is more incriminating that political aspirants in Kenya are not allowed to run without the endorsement of a registered political party. In addition, one should not forget that a number of opposition candidates were physically prevented from handing in nomination papers during the prescribed period that was limited to a mere five hours.

How should these restrictions be compared? Again, it is theoretically possible to calculate (subject to the availability of relevant figures) what percentage of the electorate is allowed to stand for office. A qualitative judgement of the restrictions might be more relevant, but it is no easy task to carry out. Tentatively, Bulgaria, Latvia and Mongolia are placed in one group, with Nepal fourth and Kenya a clear fifth.

Free and fair elections?

After the comparisons of institutional requirements *within* one country and suffrage and eligibility requirements *between* countries, this section discusses Dahl's second institutional requirement – that elections must be free and fair and be accompanied by negligible or no coercion – on the basis of four indicators. These indicators are the weight of the votes, the occurrence of electoral fraud, the degree to which the political parties have equal access to the mass media, and the occurrence of election-related violence and coercion.

As regards the weight of the votes, the suffrage is equal in four of the countries, since each voter has one vote to cast, and since each vote counts as much as any other vote cast in the same constituency or electoral district. In Mongolia, however, voters have either two, three or four votes, depending on the number of seats in their multi-member constituency.[7] This system is called the 'block vote', and the decision system is plurality. For many good reasons, this electoral system is extremely rare on the national level.[8]

The weight of the votes is not only a question of how many votes each voter can cast. One must also include the equality of chances of success as well as the size of the electoral districts, since – as Reeve and Ware (1992: 21), among others, put it – a commitment to democracy is a commitment to political equality. The size of electoral districts is particularly important in 'first-past-the-post' systems, while the equality of chances of success refers to the individual voter's influence on the overall electoral outcome, which tends to be less equal in plurality and majority systems than in PR systems.

Different objectives pursued by different electoral systems might all be seen as compatible with democratic values (Lijphart, 1984). Consequently, there is no reason to claim that any of the systems considered here is undemocratic – with the possible exception of the Mongolian block vote. One can, however, argue that the weight of the votes should be measured by looking simultaneously at all three aspects of equality of suffrage (Garonne, 1992: 5; Poledna, 1988). The equality of chances of success is most pronounced in Latvia, followed by Bulgaria, Kenya, Nepal and Mongolia. Equality of voting power (for the lower house) is found in three states, while that principle is violated in Mongolia and Kenya, where the President alone appoints twelve MPs. Districting is not a problem in countries with multi-member districts (because seats usually are allocated to districts on a proportional basis), while it is a problem of traditional concern in Kenya and Nepal.[9] These considerations entail the conclusion that the order of the countries in this respect is Latvia, Bulgaria, Nepal, Kenya and Mongolia.

The fairness of an electoral system might also be assessed on the basis of the correspondence between the parties' share of the votes and share of the seats. Table 5.2 provides measures of this kind of performance.

Table 5.2   *Measures of electoral system performance*

	Bulgaria June 1990	Bulgaria Oct. 1991	Kenya Dec. 1992	Latvia June 1993	Mongolia June 1992	Nepal May 1991
Largest party: % seats − % votes	5.7%	11.5%	**26.1%**	3.6%	**35.2%**	14.2%
Largest party: majority manufactured or earned, or minority natural?	Majority earned	Minority natural	**Majority manufactured**	Minority natural	Majority earned	**Majority manufactured**
Effective number of electoral parties	2.8	4.2	4.2[1]	6.2	2.7	3.9
Effective number of parliamentary parties	2.4	2.4	2.8	5.1	1.2	2.5
r	12%	**42%**	**34%**	15%	**57%**	37%
D	5.4%	**24.8%**	−[2]	11.3%	**35.2%**	**19.3%**
Turn-out	90.8%	83.9%	66.1%[1]	89.4%	95.6%	65.1%
Invalid votes	3%	?	1–2%	?	6%	4.4%

[1] Based on in 170 constituencies, i.e. disregarding 17 constituencies with unopposed returns and one constituency where the vote was not available at the time of writing.

[2] Not calculated; D does not convey much information, when many returns are unopposed and some seats are filled without elections.

Bold type indicates elements of particular concern.

Three measures are used: (a) for the largest party – percentage of seats minus percentage of votes, and whether the electoral system produces a manufactured majority in parliament for that party, an earned majority, or a natural minority; (b) r, the reduction in the effective number of parties, going from electoral to parliamentary parties; and (c) D, Hanby's and Loosemore's index of disproportionality. (Definitions of these measures are found, for example, in Elklit, 1992; Lijphart, 1984; or Taagepera and Shugart, 1989.)

Evidently, Bulgaria (1990) and Latvia score best on the measures of electoral proportionality used here as operationalizations of 'electoral system fairness'. It is more difficult to make a clear distinction between the performances of the Bulgarian system of 1991,[10] Nepal and Kenya, but Mongolia obviously comes last. This rank order is no surprise, since PR countries on average score better than countries with plurality systems.

Electoral fraud has been a problem in Bulgaria and Kenya, but even in Kenya it was much less of a problem than both national and international observers were expecting before the December 1992 elections. Electoral fraud is here operationalized as all kinds of *election day* malpractice, including undue sending away of voters, partisan assistance to voters, putting extra ballot papers in the ballot boxes, counting 'errors' to the benefit of one's preferred party, etc. Obviously, other kinds of malpractice can be much more important than what happens on election day, as was the case in Kenya. These other issues are not seen as instances of electoral fraud as defined here, and they are treated in connection with the relevant elements in Table 5.1. Instances of small-scale electoral fraud also occurred in the Nepalese May 1991 election, but were not significant and did not affect the final outcome.

A major problem in democratizing countries is that the mass media are not used to providing equal access for the political parties during the campaign period. This does not amount to saying that political parties should be treated equally in all respects, since journalistic criteria should still decide day-to-day news coverage. The use of such criteria will, however, often be beneficial to the incumbent government; measures should therefore be taken to redress the ensuing imbalance. Experience shows how difficult it is, but the situation was arguably better in Mongolia and Bulgaria than in Nepal and Kenya. It is remarkable that Article 21 of the Mongolian Electoral Law provides for equal access to the electronic media during the election campaign.

Election-related incidents of violence and coercion did occur in Bulgaria in 1990 as well as in Kenya and Nepal. Obviously, it is difficult to state the precise amount of such violence and coercion since the reports about the incidents are also used as campaign ammunition as well as an excuse on the side of the losers.

If the four operationalizations of electoral fairness are taken together, Latvia comes out on top, followed by Mongolia, Bulgaria, Nepal and Kenya.

Can the five countries be rank-ordered?

The four remaining institutional arrangements, which are necessary in a democracy/polyarchy and which Dahl summarizes as the liberalization dimension, are less difficult to handle. First comes 'elected officials'. This institution is operationalized by the degree to which politicians are actually held accountable. This is the case in all five countries, even though the different length of the parliamentary terms indicates slightly varying degrees of accountability. Furthermore, one can question the degree of accountability to the electors in the case of the twelve Kenyan MPs who are not elected by the voters but are appointed by the President. Even though differences are small, a comparison leads to this order: Latvia first, Mongolia and Bulgaria together in second position, Nepal and Kenya last.

As regards the extensive protection of free expression, including criticism of the government of the day, the situation in all five countries has improved considerably compared to the situation before the democratization process took off. The freedom of speech is – generally speaking – not violated and the freedom of assembly is constitutionally guaranteed in four of the countries. In Kenya, however, there was during the year prior to the elections blatant discrimination against the opposition parties as regards the de facto access to rally permits, without which parties could only with difficulty address their members and potential voters.

It should also be noted that the third operational element under the heading of protection of free expression, that is, that political parties should be allowed to contest elections, is not totally accepted in all countries. This element is closely related to the last element, which requires that the formation of political parties should not be impeded. Three countries have constitutional provisions for denying registration of political parties of a more special orientation: ethnic, racial or religious parties are not allowed in Bulgaria (but the 'Movement for Justice and Freedom' was, however, registered for the 1991 elections after international pressure[11]), religious parties cannot register in Kenya (and the Islamic Party of Kenya was consequently denied registration), and communal and sectarian parties are not allowed in Nepal (where the Terai-based Sadvabana Party was nevertheless eventually registered). The ordering on this

Table 5.3 *A rank-ordered comparison of five countries on Dahl's institutions of polyarchy*

	1st	2nd	3rd	4th	5th
1 Elected officials	Latvia	Bulgaria+	Mongolia+	Nepal	Kenya
2 Free and fair elections	Latvia	Mongolia	Bulgaria	Nepal	Kenya
3 Inclusive suffrage	Mongolia	Bulgaria	Kenya+	Nepal+	Latvia
4 Right to run for office	Bulgaria+	Latvia+	Mongolia+	Nepal	Kenya
5 Freedom of expression	Latvia+	Mongolia+	Bulgaria	Nepal	Kenya
6 Alternative information	Bulgaria+	Kenya+	Latvia+	Mongolia+	Nepal+
7 Associational autonomy	Latvia+	Mongolia+	Bulgaria	Kenya	Nepal

Note: '+' indicates a tie. Such countries are ordered alphabetically

variable is straightforward: Latvia and Mongolia in one group, Bulgaria and Nepal together in a second group, Kenya last.

The availability of alternative information is not – at least not in principle – a problem in any of the countries as the situation and the technological possibilities have improved during the last few years. It is, however, still a problem that the lack of economic resources makes the acquisition of such information a privilege for the few.

As regards the freedom to form organizations, the situation for the political parties has already been touched upon. The registration of other organizations has previously been required – and applications often declined – in all five countries. The situation is now different, even though remnants of the old systems are found in Nepal and Kenya – for example in the form that various tiny groupings were denied registration.

The rank-orderings on Dahl's seven institutions of polyarchy have been entered in Table 5.3. This table also represents a first attempt; it is therefore open for discussion whether some of the rankings (including the ties) should have been carried out differently.

Conclusion

The discussion of degrees of electoral democracy in five countries demonstrates how difficult it is to measure and compare such degrees. This assertion runs counter to the picture painted by the democracy measurement industry, which classifies political systems and their progress towards democracy with surprising degrees of precision: Freedom House uses a seven-point scale (*Freedom Review*, January – February 1993; Gastil, 1991; McColm et al., 1991), while UNDP has previously used an additive Human Freedom Index with countries obtaining scores from 0 to 38 (1991: 20). UNDP has recently published a refinement in the form of a composite Political Freedom Index (1992: 28–33), which goes a long way towards covering not only political freedom in a narrow sense, but democracy as broadly as Kusterer (1992: 23) argues the concept should be understood.

Hadenius (1992: 36–71) has presented an index of democracy. In his indexation of 132 Third World countries, he takes into consideration a considerable number of relevant factors, some of which come under the heading 'elections', others under 'political freedoms'. Hadenius' solution regarding the inclusion of the universality of the suffrage is as convincing as it is simple. The impressive degree of precision (Hadenius, 1992: 61–2) is, however, more apparent than real, since the basis is an allocation of absolute points to purely ordinal categories. Even though Hadenius discusses some of the issues, it appears that not all problems concerning dimensionality and assignment of weights to individual factors have yet been solved.

The same might be said of other recent contributions to the discussion of measurement of democracy. Bollen's (1991) rejection of ordinal scale measurement reflects his insistence on the continuous character of the variables in question. But this does not imply that the scale level is higher than ordinal. Coppedge and Reinicke (1991) follow another avenue in their unidimensional and rather crude categorization of countries according to the degree to which they approach polyarchy. Their solution is still interesting, but their lack of differentiation between countries is a serious drawback. The sample of countries used here has been subjected to their categorization scheme and Bulgaria, Mongolia and Nepal all end up in category 1. Tables 5.1 to 5.3 above have, however, documented that they are not that similar!

One of the elements in UNDP's Political Freedom Index is 'political participation', which by and large covers what is here called the degree of electoral democracy. Each element is graded on a scale from 0 to 10. Unfortunately, political considerations made UNDP decide *not* to publish gradings for individual countries, even though the grading obviously has been done.[12] Gastil has also put forward a proposal for an indicator system for democratic development (discussed in Kusterer, 1992: 31ff.), which relates very much to the field of electoral democratization.

Dahl's *ideal-type*-concept of democracy is easily understandable, and it is conceptually attractive to see systems of government as situated at various distances from perfect democracy and to conceive of democratization processes as processes which bring systems of government closer to that ideal. But the theoretical concept is not easily operationalized, partly because it is extremely multidimensional, partly because there is no agreement about levels of measurement and the weight of the various dimensions in an overall composite measure.

The insistence here on the multidimensionality of the concept of electoral democracy, and the inclination to maintain that most measurements are ordinal scale level, calls for a factorization of the correlation matrices between rankings on the fourteen dimensions in order to see if an intelligible pattern with a manageable number of factors/dimensions emerges.[13] However, the exercise revealed no such pattern.

This entails the conclusion that the theoretical concepts of democracy and degrees of approximations to that *ideal point* cannot easily –if at all – be operationalized in a manner which does justice to the many different political, administrative, social and cultural settings in which electoral democratization takes place.

The title of this chapter asked if the degree of electoral democracy is measurable. Therefore, the patient reader should expect an answer to that question, if not before, then in this final section. The answer appears to be that the question is more complicated than expected – and also more so than one should expect on the basis of recent contributions to the literature (Bollen, 1991; Coppedge and Reinicke, 1991; Hadenius, 1992; Sørensen, 1993: 17ff.).

Dahl's theoretical concept of democracy is, however, clear enough – in spite of its multidimensionality – and so is the concept of electoral democracy as an approximation to that ideal on one or more of its constituent dimensions. Operationalizations of these concepts must, however, pay attention to basic methodological considerations regarding scale level, data availability and problems of weighting the various dimensions – not to mention problems of validity and reliability (which have recently attracted some attention). And how should the dynamic of the democratization process itself be included, that is, what weight should be given to such factors as the length of the process, its progress so far, or the democratic commitment of the actors?

The weight of the various elements of the democratization process has only been touched upon, one reason being that it is not possible to defend convincingly a position saying that one element is x or y times more important for the advancement of electoral democratization than some other element. It is no solution to say – as did UNDP

(1991) – that all elements carry the same weight. But the problem remains: is the quality of voter registration less important than equal access for the political parties to the mass media? Or is a non-partisan administration of the issuance of rally permits more important than equal possibilities for registration of all would-be political parties, no matter how tiny?

One evident conclusion appears to be that detailed measurements of degrees of electoral democracy should be avoided, since that most certainly will involve serious violations of basic rules of methodology.

Nevertheless, the theoretical idea of a gradual and comparable approximation to an ideal concept of democracy is maintainable, and there is no reason to drop the idea that various processes of democratization can be compared if one remembers that such comparisons must necessarily rely on multidimensional ordinal scale measurement. Consequently, one should desist from saying more than 'This system is more democratic than that' or 'The process of electoral democratization has brought country X closer to the democratic ideal than country Y'. This is exactly what the scale of polyarchy developed by Coppedge and Reinicke (1991) permits, but only between their ten or eleven main categories, not within them.

Building on Dahl's distinction between the democratization dimensions of inclusiveness and liberalization, Svensson (1991) has argued that the liberalization dimension has been more important than the dimension of inclusiveness in the processes of democratization in Eastern Europe. The discussion here of Bulgaria and Latvia supports this interpretation. One can even argue that this preponderance of liberalization as compared to participation is also the case in Kenya, Mongolia and Nepal. Coppedge and Reinicke (1991: 51f.) arrive at the same conclusion, which almost make them dismiss this latter dimension; that, obviously, is to go too far.

It thus appears that there is no way in which one can arrive at indisputable classifications of the degree of electoral democracy. The main reason for this position is that it is not possible to agree on the weight to attach to each of the constituent factors and dimensions. How shall one compare non-allocation of voting rights to non-Latvian residents to other basic issues, especially if the solution proposed by Hadenius is not usable (even if for other reasons)?

It appears that the only way out of the impasse is to relate the systems under scrutiny to each other on Dahl's two dimensions as in Figure 5.1 (see also Svensson, 1991: 56). It goes without saying that the figure should only be seen as an illustration of the idea, while no particular importance should be attached to distances between the five data points. In this sense, the degree of electoral democracy is,

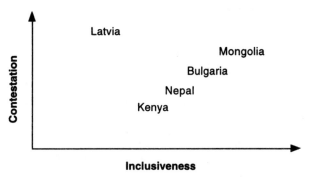

Figure 5.1 *Contestation and inclusiveness*

indeed, measurable and progress towards higher degrees of democracy/polyarchy can be illustrated graphically.

Notes

This chapter has benefited from the comments and assistance of Øystein Gaasholt, Tom Mackie, Peter Nannestad, Palle Svensson and Georg Sørensen, and from the participants in the ECPR workshop on 'Indices of Democratization'. Remaining errors and ambiguities are my own.

1 I shall, however, use 'democratic' synonymously with 'polyarchic', if for no other reason than accommodation to everyday language.

2 Or thirteen, if one considers the right to form political parties and the right to have one's political party registered for election as only one element.

3 These denials were constitutionally correct; the claim is that it is still undemocratic to deny some citizens the right to form a political party, the purpose of which is to contest elections orderly, and to deny such parties registration.

4 Most advisers advised against this clause, which in the first draft was even set at 5 per cent and which was only in the final editions suspended for the first elections! One reason for our advice was that electoral thresholds are superfluous in 'first-past-the-post' electoral systems. The function of thresholds is to discriminate against parties, which shall not be allowed to participate in the allocation of supplementary seats in PR systems.

5 I nevertheless fully agree with Diamond (1992: 36), who claims that the Nepalese democratization development is so impressive and has such inspirational potential that USAID should not slate Nepal for a cut in its development aid.

6 Rustow (1970: 350) stresses that it is a background condition of a durable and irreversible transition to democracy that questions of national unity are settled.

7 The twenty-six multi-member constituencies coincide with the administrative middle-level districts, the *aimags*.

8 It was, however, used in Nepal in the 1981 and 1986 national *panchayat* elections in 37 two-member constituencies, where each voter had two votes to cast. The remaining 38 seats were elected in single-member constituencies.

9 In both countries, the largest constituency has 15–17 times as many registered voters as the smallest.

10 A major reason for the difference between Bulgaria 1990 and 1991 is that a higher proportion of the voters in 1991 than in 1990 voted for parties which eventually got more than 4 per cent of the vote. Consequently, one cannot conclude that the 1990 electoral system produced a more proportional result than the 1991 system would have done had it been in force in 1990.

11 The former Communists still claim that the registration of MRF was unconstitutional.

12 The official explanation of the non-publication of scores for individual countries is data incompleteness and problems of methodology. If this should be taken seriously, UNDP should itself desist from publishing analyses as in Table 2.1 in *Human Development Report 1992* (1992: 32).

13 Peter Nannestad has kindly taken care of the computer work involved (using the PRELIS-program) and has also helped with the interpretation of the results.

References

Ashley, S. (1990) 'Bulgaria', *Electoral Studies*, 9: 312–18.

Barkan, J. D. (1993) 'Kenya: lessons from a flawed election', *Journal of Democracy*, 4: 85–99.

Batbayar, T. (1993) 'Mongolia in 1992: back to one party rule', *Asian Survey*, 33: 61–6.

Bell, J. D., Gould, R. A., Lasham, C. E., Sklar, M. H., Smolka, R. G., Yasharoff, N. J. and Kimball, R. D. (1990) *An Orderly Rebellion: Bulgaria's Transition from Dictatorship to Democracy*. Washington, DC: IFES.

Bollen, K. A. (1991) 'Political democracy: conceptual and measurement traps', in A. Inkeles (ed.), *On Measuring Democracy: Its Consequences and Concomitants*. New Brunswick, NJ and London: Transaction Publishers. pp. 3–20.

Borre, O., Pandey, S. R. and Tiwari, C. K. (1991) 'The Nepalese election of 1991', *Electoral Studies*, 10: 357–62.

Coppedge, M. and Reinicke, W. H. (1991) 'Measuring polyarchy', in A. Inkeles (ed.), *On Measuring Democracy: Its Consequences and Concomitants*. New Brunswick, NJ and London: Transaction Publishers. pp. 47–68.

Dahl, R. A. (1971) *Polyarchy: Participation and Opposition*. New Haven, CT and London: Yale University Press.

Dahl, R. A. (1986a) 'Procedural democracy', in *Democracy, Liberty, and Equality*. Oslo: Norwegian University Press. pp. 191–225. (First published in P. Laslett and J. Fishkin (eds), *Philosophy, Politics, and Society* [5th series]. Oxford: Basil Blackwell, 1979. pp. 97–133.)

Dahl, R. A. (1986b) 'Polyarchy, pluralism, and scale', in *Democracy, Liberty, and Equality*. Oslo: Norwegian University Press. pp. 226–43. (First published 1984 in *Scandinavian Political Studies*, 7: 225–41.)

Dahl, R. A. (1989) *Democracy and Its Critics*. New Haven, CT and London: Yale University Press.

Diamond, L. (1992) 'Promoting democracy', *Foreign Policy*, 87: 26–46.

Diamond, L., Linz, J. J. and Lipset, S. M. (eds) (1988) *Democracy in Developing Countries. Vol. 2: Africa*. Boulder, CO: Lynne Rienner.

Elklit, J. (1992) 'The best of both worlds? The Danish electoral system 1915–20 in a comparative perspecive', *Electoral Studies*, 11: 189–205. (Also in P. Gundelach and K. Siune (eds), *From Voters to Participants: Essays in Honour of Ole Borre*. Aarhus: Politica, 1992. pp. 236–54.)

Garonne, P. (1992) *Electoral Law: General Principles and Regulatory Levels.* Strasbourg: Council of Europe.

Gastil, R. D. (1991) 'The comparative study of freedom: experiences and suggestions', in A. Inkeles (ed.), *On Measuring Democracy: Its Consequences and Concomitants.* New Brunswick, NJ and London: Transaction Publishers. pp. 21–46.

Gladdish, K. (1993) 'The primacy of the particular', *Journal of Democracy,* 4: 53–65.

Hadenius, A. (1992) *Democracy and Development.* Cambridge: Cambridge University Press.

Harrop, M. and Miller, W. L. (1987) *Elections and Voters: A Comparative Introduction.* London: Macmillan.

Kenya: Pre-election Assessment Report (1992) November. Washington, DC: International Republican Institute.

Kusterer, K. (1992) 'What is it, how is it encouraged, and how is its progress measured?' Paper for the International Conference on the Democratic Process in South Asia, Colombo, Sri Lanka, 19–22 August.

Lijphart, A. (1984) *Democracies: Patterns of Majoritarian and Consensus Government in Twenty-One Countries.* New Haven, CT and London: Yale University Press.

Lijphart, A. (1991) 'Constitutional choices for new democracies', *Journal of Democracy,* 2: 72–84.

Lyager, P. P. (1991) 'Valgmaraton i Bulgarien', *Vindue mod øst,* 17: 12.

McColm, R. B. et al. (1991) *Freedom in the World: Political Rights and Civil Liberties 1990–1991.* New York: Freedom House.

Macrory, P. F. J., Elklit, J. and Mendez, R. S. (1992) *Facing the Pluralist Challenge: Human Rights and Democratization in Kenya's December 1992 Multi-Party Elections.* Washington, DC: International Human Rights Law Group.

May, J. D. (1978) 'Defining democracy: a bid for coherence and consensus', *Political Studies,* 26: 1–14.

NEMU (1993) *The Multi-Party General Elections in Kenya 29 December 1992. The Report of the National Election Monitoring Unit (NEMU).* Nairobi: NEMU.

Poledna, T. (1988) 'Wahlrechtsgrundsätze und kantonale Parlamentswahlen'. PhD thesis, University of Zurich.

Reeve, A. and Ware, A. (1992) *Electoral Systems: A Comparative and Theoretical Introduction.* London: Routledge.

Rustow, D. A. (1970) 'Transitions to democracy: toward a dynamic model', *Comparative Politics,* 2: 337–63.

Sørensen, G. (1993) *Democracy and Democratization: Processes and Prospects in a Changing World.* Boulder, CO: Westview Press.

Svensson, P. (1991) 'The liberalization of Eastern Europe', *Journal of Behavioral and Social Sciences,* 34: 54–64.

Taagepera, R. and Shugart, M. S. (1989) *Seats and Votes: The Effects and Determinants of Electoral Systems.* New Haven, CT and London: Yale University Press.

Tiwari, C. K. (1992) 'Electoral experience and process in Nepal', in P. Gundelach and K. Siune (eds), *From Voters to Participants: Essays in Honour of Ole Borre.* Aarhus: Politica. pp. 208–23.

UNDP (1991) *Human Development Report 1991.* Published for the United Nations Development Programme. New York and Oxford: Oxford University Press.

UNDP (1992) *Human Development Report 1992.* Published for the United Nations Development Programme. New York and Oxford: Oxford University Press.

United States Election Observer Report (1991) *The Kingdom of Nepal Parliamentary Elections, May 12, 1991.* Washington, DC: IFES.

6

Primary Control and Auxiliary Precautions
A Comparative Study of Democratic
Institutions in Six Nations

Stuart Weir

> But what is government itself, but the greatest of all reflections on human nature. . . . In framing a government which is to be administered by men over men the great difficulty lies in this: you must first enable the government to control the governed; and in the next place oblige it to control itself. *A dependence on the people is, no doubt, the primary control on government: but experience has taught mankind the necessity of auxiliary precautions.*
> James Madison, US democrat and President, 1788 (Hamilton et al., 1961: 322; emphasis added)

> [Constitutional codes] are meaningless unless they exist within a country which has a political culture that renders them viable . . . the greatest protector of citizens' rights in the UK are citizens themselves. . . . The protector of freedom in the end is the political culture, not some document, however weighty
> John Patten, British government minister, 1991

The appeal of democracy comes from the idea that the citizens of a country govern their own society – the original Greek, *dēmokratiā*, literally means 'people power'. In a modern liberal democracy, of course, people do not rule directly, but through a representative system of government, in which by means of fair and regular elections they have the ultimate power of the vote over their elected representatives. If that system is to fulfil its representational obligations, it ought broadly to seek to satisfy the two basic principles set out in Beetham's chapter in this volume: the first is that of popular control over political representatives and processes of decision-making; the second is that of political equality in the exercise of that control.

Previous attempts to measure the quality of democracy in different states have been based upon a description of the institutional arrangements common to the established democracies of Europe and the Anglo-Saxon world. Points are then awarded on a scale for each component that is found to be present in the various systems under scrutiny. The disadvantages of this approach are that it rarely explains precisely what is democratic about the institutions specified; that the institutions and the relationships between them are not closely inspected, thus providing an analysis that fails to consider the strengths and weaknesses of institutional processes individually and in relation to the operation of the whole system; and that the criteria are too coarse for the fine-grained analysis necessary to discriminate between the established democracies themselves.

The Democratic Audit of the UK seeks to overcome these problems by refining Beetham's two basic principles into sets of questions, which are then applied to render a descriptive analysis of a given state's institutional arrangements in systemic terms, measuring systematically how far the two principles are satisfied across a wide spectrum of institutional processes and political practice. These questions, or 'democratic criteria', necessarily elicit answers which are relative; for, as Beetham writes, democracy is not to be regarded as an 'all-or-nothing affair', which a state either has or does not have, but as a matter of degree, according to how far the principles of popular control and political equality are realized in practice (Beetham, 1993).

An 'auditing' process, based on these criteria, will make use of both 'quantitative' and 'qualitative' measuring techniques – statistical data, sociological studies, opinion surveys, comparative materials, international instruments, case law, academic analyses, the testimony of practitioners and commentators (Weir, 1993). It is, for example, possible to assemble quantitative data measuring the 'deviation from proportionality' of different electoral systems, at national and regional levels (see Dunleavy and Margetts' chapter, this volume). Such data advance the analysis of democratization beyond the 'checklist' approach to measure exactly how far each state provides citizens with votes of equal value and political parties with a return in seats proportionate to the votes they have won. But questions of 'control' and 'accountability' are not subject, as are electoral outcomes, to quantitative measurement in a context-specific setting. Answers to such questions may benefit from statistical data, but they cannot be reduced to precise figures. Ultimately, such analysis is a matter of judgement; one of the purposes of the Audit is to refine and systematize the process of judgement.

The purpose and processes of comparison

One way of improving the quality of judgement is to measure the democratic process and practice in the UK against the arrangements in other developed liberal democracies. This chapter describes a preliminary attempt to compare the institutional arrangements of the UK with those in five other democracies. The purpose is not only to provide details of process and practice against which the democratic system in the UK can be measured, but also to establish a level of 'best practice' with regard to the different aspects of democracy being audited. The tables abstract significant detailed information to provide comparative data at a glance; they will accompany extensive analysis of arrangements in the UK in the text of the Democratic Audit, with more detailed information, where relevant, about particular countries. We have chosen for comparison five liberal-democratic countries with similar (high) standards of living and relatively sophisticated, stable political systems:

1 *France*: the UK's nearest neighbour in north-western Europe, a member of the European Union (EU), and, like Britain, a former imperial power. (Further, President de Gaulle incorporated aspects of the UK tradition of 'strong government' into France's governing system.)
2 *Germany*: another EU partner in north-western Europe, with a constitution framed in part by the UK after the 1939–45 war.
3 *Denmark*: a smaller EU partner and a monarchy with a relatively peaceful political evolution over the last few centuries – an important aspect of the UK's polity.
4 *Australia*: an example of an original 'Westminster model' system being modified in a country with an advanced economy.
5 *The USA*: the most frequently cited model for liberal democracy which shares, but rebelled against, the historic political tradition of Britain.

Assembling informed judgements

The process of establishing the comparative tables is still in train. Some standard comparative texts[1], which set out the formal constitutional arrangements, were used as a base for further study. The aim was to set down how each country's institutions perform in practice; what role they play in the different political systems; and how far they, singly and in combination, are able to fulfil the Audit's basic principles. Detailed questionnaires, setting out the formal positions and posing questions regarding institutions and their relationships with each other, were distributed to political scientists, journalists and others with expert knowledge, in the five countries, and their responses were analysed and incorporated into the tables. This process was supplemented with interviews.[2] In effect, the Audit has assembled a series of 'informed judgements', all of them qualified by cross-checking and consultation among the respondents. As the Audit's resources are limited, I have been able to collect in the tables only an incomplete picture of the different institutional arrangements, particularly at local level. I would be grateful for any comments on the data assembled. These data represent at least a beginning of a type of analysis that may prove fruitful in other arenas, possibly, for example, within the context of a European Audit, taking in the member states (and possibly applicant states) of the European Union.[3]

The tables are designed specifically for comparison between the UK and other democratic polities; and although the two basic principles adopted by the Audit are intended to be universal in nature, the priorities adopted for the tables and the phraseology inevitably reflect culturally specific preoccupations. Nevertheless, in principle, the tables should be capable of use in any comparable polity, and the Audit is organizing joint seminars with academics and others from India, Australia and elsewhere to test their general applicability, and to develop more universal criteria.

The question of political cultures

The tables published with this commentary concentrate entirely upon electoral processes and institutional arrangements. They do not deal with the political culture of the various countries. The political culture of a nation is as crucial to its democratic qualities as its institutional arrangements, though there is, of course, a complex interaction: the political culture shapes the institutions and will in turn be affected by the institutional arrangements. Danish political culture, for example, exhibits a strong desire for forms of direct democracy, evident in local networks of elected authorities and participatory service agencies. In 1953, this tendency led directly to the abolition of the second chamber and the introduction in its place of national referendums as a check on controversial or potentially unpopular measures by the popular chamber. In Germany, the initially unpopular Basic Law, imposed by the allied forces after 1945, has contributed to a culture of concern for constitutional values and has itself become the national institution in which German people take most pride.[4] In France, the instability of parliamentary regimes under the postwar Fourth Republic led to widespread frustration with 'weak government' and Charles de Gaulle came to power in 1958 not only to deal with the Algerian crisis, but also with a broad mandate from the French people to introduce constitutional changes creating a stronger presidency and executive.

An aggregate assessment of the UK's democratic institutions

The tables largely deal with two aspects of representative democracy: the means by which what Madison describes as the 'primary control' of fair and regular elections is brought to bear upon government; and the 'auxiliary precautions' taken to buttress popular control between elections. Within the rubric of the Audit, these precautions concern the rules for distributing powers between the different institutions of government, defining how those institutions exercise their powers and are made accountable for their use – rules which, for example, ensure that the government, or executive as a whole, is made democratically accountable to parliament, on the one hand, and subject to the rule of law, via the judiciary, on the other. The legislature's powers of scrutiny, the transparency of government decision-making, the existence of countervailing institutions and 'checks and balances', and the extent of executive consultation and responsiveness are all significant indicators of the degree of popular control in any representative system of government.

For any government, the bite of democracy lies ultimately in the prospect of losing office after an election; as the Irish writer Joyce Cary observed, 'The only good government is a bad government in the hell of a fright' (1944). But elections normally occur at intervals of up to four or more years. If democracy is to take a lasting hold on the executive, the mechanisms of popular control between elections must be effective on a continuing basis, as well as the electoral system itself providing an effective instrument of direct accountability.

Protecting the constitution and political rights

The tables overall confirm the well-known 'exceptionalism' of the British system of government. Britain is the only state without a written constitution; many constitutional rules of its 'unwritten' constitution are embodied in non-legal 'conventions' which a government may modify, tear up or ignore. The UK is the only state of the six in which there is no judicial body charged with the defence of its constitutional arrangements; in which legal-constitutional rules are not given enhanced status and special protection by the courts; and in which constitutional laws may be changed or abolished as easily as any other laws. (Tables 6.1 and 6.2.) The two 'Westminster model' countries – Australia and the UK – are again exceptional in having no specific domestic guarantee in writing of political and civil rights.[5] In Australia, the High Court has creatively construed the original act establishing the state as a democracy to uphold the political rights and freedoms it considers to be constitutive of democracy. The UK is a signatory of the European Convention of Human Rights. Thus, the political and civil rights of UK citizens are protected, albeit at a considerable remove in terms of time and costs as well as distance, by the European Court of Human Rights in Strasbourg (Table 6.3). The UK is alone among the six nations in leaving high judicial appointments to the discretion of the executive alone (through the Lord Chancellor, a cabinet minister, who takes professional advice) (Table 6.4).

'Primary control': electoral arrangements

In analysing electoral arrangements, we have left aside certain basic matters, such as the safety and secrecy of the ballot, and largely concentrated on electoral *systems*. The results reflect the diversity of electoral systems in use among democratic states, though the divide between the Anglo-Saxon (Westminster) and European models is also evident. Broadly, elections in both the UK and USA are conducted on the early nineteenth-century plurality rule (or 'first-past-the-post') system in individual constituencies. Australia employs the alternative vote (AV), a variant of plurality rule systems, for elections to the popular chamber (and for senate elections, a rarely used proportional system, the single transferable vote (STV), devised in nineteenth-century Britain). For elections to the popular chamber, Denmark and Germany both combine very different constituency-based elections with a 'top-up' element – in Denmark, national; in Germany, regional – to achieve a broadly proportional result. France employs the non-proportional 'double ballot' system (Table 6.5).

British political culture is the product of a historic tradition of 'strong government', which has given 'legitimacy' to the existence of a very powerful executive and an electoral system that has disproportionately swollen the parliamentary majority of the leading party in an election. The argument is that a single-party executive commanding a working majority in the legislature will provide more effective government and will be the more clearly accountable at the subsequent election. This reckoning can produce rough justice in a two-party polity, so long as the electoral bias is 'neutral' as between two well-matched parties. In Britain, the 'swing of the pendulum' is especially important; for in the absence of legally entrenched guarantees of democratic practice and political and civil rights, strict electoral discipline is necessary to ensure that neither party abuses the 'conventions' that serve in place of such guarantees.

Table 6.1   *Basic constitutional structures*

Country	State form	State structure	Head of state	Effective executive head	Executive–legislative relationship	Second chamber	Second chamber's powers	Voting systems[1]
Australia	Monarchy	Federal	Hereditary monarchy (UK Crown represented by Governor-General)	Prime Minister	Unified	Directly elected. Equal representation for states not electors.	Equal with popular chamber but cannot amend budget	Mixed: single transferable vote (proportional) for second chamber; alternative vote for popular chamber
Denmark	Monarchy	Unitary	Hereditary monarchy	Prime Minister	Unified	None	No second chamber	Proportional: complex system of multi-member constituencies with national 'top-up'
France	Republic	Unitary	President, elected by popular vote	Hybrid – President and Prime Minister	Partial unification – no assembly powers over executive actions of President	Indirectly elected	Equal with popular chamber – depending on government	Double ballot in single-member constituencies

Table 6.1 *Continued*

Country	State form	State structure	Head of state	Effective executive head	Executive–legislative relationship	Second chamber	Second chamber's powers	Voting systems[1]
Germany	Republic	Federal	President elected by legislature	Prime Minister	Unified	Appointed by state governments	Equal for certain matters – otherwise qualified veto	Proportional: party list 'top-up' to balance constituency results
UK	Monarchy	Unitary	Hereditary monarchy	Prime Minister	Unified	Hereditary, plus bishops of established church, law lords and 'life peers' appointed by government	Suspensory powers only	'First-past-the-post' elections in single-member constituencies
USA	Republic	Federal	President, elected by popular vote[2]	President	Separation of powers	Directly elected by state electorates	Equal – but the chambers have primacy in different areas	'First-past-the-post' in single-member constituencies

[1] See Table 6.5 for further details of electoral systems.
[2] Through an electoral college.

Table 6.2   *Protection for the constitution*

Country	What body protects the constitution against unconstitutional laws?	How do laws get challenged on their constitutionality? How easy is it for ordinary citizens to do this?	How easy is it for the government to amend the constitution?
Australia	The High Court*	In the course of hearing cases. Technically this is open to all citizens although in practice expense may limit access.	**Difficult** Must be approved in a referendum both by a majority of voters in the country as a whole and by majorities in at least 4 out of the 6 states
Denmark	The Supreme Court	If cases are brought. In practice, the court has never found a law to be unconstitutional.	**Very difficult** Must be passed by successive parliaments with an intervening election and approved by a majority of at least 40% of the electorate in a referendum
France	The Constitutional Council (the Council of State for administrative matters)	On appeal by the President of the Republic, the Prime Minister, or the President of or 60 members of one of the chambers of parliament	**Not easy** Can either be passed by a simple majority in both chambers of parliament and then validated in a referendum or be passed with a 60% majority in a joint session. (If change is proposed by parliament, a referendum is compulsory.)

Table 6.2 *Continued*

Country	What body protects the constitution against unconstitutional laws?	How do laws get challenged on their constitutionality? How easy is it for ordinary citizens to do this?	How easy is it for the government to amend the constitution?
Germany	The Federal Constitutional Court*	Through litigation, complaints from individual citizens or referrals from governments (state as well as federal) or the lower chamber of parliament. Help with legal costs is available.	**Part immutable, part difficult** The constitution has two parts: the first can never be changed (it includes protection for democracy and freedoms and rights); changes to the second part require two-thirds majorities in both chambers of parliament
UK	No such body	It is not possible to challenge laws on their constitutionality	**Easy** No written constitution. Any government can change the constitutional arrangements in the course of a parliament.
USA	The Supreme Court*	In the course of hearing cases	**Very difficult** Constitutional changes require a two-thirds majority in both houses of Congress as well as ratification by at least 38 of the 50 states

* State courts protect the constitutions of each state.

Table 6.3   *Protection for political and civil rights*

Country	Does the constitution contain protections for individual political and civil rights?	Have the domestic courts been active in protecting rights and freedoms?
Australia	Not formally. The constitution is a skeletal document which has no Bill of Rights, but contains provisions relating to discrimination by state governments between Australian citizens, freedom of religion and trial by jury.	An activist High Court has recently ruled that the original act intended to set up a democracy and has used this interpretation to uphold the rights and freedoms it considers necessary to a democracy
Denmark	Yes	The Supreme Court may overturn a decision by a minister if it contravenes customary or written rules but will not go beyond interpreting such existing rules. It is not an active court in the American sense.
France	Yes, by virtue of the 1789 Declaration of Rights and the preamble to the 1946 constitution	On occasion
Germany	Yes, afforded extra protection because they are in the immutable part of the constitution	Yes, active with generous interpretation of rights but also balancing them against 'practical political reality' and security requirements (such as in the 1962 *Spiegel* affair)
UK	No – there is no constitution	Ad hoc and unsystematic support, which relies on the common law
USA	Yes	Yes, very active, sometimes with very wide interpretation

Table 6.4 *Appointments to the highest court*

Country	How are the members of the highest court selected?	Who controls these appointments?	What is their normal term of office?	Can they be removed prematurely? and, if so, how?
Australia	The federal cabinet chooses them after consultation with state governments	The government	Must retire at 70	Only by a resolution by both chambers of parliament on the grounds of 'proved misbehaviour or incapacity'. This has never been done.
Denmark	They are chosen by the cabinet (on the nomination of the Minister of Justice) and formally appointed by the monarch. The nominee has to lead 3 cases before the court which has a (so far unused) power of rejection.	The Supreme Court	Must retire at 70	Judges under 65 can only be removed by judicial sentence of the court itself. Judges between 65 and 70 can be forced to retire (but continue to receive a salary until they reach 70).
France	The President and presidents of the two chambers of parliament each appoint one-third of the members. Former Presidents are ex officio members but never sit.	The three presidents (these are personal appointments)	9-year non-renewable terms	No provision in the constitution – they serve relatively short terms anyway
Germany	The two chambers of parliament each appoint half of the judges. A judge needs a two-thirds majority in the Bundestag or in the appropriate Bundesrat committee to be appointed.	Parliament	12-year terms	They can only be removed on the motion of the Court itself
UK	The monarch appoints them on the recommendation of the Lord Chancellor and the government	The government	Must retire at 70 (with provision for five-year extension)	They may be removed by the Queen (i.e. the executive) on an address presented by both Houses of Parliament
USA	The President selects them but they must then be confirmed in office by a majority of the Senate	The government and Congress	Life, on good behaviour	Congress can remove them by means of impeachment

Note: The two 'Westminster model' countries stand out for the total discretion afforded to their executives in appointing top judges.

Table 6.5   *Elections to the popular chamber*

Country	Electoral system (all are directly elected)	Deviation from proportionality (%)*	Election year
Australia	**Alternative vote** Single-member constituencies. Voters rank candidates in order of preference. The votes for the lowest-scoring candidate are redistributed to their next preferences and this process is repeated until one candidate has an absolute majority.	16.7	1990
Denmark	**Proportional** 185 seats are distributed between multi-member constituencies of 2–21 members. Ballots are complex, allowing voters different ways of registering a preference. Then 40 'top-up' seats are distributed nationally to ensure proportionality, subject to a 2% threshold.	4	1988
France	**Double ballot** People vote in single-member constituencies. If no candidate wins an overall majority in the first ballot, candidates with less than 12.5% of registered votes are eliminated and there is a run-off ballot.	17.3	1988
Germany	**Party list** People cast two votes: the first for an MP in a single-member constituency, and a second 'list' vote for party lists. Half the seats are allocated in constituency contests on the basis of the first ballot; the rest are then allocated within each state to rebalance the parties so that each ends up with seats in proportion to their 'list' vote in that state (not their national vote). Parties must win 5% of the national vote, or 3 seats, to qualify for 'top-up' representation in the chamber.	8	1990
UK	**First-past-the-post** People vote in single-member constituencies. The candidate who gets the most votes takes the seat.	16.9	1992
USA	**First-past-the-post** People vote in single-member constituencies. The candidate who gets the most votes takes the seat.	6.7	1988

* For definition of Deviation from Proportionality (DVP), see Dunleavy and Margetts' chapter in this volume. Broadly, the larger the percentage figure, the greater is the deviation from a proportional result. The DVP figures given are for the latest election for which analysis is available.

This system has broken down. At least three major parties now challenge each other nationally, and nationalist and sectarian parties participate in the elections in Scotland, Wales and Northern Ireland. Plurality-rule elections inevitably produce 'split' and 'wasted' votes and unstable and disproportionate results in such circumstances. Moreover, population shifts have combined with the UK network of small constituencies to reshape the prevailing electoral bias in favour of the Conservatives. Thus Britain's plurality-rule elections produce highly disproportional results at national level (Table 6.5), with even more strongly disproportional results regionally (see Dunleavy and Margetts' chapter, this volume).

Such disproportionality can be criticized on both the democratic criteria we are employing. First, it offends against the basic principle of political equality: each vote should have an equal value, wherever one lives and whichever party one votes for. Secondly, the continuing disproportionality of electoral outcomes in the UK has significantly diminished the degree of direct popular accountability of governments, as the party securing two-fifths of the popular vote is normally able to achieve unbroken power between elections, and power exercised without reference either to other parties or to any other section of the electorate.

A British Prime Minister's opportunities to maintain continuous power are enhanced by her or his discretionary power over the timing of a general election (Table 6.6). In Australia, Denmark and the UK the Prime Minister may take the initiative over the timing of an election by asking the monarch (or her or his representative) for a dissolution of parliament. But a Prime Minister in the UK has more power than either of her or his counterparts in Denmark and Australia. A British monarch will customarily accede to the request for a dissolution, as the premier's party will normally have a majority in the popular chamber. The Danish monarch may consult other party leaders to see whether they have any prospect of forming a workable government in a chamber where the Prime Minister's party does not have an automatic majority. The five-year parliamentary term in the UK gives a British Prime Minister more room for manoeuvre in the timing of an election, especially in relation to economic circumstances, than an Australian premier has within a three-year cycle. In Australia, too, the Senate can force a dissolution if it is opposed to a budget or legislative proposal.

The Conservatives have now exercised single-party rule in the UK over the past fifteen years, based on workable or large majorities in the popular chamber won on a minority of the popular vote in four successive elections (Table 6.7). This unbroken period of single-party power is unrivalled among the five other polities. Moreover, as

Table 6.6   *Control of the election process*

Country	Maximum parliamentary term	Premature dissolution: the formal procedure	Who/what really decides when elections happen?
Australia	3 years	The Governor-General has the formal power. By convention it is done at the request of the Prime Minister or if there is a persistent disagreement between the two chambers over a bill; generally, the Senate rejecting a bill twice constitutes grounds for a double dissolution, but in 1975 the Governor-General exercised reserve powers to impose an election on an unwilling prime minister.	Prime Minister (though Senate can force double dissolution)
Denmark	4 years	The monarch, on the advice of the Prime Minister, can call an election at any time. However, if the PM resigns, the monarch will consult the heads of all the parties to see if one of them has enough support to form a workable government.	Prime Minister
France	5 years	The President of the Republic can, as long as it is at least a year since the last dissolution and the President has not taken emergency powers. The President has dissolved the chamber prematurely four times:[1] in 1962, 1968, 1981 and 1988.	President of the Republic and the constitution
Germany	4 years	The popular chamber may be dissolved by the Federal President if it fails to elect a chancellor or if a government motion of confidence is rejected – this has happened twice since 1945, in 1972 and 1983[2]	Parliament and the constitution
UK	5 years[3]	The monarch may at any time dissolve parliament at the request of the Prime Minister. Parliament can also dissolve itself by statute (it last did so in 1911). No peace-time parliament has run its full term since time limits were introduced in 1715.	Prime Minister
USA	2 years	Fixed term: cannot be dissolved	The constitution

[1] Under the French Fifth Republic.

[2] On both occasions it was actually the German government which introduced and contrived to lose the confidence motion.

[3] The UK Parliament can legislate to extend its tenure (as it did during both world wars).

Table 6.7 illustrates, power in the other nations may be formally split between the executive and legislature (as in France and the USA), with different parties in control in each; or in other 'unified' systems, a second chamber may represent different party political or counter-vailing interests. The fusion of executive and legislature in the UK, and the unvarying Conservative majority of the Lords (actually enhanced since 1979), makes for an unprecedented concentration of power.

Further, under proportional systems, as in Denmark or Germany, the Conservatives, while at each election since 1979 the largest single party, would have been obliged to share power, acting as a minority government, or in coalition, throughout the period.[6] The electoral system would, in effect, have built in two constraints: first, the fear of losing power at an election; and secondly, the need to negotiate policies with other parties, either through understandings in the popular chamber or formal agreement in coalition. In Australia, the AV system produces more proportionate electoral results for the popular chamber, largely because Australia has retained an effective two-party system, in which power does switch between parties at more frequent elections (held at least every three years; see Tables 6.6 and 6.7). In Britain, the failure of the electoral system to give due weight to the parliamentary representation of rival parties has increasingly reduced the impact of Madison's 'primary control' over that party's conduct in office, and renders even more serious the comparative weakness of the UK's 'precautionary measures' of indirect control over the executive (see below).

Governing the electoral process

Equity between both parties and candidates is a necessary condition of political equality and choice. The UK is again out of line with the majority (Tables 6.8 and 6.9). The other nations, including Australia, provide public funds towards campaign costs (and tend to impose spending ceilings to encourage equity between rival campaigns). The UK does not require political parties to disclose large donations, or limit or prohibit them in certain cases, as Australia, France and Germany do, and a select committee has recently rejected proposals to enforce such disclosure (Home Affairs Committee, 1994). Public funding for election expenses, especially where combined with spending limits, does provide a more 'equitable' system; and research at constituency level in Britain has shown that the more parties spend, the more seats they win (Johnston and Pattie, 1993). In Britain, the Conservatives outspend Labour, and both outspend the Liberal Democrats. However, elections in the UK remain relatively

Table 6.7   *Changes in power, 1968–93*

Country	President/Chancellor	Popular chamber	Second chamber
Australia	N/A	69–72 Liberal–Country majority govt 72–75 Labour majority govt 75–83 Liberal–Country majority govts 83–93 Labour majority govts	69–74 Liberal–Country majority 74–75 No overall majority 75–80 Liberal–Country majority 80–93 No overall majority
Denmark	N/A	68–71 Rad. Lib.–Con.–Lib. majority govt 71–73 Soc. Dem. minority govt 73–75 Liberal minority govt 75–78 Soc. Dem. minority govts 78–79 Soc. Dem.–Lib. minority govt 79–82 Soc. Dem. minority govts 82–84 Lib.–Con.–C. Dem–CPP minority govt 84–87 Lib.–Con.–C. Dem–CPP majority govt 87–88 Lib.–Con.–C. Dem.–CPP minority govt 88–90 Lib.–Con.–Rad. Lib. minority govt 90–93 Con.–Lib. minority govt	N/A
France	(President) 69–74 George Pompidou (UDR) 74–81 Giscard d'Estaing (UDR) 81– François Mitterrand (PS)	68–81 UDR majority govts 81–86 Socialist majority govts 86–88 RPR–UDF majority govt 88–93 No overall majority	Regional representation

Table 6.7 *Continued*

Country	President/Chancellor	Popular chamber	Second chamber
			Länder representatives
Germany	(Chancellor) 69–74 Willy Brandt (SPD) 74–82 Helmut Schmidt (SPD) 82– Helmut Kohl (CDU)	69–76 FDP–SPD majority govts 76–80 FDP–SPD minority govt 80–83 FDP–SPD majority govt 83–93 CDU/CSU–FDP majority govts	
UK	N/A	70–74 Conservative majority govt 74–79 Labour minority govt 79– Conservative majority govts re-elected in 1983, 1987 and 1992	Effective Conservative majority throughout
USA	68–74 Richard Nixon (Rep.) 74–76 Gerald Ford (Rep.) 76–80 Jimmy Carter (Dem.) 80–88 Ronald Reagan (Rep.) 88–92 George Bush (Rep.) 93– Bill Clinton (Dem.)	68–93 Democratic majority	68–80 Democratic majorities 80–86 Republican majorities 86–93 Democratic majorities

Key to Abbreviations:

Australia:
Labour   Australian Labour Party (ALP)
Country   formerly Country Party, now National Party
Liberal   Liberal Party

Denmark:
C. Dem.   Centre Democratic Party
Con.   Conservative Party
CPP   Christian People's Party
Lib.   Liberal Party
Rad. Lib.   Radical Liberal Party
Soc. Dem.   Social Democratic Party

France:
PS   Socialist Party
RPR   Rally for the Republic
UDF   Union for French Democracy
UDR   Union for the Defence of the Republic

Germany:
CDU   Christian Democratic Union
CSU   Christian Social Union
FDP   Free Democratic Party
SPD   Social Democratic Party

Table 6.8   *State regulation of political parties*

Country	The parties in law	Financial controls
Australia	Parties are not mentioned in the constitution, except in a 1977 amendment for filling Senate vacancies. They have to register with the Electoral Office if they want formal recognition. Otherwise they are simply treated as voluntary associations – so their internal organization is largely their own business. Candidates need not belong to a party.	Parties and candidates are supposed to make annual returns of all campaign expenditure, debts and donations, including the names of donors who make gifts of more than about £680. (Anonymous gifts to be returned to the treasury.) In practice, parties (including the Labour Party, which introduced this legislation) get round these rules, e.g. by using 'front' organizations. There is no evidence of corruption at federal level, but several instances at state level.
Denmark	Parties are not mentioned in the constitution, only in the parliament's standing orders. Candidates need not belong to a party. But parties that want to take part in elections must be represented in the outgoing parliament, or petition for recognition.	Parties do not have to disclose individual donations but must publish annual accounts. Given the large number of parties in parliament and the compromise/consensus style of the coalition politics, it is relatively hard to buy influence. Party funding has not (yet) been a matter of great controversy. Denmark is a small country so campaign costs are not large.
France	The constitution states that parties must 'respect the principles of national sovereignty and democracy' (the rule was aimed at, but not used against, the Communists). Parties are nominally regulated by very permissive laws covering all associations and by the frequently evaded electoral law. Candidates need not belong to a party.	Candidates for national office must make a declaration of assets at the beginning and end of their terms of office. The amount of private donations to candidates is subject to limits. Donations from public bodies and gambling organizations and foreign donations are prohibited. After scandals over illegal fund-raising, a 1990 law sought to make funding more transparent by increasing state aid to parties.

Table 6.8 *Continued*

Country	The parties in law	Financial controls
Germany	The constitution rules that parties must not be anti-democratic or endanger the state. The Constitutional Court has banned parties of the extreme left and right – but not since 1956. The 1967 Party Law seeks to make sure that parties are democratic: it stipulates that officers should be democratically elected and that the process of selecting candidates should be open to members – by means of a responsible selection committee or party convention.	Donations are forbidden from political foundations, public, charitable or religious organizations, professional associations receiving money collected for political parties or those who expect advantages from their donations. Also forbidden are most foreign donations and anonymous donations of more than DM1,000. The names and addresses of those giving more than DM40,000, together with amount donated, must be published together with statements of expenditure. Illegal donations can be deducted from the state subsidy the party receives (parties represented in the Bundestag get payments to support the work of the parliamentary party).
UK	British law is virtually silent on parties. They are governed by general legislation on associations. Electoral law is almost entirely aimed at candidates (party affiliations could not be mentioned on ballots until 1969). Candidates need not belong to a party.	If parties are legally incorporated they must publish annual accounts. If not (the Conservative Party is not), this is not required. There are no specific rules of disclosure of political donations to parties; though individual candidates must submit an account (which will be open to public inspection) after an election which includes the names of every donor to the campaign.
USA	The existence and rights of political parties are constitutionally protected under freedom of association. Other than laws relating to finance (see right), rules for parties are laid down in state laws, which concentrate mainly on rules about primary elections, and court decisions, which have determined that parties have virtually unlimited freedom to make their own rules and that these rules take precedence over state law. Candidates need not belong to a party.	Campaign contributions to individual candidates are subject to ceilings of $1,000 for contributions from individuals and $5,000 for those from committees which are supporting more than one candidate. This has led to a proliferation of political action committees (PACs) which pass on huge sums and gain influence thereby. Political donations qualify for tax credits. Candidates must make 'full and timely disclosure' of their campaign receipts and expenditure.

Table 6.9   *Equalizing electoral opportunities*

Country	Election expenditure	Access to the broadcast media
Australia	Election expenses of candidates who get 4% of the first preference votes are reimbursed up to a maximum which is calculated according to the number of votes they receive (at the 1993 election it was approximately A$1 for each vote for candidates for the House of Representatives).	Parties usually treated equally in programmes but there is no compulsory regulation. Parties are free to buy advertising on commercial channels – a government attempt to regulate this was struck down by the High Court. It is the policy of state-run channels to provide equal time to major party groups.
Denmark	Annual grants are given to parties and individuals who won at least 1,000 votes in the most recent general election (calculated according to the number of votes received at a rate of 5DKr per vote).	All parties approved for candidacy must be equally treated in election programmes on TV and radio in terms of time. All get plentiful airtime.
France	Candidates who win at least 5% of the first-round vote and stay within the authorized spending ceiling can claim a refund of their campaign expenses to a maximum flat rate. Parties who run at least 50 candidates get aid calculated according to the number of votes they receive (FFr 9.10 per vote in 1993). Presidential candidates also receive help.	On public TV channels, airtime for election broadcasts is allocated 50–50 between the government and the opposition parties already represented in parliament; parties which are not, but which run at least 75 candidates, get short broadcasts. On commercial TV, there is an equal-time rule for programmes and parties cannot buy time for political broadcasts.
Germany	'Necessary expenses of an equitable election campaign' are reimbursed. Candidates get DM5 per vote from a 'refund fund' if their parties have polled at least 0.5% of the vote. Additional funding is granted to political parties which poll at least 2% of the list votes.	Free access to the media during election campaigns. Airtime is allocated according to 'the importance of parties' – judged mainly on the basis of their previous electoral performance.
UK	No system of state funding. Strict (and low) limits on election expenditure in constituencies. Candidates are allowed one free mailing in their constituency during the election campaign.	Free 'party political broadcasts' on radio and TV (the only partisan broadcasts permitted). No strict rules but allocated on basis of presence in parliament and number of candidates. Otherwise, terrestrial TV channels try to give two main parties equal time in programmes and news broadcasts, and a 'fair' allocation to other parties.

Table 6.9   *Continued*

Country	Election expenditure	Access to the broadcast media
USA	Presidential candidates may receive matching funds in the pre-nomination period if they accept expenditure limits (Supreme Court has ruled that expenditure limits can only be applied to publicly funded campaigns). The Democrats and Republicans receive grants for their nominating conventions and for their general election candidates. Minor party candidates who won at least 5% of the votes at the last election get grants; those who win 5% of the votes in the current election get a retrospective grant.	Candidates are free to purchase as much or as little airtime as they can afford. Given the overwhelming influence of TV, this accounts for the supreme importance of fund-raising in US politics.

Note: This table deals with state funding for parties and/or candidates; official limits on election expenditure at national or local level; and rules governing access to the media and media election coverage during elections.

The UK is unique in offering absolutely no grants or reimbursements to help cover election expenses. However, the costs of campaigning in the UK are reduced by free mailings and party political broadcasts. The USA is unique in its total lack of regulation of access to the broadcast media, allowing candidates to purchase as much airtime as they can afford – accounting, perhaps, for the supreme importance of fundraising in US campaigns.

cheap; and Britain, like Denmark, France and Germany, provides for free and equitable access to the single most important medium during elections – the major terrestrial television channels – as well as applying rules for impartial TV news coverage of elections. This equalizing provision will be rendered less valuable, however, by the proliferation of rival satellite and cable TV channels in Western Europe.

The role of second chambers

Most modern democracies regard the existence of a second chamber as an important practical check on the popular legislative house. In common with four of the 'peer' countries, the UK has a bicameral legislature. (Denmark has a single popular chamber.) In the four other nations, the second chamber is representative of the federal nature, or regional dimension, of their polities, and is either directly or indirectly elected via the states or regions. In the UK, it is a unique anachronism. Britain's House of Lords represents the landed and financial aristocracy, by way of the hereditary principle; the established church (of England alone); the judiciary, by virtue of office; and appointed life members, by way of executive patronage, past and present (Tables 6.1 and 6.10). Hereditary peers (and, by extension, the Conservative Party) have an inbuilt majority in the Lords, whereas the political composition of the other second chambers varies with the fortunes of the political parties (Table 6.7).

The power of the four other second chambers to check the executive and modify its legislative programme varies considerably, though all are formally equal in most respects, other than budget-making, with the popular chamber. The US and Australian Senates are well resourced and have powers of approval over all legislation and budgets. The Australian Senate can take its opposition to a budget or law to the point of dissolution. The French Senate and German Bundesrat both give way to the lower house's budgets, but the Bundesrat, as guardian of the states' interests, must approve any laws which affect state governments. By contrast, largely because of its 'amateur' and unrepresentative nature, the House of Lords is subordinate to the Commons (and thus to the executive). The Lords may at times exercise influence over a government, but may not intervene over the budget and has a limited power to delay other legislation which it is reluctant to use for fear of calling its remaining powers or its very existence into question (Table 6.11).

Table 6.10 *The role of the second chamber*

Country	Name of second chamber	Who or what is represented in it?	No. of members	How are members selected?	Term of office?	How well resourced are members?
Australia	Senate	States and territories	76	*Directly elected* using proportional single transferable vote (STV) in multi-member constituencies. All states have equal representation, regardless of population size.	The maximum term is 6 years: normally half are elected every 3 years, but the Senate can be dissolved, along with the popular chamber, if there is persistent disagreement between them on a Bill	Basic salary about £30,000, plus electorate allowance of £11,000
Denmark	No second chamber	–	–	–	–	–
France	Senate	Regions	321	Senators are *indirectly elected* by electoral colleges in the departments using a mixture of electoral systems	Senators serve 9-year terms: a third being elected every 3 years. The Senate cannot be dissolved prematurely.	Salary of £54,000, plus large allowances for secretarial and office expenses
Germany	Bundesrat	States	68	State governments (not assemblies) send representatives	No fixed term – the representatives change as the composition of the state governments change.	Salary from state government continues – will be generous
UK	House of Lords	Aristocracy and establishment	1,196	The House of Lords consists of: hereditary peers; government-appointed 'life' peers; 26 archbishops and bishops; 20 law lords	Peers serve for life and the House cannot be dissolved	No salary – daily attendance allowance claimable (£24 plus help with secretarial and accommodation expenses)
USA	Senate	States	100	Two senators from each state are elected on a 'first-past-the-post' system	Senators serve 6-year terms: a third are elected every 2 years. The Senate cannot be dissolved prematurely.	Salary of approx. £70,000 plus office suite and very generous allowances (can be as much as £2,000,000 depending on population of their state)

Table 6.11   *Relationship between chambers*

Country	Legislation (other than constitutional amendments)	Budgets
Australia	To become law, legislation must be passed by both chambers.	Budgets need the approval of both chambers. The Senate can reject the budget but it cannot amend or initiate it.
Denmark	N/A	N/A
France	The popular chamber's decision is final on all non-constitutional legislation.	The real decision lies with the popular chamber. The Senate can delay the budget for just 70 days.
Germany	Laws affecting the powers of the state governments require the consent of the second chamber, otherwise the decision of the popular chamber is final. However, the wide scope of state competence means that a very high proportion (around two-thirds) of federal legislation affects states and thus requires the assent of the second chamber.	Budgets only need the approval of the popular chamber; though they are submitted to both chambers.
UK	The popular chamber's decision is final in all cases.	Budgets require only the approval of the popular chamber.
USA	Laws must be passed by both chambers	Budgets must be approved by both chambers.

Note: Charles de Gaulle decided to curb the power of the French Senate of the Third Republic, using the House of Lords as a model. But the impotence of the UK second chamber is unrivalled.

Parliamentary control of the executive

In the four 'unified' states, the formal parliamentary check on executive conduct lies primarily in the popular chamber's ability to reject a prime minister or government. In Denmark and Germany, the head of government is obliged to negotiate with other parties to maintain the government's programme.

The German Bundestag maintains real power over the legislative process, which is more open and consensual than in the UK. In Denmark, a third of the members of the Folketing may force a referendum on legislation, other than financial, which they oppose (Table 6.12). In Australia and Britain, single-party government based on disciplined party majorities in the popular chamber gives the executive control of parliament rather than the other way round. The presence in France of a President and Prime Minister with complementary powers complicates the position; when they are of different parties, they act as a check on each other. The popular assembly has no power to check the President's exercise of defence and foreign policy powers. While the directly elected President has certain powers over the Prime Minister and cabinet, they retain charge of the everyday conduct of government unless the President's party links give him de facto power over the Prime Minister. The National Assembly may in theory reject a government's programme, but does so only with great difficulty in practice. In the USA, the President is independently elected and does not depend on Congress to stay in office (though Congress has the power to impeach the President for serious wrongdoing). However, as the two houses control the legislative and budget-making processes, the President must in practice seek to gain their approval for major financial and legislative proposals, or face deadlock. In all cases, the major constraint is electoral, though the danger of losing office varies greatly (Table 6.12).

The legislature's struggles to scrutinize and reject budgets and to control the armed forces lie at the heart of the democratization of power in many countries. The powers of modern legislatures over budgets vary greatly among the six 'peer' nations (Table 6.13), but in three (Denmark, Germany and the USA), the legislature has considerable powers over the budget. In Australia, the Senate often makes the budget process difficult for an executive which commands the lower house. In France, parliament may only reduce the budget and increases over 'base spending' are closely scrutinized. In Britain, by contrast, even the cabinet has little prior influence over the contents of the budget, opposition 'budget days' are expressive political occasions, and the government's majority renders futile any detailed scrutiny. The executive's freedom to make treaties, deploy military forces and declare war in the UK (and Australia) is far less constrained by parliament than in the four other nations, including France with its own imperial legacy (Table 6.14).

All legislatures have parliamentary committees which are designed to scrutinize the actions of the executive and legislative and financial proposals. In Australia and the UK, the executive's relationship with a usually loyal party majority in the popular chamber greatly reduces the effectiveness of these committees, as the composition of the committees reflects that of the chamber and party loyalty ultimately tends to prevail. The Australian Senate, however, deploys special committees of inquiry into legislative proposals and other issues. These committees are bipartisan in spirit and, though poorly resourced, have the power to influence and embarrass government; so much so, that recently government ministers and their officials have begun refusing to appear before them.

By contrast, parliamentary committees in Denmark and Germany

Table 6.12 *The executive and parliament*

Country	Who is the chief executive?	How is the chief executive selected?	How is the cabinet selected?	Formal checks on the executive's conduct?	Main practical check on executive?
Australia	The Prime Minister	They lead the majority party (or coalition) in the popular chamber	Depending on the party in power, the cabinet is chosen by the PM or the party caucus	Senate rejection of budget or defeat on issue of confidence in the popular chamber will lead to resignation of government, or dissolution of parliament	Wants to win the next election to the popular chamber – elections at least every 3 years
Denmark	The Prime Minister	The monarch consults all party leaders and appoints the one least likely to be met with a motion of no confidence by the parliament	Other ministers are chosen by the PM (in consultation with coalition partners) and then formally appointed by the monarch	The PM or minister may be forced to resign by a no-confidence vote (though the PM may opt for a general election). A third of members may force a national referendum on any bill (other than a finance or nationality measure); the bill will be rejected only if a majority against it comprises of at least 30% of the electorate.	Needs to maintain a coalition of different parties to stay in power. Parliamentary standing committees also play a role as does a desire to build consensus for major initiatives.
France	The President and the PM. The President has primacy in defence/foreign affairs, the PM in the day-to-day running of government – but real power comes with control of parliament.	The President is directly elected and appoints the PM but the PM must seek the approval of the popular chamber. The President cannot contradict election results or impose a PM on a united majority party.	Members of the Council of Ministers are nominated by the PM but appointed by the President. This can become a battle for influence, as in 1986 when Mitterrand refused to accept a nomination. However, he had no power to impose his own choice.	The government must resign if the popular chamber passes a motion of censure or rejects a general policy or programme by an absolute majority of members. But the drafters of the constitution deliberately made this very difficult!	When President and PM are of similar political views the main check is the next election. If they do not agree, then they are a check on each other.

Table 6.12 *Continued*

Country	Who is the chief executive?	How is the chief executive selected?	How is the cabinet selected?	Formal checks on the executive's conduct?	Main practical check on executive?
Germany	The Federal Chancellor	The popular chamber elects the Chancellor	The cabinet is appointed on the advice of the Chancellor, whose choice is, however, heavily constrained by coalition politics. By convention, the coalition partner has a prerogative over the Foreign Affairs and Economics ministries.	The Chancellor can be forced to resign by a 'constructive no-confidence vote', i.e. election of a new Chancellor by an absolute majority of the popular chamber. An election usually follows shortly.	The Chancellor needs to maintain the coalition to stay in power. In practice, this means bargaining over key decisions with the coalition partner(s).
UK	The Prime Minister	They lead the majority party (or largest party) in the Commons	Other ministers are chosen by the PM	Defeat in the Commons on an issue of confidence would force the government to resign. No clear definition of what constitutes an issue of confidence.	The majority party wants to win the next election to popular chamber. In practice, this sanction is weakened by PM's effective power to decide election date.
USA	The President	Popularly elected via an electoral college. In practice, the candidate must be the choice of one of the two major parties.	Government appointments are made by the President, but require Senate approval	Constitutional checks and balances administered by the Supreme Court, and Congressional scrutiny of governmental departments. The President cannot be made to resign – only impeached for serious wrongdoing.	Necessity to compromise with Congress in order to achieve anything! Congress controls both fiscal and legislative progress.

Table 6.13   *Parliamentary approval of the budget*

Country	What kind of parliamentary approval does the budget require?	How easy is it for the parliament to amend the budget?	How easy is it for the government to get its version of the budget through?
Australia	Needs the approval of both chambers of parliament. The government controls the lower house but may have problems in the Senate if it does not have control.	The Senate cannot amend at all but can reject or recommend amendments to the House of Representatives, where only amendments to reduce appropriations are valid	The government controls the popular chamber but it can have problems getting the budget through the Senate. Failure to do this in 1975 resulted in the government's dismissal by the Governor-General.
Denmark	Needs the approval of parliament: at least half the MPs must take part in the voting, but they cannot call for a referendum on the bill. Parliament may rewrite budget and/or policy but will not do so in detail.	Parliament can amend the budget like any other bill but refrains from detailed revision. It can also sub-divide the bill and vote on individual parts of it, which allows the government to use support from different parties for different parts of the bill.	The budget is an annual testing ground for the coalition government. The government (usually only with a minority in parliament) often has to struggle to keep the budget as close as possible to its target. However, the budget may be used as a means of overturning the cabinet by rejecting the whole bill or important sections of it.
France	Needs the approval of the Assembly. But if the Finance Bill is not considered by parliament within 70 days, the government may implement it by decree.	Parliament can only amend to reduce, not increase, expenditure or revenue	The base budget is normally approved without scrutiny and is difficult to change. But increases in spending are scrutinized.
Germany	Must be approved by the popular chamber of parliament. Unlike most other financial legislation, the budget does not require the formal consent of the second chamber, although it is submitted to both chambers.	Parliament can amend as for any ordinary bill	The shape of the budget is determined by intra-coalition bargaining. Monetary policy controlled by the politically independent Bundesbank.

Table 6.13 *Continued*

Country	What kind of parliamentary approval does the budget require?	How easy is it for the parliament to amend the budget?	How easy is it for the government to gets its version of the budget through?
UK	Finance bills need only the approval of the Commons, which the government normally controls	The House of Lords cannot amend financial bills. MPs can only amend to reduce taxes and expenditure. Amendments are rare.	The government controls the lower house and opposition 'budget days' are just used for general policy debates. Thus there is little detailed scrutiny.
USA	The presidential budget may be influential but the real budget is totally controlled by Congress: it is drafted by the budget committees of each chamber and must be passed by both	Members of congress can, and do, amend the budget, rewriting it in great detail	The government has no control over the budget. Congress calls in many witnesses to account for expenditure and can even force the government to spend money ('mandatory expenditure'). The President has power to veto the budget; however this power is too weak to be of much use. Large parts of the budget (such as the social security fund) are controlled by the Ways and Means Committee alone.

Table 6.14   *Executive discretion*

Country	Making treaties	Use of military force/declaring war
Australia	Treaties do not have to be ratified by parliament. They are ratified by the Governor-General in Council (Executive Council). The only exception is where a treaty requires parliament to enact legislation to implement it.	The executive has the power to declare war. The Governor-General is formally Commander-in-Chief but acts on the advice of the Prime Minister and cabinet. The last formal declaration of war which committed Australia was the British declaration of war on Germany in 1939 (this arrangement no longer applies!).
Denmark	Treaties have to be ratified by parliament. If sovereignty is ceded to an international authority, a five-sixths majority is needed or a referendum will be required as well.	Parliament must approve any use of military force against a foreign state unless it is in defence against an armed attack (e.g. the despatch of a naval vessel to the Gulf War)
France	The President negotiates and ratifies treaties, but significant treaties require parliament to pass a law authorizing them before they can be ratified	According to the constitution, parliament must authorize the declaration of war, and the PM is responsible for national defence. But the President is chief of the armed forces and has wide emergency powers.
Germany	Some treaties (regulating political relations of the federal state or relating to federal legislation) require parliament to pass a law. Some administrative agreements require the assent of the Bundesrat on behalf of the states.	The constitution prohibits the deployment of force outside NATO countries – the idea being to limit its use to defensive purposes. There is pressure to change this to allow Germany to participate in UN operations.
UK	Treaties do not need to be ratified by parliament. By convention a treaty is usually laid before parliament 21 days before ratification to 'enable views to be expressed'.	The government can deploy military forces and declare war without parliamentary approval
USA	The President has the power to make treaties but only with the advice and consent of the Senate; ratification requires the assent of a two-thirds majority	This is an area of continuing conflict. The constitution gives Congress the power to declare war, but President Johnson used Congress' Gulf of Tonkin resolution legally to justify waging war in Vietnam. In practice, the President has considerable leeway in the use of military force, although prolonged engagement would be difficult without Congressional support (e.g. the invasion of Grenada; 'counter-insurgency' initiatives in Central America).

Note: All executives require some area of discretion in order to function, but the precise degree of discretion varies considerably. The UK and Australia stand out for the total lack of parliamentary control over treaty-making or declarations of war by the executive, severely limiting democratic control over foreign policy.

American problems with who controls involvement in conflicts may reflect a modern trend for conflicts to be the result of insurgency or secessionist movements within one state rather than formal wars.

are not dominated by the government party, reflecting as they do the results of proportional elections and political traditions of widespread debate in advance of major legislative proposals and policy decisions. In both countries, these committees have considerable influence. In Denmark, civil servants are directly responsible to the committees, not to ministers (as in the UK). In Germany, the committees are major policy-making bodies and their chairs are political figures in their own right. In the USA, the doctrine of 'separation of powers' confers real powers of scrutiny and legislation on both houses, and thus upon their many committees (Table 6.15).

Freedom of information

'Openness' and 'transparency' are important keys, both to popular control and political equality at the level of principle, and to scrutiny of the executive in practice. One comparatively recent feature of democratization has been the development of 'right to know' regimes among democratic nations, including those with 'Westminster model' constitutions (Table 6.16 (a) and (b)). While the UK has given individuals certain individual rights of access to official personal files, it and Germany are in a minority among the six 'peer' nations in having failed to introduce such a system, with rights of access to official information and enforcement procedures through the courts. In Britain, there is merely a non-statutory code of practice, governing the release of official information rather than the disclosure of documents. The code is interpreted at the discretion of officials. Their decisions may be investigated by the ombudsman, who has no power to enforce disclosure; he may only make recommendations and report to the parliamentary ombudsman committee. In Germany, too, the release of official information is discretionary. Historically the regime has been more positive in providing information than Britain's Whitehall, but decision-making processes are equally protected. The Bundestag's powerful legislative role, however, means that data and expert advice on new legislation is publicly available. Far more official information is available in the four other countries, much of it directly relevant to government decisions and policies, and to political controversies. It is easy to exaggerate the power of such FOI laws. Advice and documents in the entrails of the executive generally remain secret; officials obstruct and evade the access provisions and delays in providing documents are widespread. But at least the principle of making disclosure independent of official discretion and enforceable by the courts is in place.

Table 6.15   *The role of parliamentary committees*

Country	Committee system	Influence of committees
Australia	Quasi-permanent standing committees which lapse when chamber is dissolved for an election, plus special Senate committees of inquiry into legislative proposals and political issues	The lower house committees have a 'worthy' influence, but are very much bound up in party politics. Even though their powers and resources are limited, the Senate committees have the power to influence public opinion and embarrass governments.
Denmark	Standing committees cover policy areas roughly coterminous with ministries. Committees correspond with ministries in depth and cross-examine ministers. Civil servants are directly responsible to the committees. Concern that MPs who tend to specialize by committee may be influenced by close relationships with 'their' ministries.	Important means for opposition parties to exert pressure on executive and extract information. Membership reflects the relative strengths of the parties in parliament, so coalition governments must negotiate broad support to get their policies through. The finance committee is very powerful, as it essentially controls amendments to the budget during the fiscal year.
France	The constitution restricts the number of standing committees to six in each chamber. The committees vet legislation and exercise limited oversight of government departments. Committees are large and unwieldy, with most of the practical work being done in working groups.	Governments control the legislative process, the timing and content of any bill presented in the Assembly; if it also has a working majority in the Assembly, it also controls the committees. But governments prefer to make amendments in committee and will revise poorly drafted texts. The finance committees in both houses are the most important.
Germany	About 20 committees cover the departmental structure. Ministers and senior bureaucrats attend their sessions. Committee chairs are senior political figures in their own right.	The Bundestag (lower house) committees are the focal point of parliamentary activity. They are regarded as 'expert' bodies and play a significant part in the legislative process, often substantially amending government bills. They benefit from a political culture in which prior debate of legislative proposals is the norm.

Table 6.15 *Continued*

Country	Committee system	Influence of committees
UK	Some 16 departmental select committees in the Commons exercise limited oversight over the policies and decisions of departments and their associated public bodies. Their composition reflects that of the Commons and is heavily influenced by the whips (party managers) of the two major parties. The Lords has a major and highly respected committee on the European Union and another on science and technology.	The committees play a 'worthy' role, except for the Public Accounts Committee, which draws upon the investigations and resources of the National Audit Office. They have no power to compel ministers to attend and ministers control the attendance and evidence of senior officials. A few committees command respect, and occasional reports have a political influence, but the majority of their reports go undebated (and often unreported). Majority party interests often blunt their findings.
USA	Powerful standing committees (22 in the House; 16 in the Senate) have permanent staffs and considerable resources. Their chairs are often major political figures and sub-committees have proliferated in an attempt to limit their powers. Select committees, created to examine a specific issue, occasionally have long lives lasting over several sessions.	Under the separation of powers between the US executive and legislature, standing committees have a mandate to draft legislation in their policy areas and their approval is required for all legislation. They control the passage of legislation, providing the necessary appropriations to fund programmes.

Table 6.16(a)   *Freedom of information: the law and the courts*

Country	What freedom of information legislation has been introduced?	Arbitration	How easy is it to get supposedly available information?
Australia	The Freedom of Information Act 1982 gives the public a right of access to documents held by the national government but not state governments (although some have also introduced their own legislation).	Decisions to refuse access must be accompanied by reasons. Appeals can be taken to the Ombudsman and the Administrative Appeals Tribunal and the Federal Court also enforces the legislation.	Exemptions from disclosure are broader and less challengeable than in the US. The Act is criticized for providing only limited access to official documents and failing to throw light on government decision-making. Also complaints about delays. There is a discretionary waiver on fees for access.
Denmark	Access laws in 1970 and 1981 grant a limited legal right of access to government documents, with broad exemptions for areas of 'major concern' regarding defence and security, international relations, the economic interest, 'other interests in which secrecy is needed because of the character of the case', etc.; for *statsrader* minutes of meetings between the monarch and government; and for minutes, records and papers of most ministerial and internal meetings.	The laws are enforceable in the courts, but an effective Ombudsman service provides a cheaper and more accessible legal remedy and, on occasion, a non-legal remedy employing his/her ability to criticize officialdom.	Legally, Danish FOI law is weak and some ministries (e.g. the foreign ministry) interpret the exemptions broadly. But in general the law has contributed to a far more open administrative culture and has justified many officials' attempts to pursue open policies. Complaints about delays.
France	A series of laws (1978–9) provide for the publication of documents and access to public archives, and require the administration to justify decisions refusing access.	The administrative courts can enforce the laws in the last resort, but the Commission of Access to Administrative Documents (CADA) arbitrates between the public and the administration.	CADA has no legal power to oblige government to pass the documents required on to individuals. Complaints about 'excessive' delays – the proceedings can take a minimum of 5 months.
Germany	No FOI law. The German Basic Law (article 5) guarantees freedom of information, which means only a right to inform oneself from accessible sources. Government and administrative bodies generally provide the public with extensive information that they wish to be known. The constitutional protection of the media includes a press right to be informed by public authorities (so long as the information is not classified as secret, or its release would not harm an overriding public or private interest). Press laws passed by the German states grant a right of access to information, but not a right of access to public records or particular information. There is a special right of access to records of the former East German state security service, especially for people on their files.	The courts will rule on refusals to divulge information, but regard limits on access to information to protect the orderly functioning of the army and public administration as given in the context of the constitution	Relatively straightforward, but the information available is limited. The open procedures of the Bundestag, which has a major legislative role in its own right and also evaluates executive decisions, place a great deal of relevant 'expert' information in the public domain. Virtually all information about executive decision-making is kept confidential for at least 30 years.

Table 6.16(a) *Continued*

Country	What freedom of information legislation has been introduced?	Arbitration	How easy is it to get supposedly available information?
UK	No legislation. A non-statutory code of practice for the release of official information but *not* official documents was introduced in 1994. This discretionary scheme does not provide for a public right of access.	The code is not enforceable in the courts. The ombudsman can investigate complaints but has no power to enforce his decisions. He may make recommendations and report cases to a Commons select committee.	Untried – it all depends on the government and its officials. Denial of access for the public or media is ultimately judged not by the courts but in a parliamentary chamber dominated by the executive.
USA	The Freedom of Information Act 1966. Courts decisions over time have made exemptions from disclosure more specific than in other countries' FOI laws. The right of access covers the executive branch of the federal government but not the White House, Congress or state governments. Some states have their own FOI laws.	Denial of access can be taken to the Federal Court, which has strengthened rights of access. The government may pay the legal costs of litigants who prove their case.	As elsewhere, government agencies adopt a variety of strategies to prevent the release of information. But it is generally easier to challenge the government in the courts. The courts are often reluctant to overrule the executive on issues of national security and foreign policy but otherwise active media pressure and public interest groups have improved the FOI Act in practice. Delays here too – the State Department may take 2 years to yield up information, and the CIA is even slower. There is a fee waiver in public-interest cases.

Note: European data protection laws limited to individual citizens' access to personal files are not included.

Table 6.16(b)   *Access to policy documents*

Country	Is the public able to gain access to:	
	the 'expert', technical or factual data on which advice to the executive for decision-making is based?	strategic policy advice, cabinet minutes and other documents in the executive decision-making process?
Australia	Yes, immediately, except for exemptions (e.g. sources, commercial confidentiality, etc.) if technical or 'scientific'; general 'expert' advice not so freely available.	Cabinet papers are exempt from disclosure and a 30-year rule applies. The rule is extendable (i.e. some papers not to be released for a very long time, if at all).
Denmark	Internal documents and data which are not legally available are often made public anyway. Information, including that preceding the act (i.e. before 1971), is generally subject to a 50-year rule. Classified documents (e.g. about the royal family, security, international relations, etc.) are normally released after 80 years, and in some cases, after 100 years. But documents subject to these time limits may be released on request, not least for research purposes. However, the *Rigsarkivaren's* [head of state archives] use of discretionary powers has been heavily criticized.	Strategic policy papers and most internal documents are subject to the 50-year and 80-year rules, though they may be released earlier on request. However, cabinet minutes and papers are by tradition 'private' (originally they were taken home by the minister taking them for secrecy's sake) and so they never formally enter the public sphere. Again, access may be given on request.
France	Yes, immediately, through FOI legislation, but complaints about delays in producing the information.	Never
Germany	The executive's own sources of advice and information are not released for at least 30 years. The hearings and findings of the Bundestag's powerful committees, which hear expert evidence on legislative proposals and executive policies, and examine ministers and senior bureaucrats, are published. But the Bundestag reports vary from case to case in how much material they contain.	The Federal archive statute gives everyone the right to see public documents after periods varying from 30 to 110 years, as laid down in the statute. Public authorities must deliver documents to the Federal archive.

Table 6.16(b) *Continued*

Country	Is the public able to gain access to:	
	the 'expert', technical or factual data on which advice to the executive for decision-making is based?	strategic policy advice, cabinet minutes and other documents in the executive decision-making process?
UK	No, government promise to publish relevant 'facts and analysis' when policies and decisions are announced, as well as 'factual information on request', subject to extensive restrictions. There is no right to know. Otherwise, 30-year rule applies.	A 30-year rule applies, with provision for a longer, or indefinite ban on sensitive information. Much information is simply not archived. An attempt is being made to 'liberalize' the release of withheld information for historical research.
USA	Yes, immediately, through the FOI Act, but access not as broad as in, say, Denmark. Intra-governmental memoranda and advice withheld until executive decision or policy announced.	White House, presidential and cabinet papers are all exempt from disclosure. Files enter a presidential archive at the end of an administration and are then continuously declassified (unless there is a national security bar). There is no time limit (like a 30-year rule).

Note: European data protection laws limited to individual citizens' access to personal files are not included.

Regional and local government

Both France and Germany have elected assemblies at regional (or 'state') level, which is also represented at the centre in the second chamber. (Denmark, being a smaller state, has a sub-regional set of 'counties' above its local authorities.) Australia and the USA are federal nations, both giving considerable autonomy to the constituent states. The UK, being a unitary state, is unique in Western Europe generally for the absence of elected, or any political, expression at the regional level, even though the 'home nations' of Scotland and Wales, and the province of Northern Ireland, have distinct socio-political identities of their own. In the UK, the central bureaucracy administers the English regions, Scotland, Wales and Northern Ireland (the latter three through dedicated Departments of State).

In 1872, Walter Bagehot, the Victorian authority on the 'English' constitution, celebrated 'our tolerance of those "local authorities" which so puzzle many foreigners' (Bagehot, 1993: 264); and the major official postwar inquiries into local government in the UK have all confirmed its historic role as a 'counterweight' to central government (see, for example, the Widdicombe Report, 1986). Yet uniquely, again, among the European 'peer group' and in Western Europe, the UK fails to give local government either constitutional protection or general powers to act independently of central government (Table 6.17). And whereas in the 1980s and 1990s other European nations have been developing 'local democracy', and conducting experiments in more direct representation, central government in the UK has been reducing the financial and general autonomy of local authorities and transferring responsibility for core services, such as education, housing, urban renewal, employment training, etc., to non-elected bodies at national, regional and local level. The constitutional conventions, which have hitherto protected local government, have had no effect on a government determined to enforce its view of the subordinate role of local government.

Summary

Britain's tradition of 'strong' government leaves no room for doubt about the executive's ability to 'control the governed'. What is more in doubt is the reality of the people's 'primary control' of government, and, secondly, the presence of adequate 'auxiliary precautions' to reinforce that control of government and quasi-governmental activity. The doctrine of 'parliamentary sovereignty' cloaks the reality of executive supremacy, to which a single party may

Table 6.17 *Independence of sub-national government (European states only)*

Country	Is there constitutional protection for any form of sub-national government?	Can sub-national government act independently of central government?
Denmark	The constitution states 'the right of municipalities to manage their own affairs independently, under state supervision, shall be laid down by parliamentary law'.	Local authorities have general competence, so they may perform any function which relates to their area and is not prevented by administrative law or other rules set by parliament or the state administration
France	Communes were given constitutional status in the 1884 basic law which was incorporated into the municipal administration code in 1957 (amended in 1979 and 1982 to include rights and freedoms).	Local authorities have general powers unless specific fields are reserved to other levels of government. A law lays down the division of competences between central and local authorities.
Germany	The Basic Law protects the status of each layer of authority (the federal government, the states and the local authorities). State governments have considerable autonomy based on the constitution, and financial rights (income and corporation tax are shared equally between federal and state governments). The specific form of local government is determined at state level and state legislation determines the scope of local government activities. The states of Hamburg, Bremen and Berlin are effectively also local authorities with no 'autonomous' local councils within them.	Under the Basic Law, state authorities have general powers to act within the law and municipalities have the 'right to regulate all the concerns of the local community within the framework of the law'. In the case of municipalities, the legal framework includes state law which effectively limits their scope for action. State governments supervise local authorities and expect local actions to be consistent with their own policies.
UK	No constitution. The protection offered by constitutional convention has been overturned in the past 15 years.	Local authorities may only undertake functions allocated to them by statute, but these functions are often defined in very broad terms, allowing some measure of discretion (doctrine of *ultra vires*). They also have a right to spend comparatively small amounts on non-statutory proposals of public benefit.

ascend via a majority in the House of Commons obtained on a minority of the popular vote. The executive's freedom from constitutional restraint, or legal checks and balances, is unique among the peer group studied in this limited comparative exercise. This freedom is the result of a political tradition which relies too much upon the swing of the electoral pendulum and the force of unwritten conventions to hold the executive in check. The result, as this exercise has shown, is to leave the polity in a state of systemic weakness. Britain is exceptional in the ease with which the executive can change the law to which it is itself supposedly subject; in the absence of legal protection for its constitutional arrangements and the civil liberties of its citizens; in its lack of pluralism of powers, shared by law between central, regional and local governments; in the weakness and unrepresentative nature of its second chamber; in the comparative weakness of parliamentary control over executive action and parliamentary committees; in the absence of efforts to promote open government through an enforceable 'right to know'; in the executive's unconstrained powers to enter into treaties and wars with no parliamentary oversight.

It is common in the robust traditions of political life in Britain to ask whether the absence of such formal checks and balances matters within the broader context of electoral accountability. We have argued above that they are required, between elections, to conduct the continuous scrutiny and monitoring checks upon government that are necessary to give substance to the electoral choice. In Britain, however, the electoral system which is supposedly designed to make that choice clear-cut now obscures and frustrates it. A party in government that can calculate on remaining in power after an election if it wins the votes of a readily targeted 42 per cent of the electorate is de facto not electorally accountable; and will be not a representative, but potentially a sectarian, government. In these circumstances, the current longevity of Conservative Party rule, allied with the exceptional freedom of executive power at its disposal, is full of dangers to the democratic process. The absence of 'auxiliary precautions' magnifies those dangers.

Notes

Preliminary research and compilation work was carried out by Amanda Dickins, research assistant on the Audit. Further research was carried out by Wendy Hall, current research officer.

  1 The following texts proved particularly useful in the initial stages: Article 19 (1991); Delury (1987); Goldsmith and Newton (1986); Humana (1986); Inter-Parliamentary Union: various publications; Lane et al. (1991); Smith (1989).

  2 The respondents were as follows: *Australia*: John Craig and Michael Muetzelfeldt, Political and Policy Studies, Deakin University; Rob Elder and Kate

Darian-Smith, Sir Robert Menzies Centre for Australian Studies; *Denmark*: Peter Bogason, Institute of Economics and Planning, Roskilde University; Jørgen Elklit, Institute of Political Science, University of Aarhus; Tage Kaarsted and Poul Erik Mouritzen, Department of Commercial Law and Political Science, Odense University; Morten Kelstrup, Institute of Political Science, Copenhagen University; Tim Pearce, Reuters; *France*: Anne Corbett, journalist, Paris; Vincent Hoffman-Martinot, CERVIL, Institut d'Études Politiques de Bordeaux; Stephen Jessel, BBC Radio correspondent in Paris; *Germany*: Eberhard Bort and Christopher Harvie, Seminar für Englische Philologie, University of Tübingen; Udo Bullmann, Justus-Liebig-University, Giessen; Allan Cochrane, Faculty of Social Sciences, Open University; Michael Fehling, Institute for Public Law, Albert Ludwigs University, Freiburg; Stephen Padgett, Department of Government, University of Essex; *UK*: David Beetham, Department of Politics, University of Leeds; Amanda Dickins, Wendy Hall and Stuart Weir, Democratic Audit; Patrick Dunleavy, Department of Government, LSE; *USA*: Patrick Dunleavy, Department of Government, LSE, London; Kelly D. Patterson, Department of Political Science, Brigham Young University, Utah; Kent Worcester, Social Science Research Council, New York; *general*: Patrick Dunleavy, LSE; Maurice Frankel, Campaign for Freedom of Information, London; Wendy Hall, Democratic Audit; Paul Hirst and Helen Margetts, Birkbeck College, London; Ken Newton, Department of Politics, Essex.

3 Preliminary work has begun on a democratic audit of the European Union and member state–EU mechanisms of accountability. The European Consortium for Political Research funded an exploratory seminar in Trondheim in November 1993.

4 The Basic Law was the first choice of (West) Germans as an object of national pride in a 1988 poll, with 51 per cent choosing it; in the UK, the monarchy came first (65 per cent). See 'Pride in one's country', Topf et al. (1989).

5 The second volume of the Democratic Audit, to be published in 1995 by Routledge, analyses the protection of political and civil rights in the UK in the context of international rights instruments. See Klug (1993).

6 Dunleavy et al. (1992) shows, for example, that the Conservatives would have been reduced from 336 seats under 'first-past-the-post' in 1992 to 268 under the proportional German additional member system (AMS) (Table 6.5), thus losing their overall majority and being obliged to form a minority government, enter into coalition, or go into opposition to a Labour – Liberal Democrat coalition or a Labour minority government with Liberal Democrat support.

References

Article 19 (1991) *Information, Freedom and Censorship: World Report 1991*. London: Library Association.

Bagehot, W. (1993) *The English Constitution* (2nd edn). London: Fontana. (Original work published 1872.)

Beetham, D. (1993) *Auditing Democracy in Britain*. Democratic Audit Paper No. 1. Human Rights Centre, University of Essex, Colchester/Charter 88 Trust, London.

Cary, J. (1944) *The Horse's Mouth*. London: Penguin.

Delury, G. (1987) *World Encyclopedia of Political Systems and Parties*. London: Longman (2nd edn). New York: Facts on File Inc.

Dunleavy, P., Margetts, H. and Weir, S. (1992) *Replaying the 1992 General Election: How Britain Would Have Voted under Alternative Electoral Systems*. LSE Public Policy Paper No. 3. London: Joseph Rowntree Reform Trust/LSE Public Policy Group.

Goldsmith, M. and Newton, K. (1986) 'Local government abroad', in *Aspects of Local Democracy*, Research Volume IV of *The Conduct of Local Authority Business* (Widdicombe Committee report), Cmnd 9797. London: HMSO.

Hamilton, A., Madison, J. and Jay, J. (1961) *The Federalist Papers* (ed. Clinton Rossiter). New York: Mentor/Penguin. (Original work published 1787–8.)

Home Affairs Committee (1994) *Funding of Political Parties* (Second Report), HC Paper 301, Session 1993–4. London: HMSO.

Humana, C. (1986) *World Human Rights Guide*. London: The Economist.

Johnston, R. J. and Pattie, C. J. (1993) 'The effectiveness of constituency campaign spending at recent general elections', in Home Affairs Committee, *Funding of Political Parties*, HC Paper 726, Session 1992–3. London: HMSO.

Klug, F. (1993) 'Human rights as indicators of democracy'. Paper presented at ECPR Workshop 16, 'Indices of Democratization', University of Leiden, April 1993 (available from ECPR archive, University of Essex).

Lane, J.-E. et al. (1991) *Political Data Handbook: OECD Countries*. Oxford: Oxford University Press.

Patten, J. (1991) '*Political culture: Conservatism and rolling constitutional changes*'. Conservative Political Centre lecture, London, 7 July.

Smith, G. (1989) *Politics in Western Europe: A Comparative Analysis* (5th edn). Aldershot:Gower.

Topf, R., Mohler, P. and Heath, A. (1989) 'Pride in one's country', in R. Jowell et al. (eds), *British Social Attitudes: Special International Report*. Aldershot: Gower/Social & Community Planning Research.

Weir, S. (1993) 'Auditing democracy in Britain: objective and subjective elements'. Paper presented at ECPR Workship 16, 'Indices of Democratization', University of Leiden, April 1993 (available from ECPR archive, University of Essex).

Widdicombe Report (1986) *The Conduct of Local Authority Business*. Cmnd 9797. London: HMSO.

7

The Experiential Approach to Auditing Democracy

Patrick Dunleavy and Helen Margetts

Can the level of democracy in a country be measured systematically? Empirical political scientists have generally avoided this issue, focusing instead on much narrower indices of their own devising whose meaning is less ambiguous but whose applicability to 'real life' is unclear (Bollen, 1991). Despite vigorous normative controversy about the concept of democracy, some far-reaching critiques of the limitations of Western liberal democracy, and extensive practitioner debates about applied institutional arrangements, during the Cold War era relatively little work was done on systematically evaluating democratic performance. Most quantitative work focused on quite broad-brush measures applied to all states and designed to establish whether a particular country's regime could be classified as a liberal democracy at all – for example, in terms of genuinely competitive elections and basic protection of human rights. These indices were generally ineffective in discriminating *between* pluralist polities themselves in terms of better or worse performance on key democracy dimensions.

The audit approach to assessing democratic performance is innovative in several respects. Instead of seeking a single aggregate scale (or a few such measures), the audit concept stresses a multi-criteria, multi-sectioned evaluation (Beetham, 1993). And instead of being solely quantitative in approach, an audit mode of analysis recognizes that many issues can only be tackled by qualitative investigation, where the detailed arguments used and conclusions reached are both likely to be contested. Quantitative analysis has a (relatively small) part to play in generating an improved consensual basis for debate about qualitative evaluations. Since any single performance measure will capture only a fraction of potentially relevant information, the production of multiple indicators is a key step in quantitative work.

Institutional and experiential approaches to measuring political behaviour

The indices used in auditing democracy should tap different and diverse aspects of the political and civil life of liberal democracies. Yet most political science work has been undertaken from a single predominant viewpoint, which might be labelled the 'institutional' approach. In this perspective, political phenomena are ascribed significance to the extent that they shape or influence control of political power and the state apparatus. Developments, trends and changes which determine the operations of key political institutions are typically measured by numerous, carefully designed and well-studied indicators. But political phenomena which are screened out of institutional influence are less likely to be studied, or are measured infrequently, crudely or inadequately. Hence the institutional approach is implicitly system-biased, fostering the growth of knowledge about issues which are salient within the status quo, rather than the autonomous development of knowledge about political processes (Dunleavy, 1990).

To combat this weighting of priorities, we argue for the addition of a way of auditing democratic performance focusing on people's experiences of liberal democratic politics. 'Experience' is defined by the *Concise Oxford Dictionary* as 'actual observation of or practical acquaintance with facts or events; knowledge or skill resulting from this; an event regarded as affecting one ([as in] 'an unpleasant experience'); the fact or process of being so affected ([as in] 'learning by experience')'. The hallmark of an *experiential* approach then is to compile measures and indices which capture how people are affected (consciously or unconsciously) by events or developments in the civic life of a country or community, by their own political participation, and by the knowledge, skills or adaptation mechanisms which they consequently develop. If we are to develop a political science which is not system-biased, political experiences need to be studied as important phenomena in their own right, whether or not they translate directly into changes in the control or operations of state institutions.

Similarly the experiential approach insists that there is no necessary correlation between the salience of experiences in shaping political outcomes, and their salience for citizens or other political actors involved. Both game theory and the study of collective action problems have repeatedly demonstrated that the logic of political interactions and interdependencies can often prevent strong and consistently held preferences from finding effective expression (Dowding, 1992). Moreover, many political outcomes may be the products of interactions and interdependencies beyond the capabilities of individual actors to manage. In this sense, these outcomes may be willed by no one.

Nor are citizens' experiences the same as their subjective perceptions of political processes or their attitudes. Just as rational actors can misperceive their interests in complex interactions and interdependencies, so citizens may not perceive all their experiences, or may misperceive them. Innovative ways of generating attitudinal data can form an important element of the experiential approach. But people's subjective perceptions and responses in opinion surveys must not be seen as capable of accurately capturing all their political experiences, or as necessarily decisive or authoritative indicators of the character of these experiences. Many political experiences build up bit by bit over long time periods or across diverse contexts, all the while generating adaptive responses as they do so.

An analogy may be useful here. Suppose that a woman A and a man B are living together. Every night B takes all his change (coins and loose money) out of his pocket and puts it on their dressing table. Each night, A takes a pound coin from the pile without B's noticing. B 'experiences' a reduction in finance. He will always have slightly less money than he thinks and may even adjust his behaviour because of it, for example by buying a cheaper lunch. But because he is not aware of what is going on, has not recognized it explicitly, B cannot form an attitude about it. Experiential indicators endeavour to incorporate effects of this kind, stressing the importance of voters' objective situations in defining their experience of democratic involvement or political participation. A further reason why experiences and attitudes are not equivalent is that citizens' perceptions will often be heavily influenced by the institutional approach to measuring democracy which we criticize in the remainder of this chapter.

To demonstrate the implications of the experiential approach we briefly consider four areas where the approach suggests a divergent method and produces different results from the dominant institutional orthodoxy:

1 comparing voters' experiences of electoral participation across countries;
2 developing 'benchmark' indicators and using them intelligently to highlight interesting or deviant cases;
3 tracking democratic experiences through time; and
4 capturing the *overall* character of democratic experiences in a liberal democracy.

Empirically we concentrate mainly on two important indicators of the democratic quality of elections, deviation from proportionality and the relative reduction in parties, demonstrating the different ways in which an experiential approach deploys these indicators.

Comparing voters' experiences across nations

Cross-national comparisons, between one country and other liberal democracies or similar countries, are a key component of any effort at measuring democratic performance. The audit method here is explicitly relativist: feasible standards of democratic performance are those demonstrably achieved elsewhere. We first show why the institutional approach has restricted the scope of these comparisons to country-level data, before refuting the arguments for focusing simply on nation-states. Second, we show why the experiential approach fosters more disaggregated comparisons, demonstrating the differences between the institutional and experiential perspectives in practice by looking at deviation from proportionality.

Aggregate comparisons

The institutional approach has created and maintained an almost exclusive focus on national-level data in comparing democratic performance. Despite the huge variations in the size of liberal-democratic countries, each state is treated as an equivalent 'case' to all others. And despite the small number of relevant countries, which severely constrains cross-national quantitative analyses, there has been little or no effort to assess democratic performance at a more disaggregated level, such as a regional level (Dunleavy and Margetts, 1993). Nation-states have been taken as the basic units of comparative analysis, almost unsplittable explanatory atoms.

The rationale for this exclusive focus on country-level data has four main roots – an emphasis on the state, an argument from sovereignty, a focus on distinct public policy regimes and reliance on unitary explanations.

An emphasis on the state is inherent in the institutional approach. Countries are nation-states, and it is at national level that the organizations, offices and roles which constitute a state are established. Modern studies stress an extended, multi-criteria view of statehood as a unique combination of necessary characteristics. Thus 'the state' is:

1 a set of organized institutions with a level of connectedness or cohesion, justifying short-hand descriptions of their behaviour in 'unitary' terms;

2 operating in a given spatial territory, inhabited by a substantial population organized as a distinct 'society';
3 these institutions' 'socially accepted function is to define and enforce collectively binding decisions on the members of [that] society'. . . ; and
4 their existence creates a 'public' sphere differentiated from the realm of 'private' activity or decision-making.

Each such state (ensemble of institutions) must also:

5 claim sovereignty over all other social institutions and effectively monopolize the legitimate use of force within the given territory . . .;
6 be able to define members and non-members of the society, and control entry to and exit from the territory;
7 make strong ideological/ethical claims to be advancing the common interests or general will of members of the society;
8 be accepted as legitimate by significant groups or elements in the society;
9 command bureaucratic resources . . . so as to be able to collect taxation . . . and order governmental affairs effectively, given prevailing transactions costs . . .;
10 substantially regulate societal activities by means of a legal apparatus, and government activities by means of a constitution;
11 be recognized as a 'state' by other states. (Dunleavy, 1993).

Arguably most of these criteria can only be actualized at the whole-country level, where the appropriate institutional apparatus exists. They can certainly only be *simultaneously* present at national government level, whereas it is possible (but controversial) to identify a 'regional state' or 'local state' at sub-national levels possessing some but not all of these features. The substantial common characteristics of nation-states are obviously increased by narrowing the focus to connected sub-sets or families such as liberal democracies. The recent revival of 'new institutional' modes of thinking and state-centred theory more generally in political science both stress the independent significance of organizational structures and cultural traits for the political and policy behaviour of governments. States as relatively unified institutional clusters make sense as units of analysis because their arrangements have powerful consequences in their own right.

The argument from sovereignty is the second part of the institutional rationale for focusing on countries as units of analysis. It relies on the external and internal 'sovereignty' of national states –

their ability to review and reconstitute their internal operations in radically new ways, as well as to freely change their external behaviour or relations. In liberal theory, sovereignty is essentially linked to statehood. It is the potential for autonomous action which ultimately resides with each separate nation-state, and respect for which provides a fundamental basis for international law. Nation-states retain the capacity to vary their policy responses in a distinctive fashion to respond to their situation. However reduced the scope for independent action by a given state may seem, and however little it may have acted autonomously in the past, the sovereignty concept insists that each state retains the potential for such action in future. In practical terms, the institutional rationale argues that underlying sovereignty is episodically expressed in crises or by radical developments of distinctive policy strategies. These factors confirm the importance of the nation-state as the basic unit of analysis, however similar or parallel developments may routinely seem across countries.

A focus on distinct public policy regimes supports an exclusive focus on country-level comparisons if it is true empirically that policy variations between nation-states are primary, while intra-country differences are secondary. Over time countries have evolved distinctive relations of substitution and complementarities between policy areas, shaped by numerous different historical, cultural, societal and political influences. Even where convergence in state provision has apparently occurred (as with the generalization of welfare state policies across industrialized nations, the expansion and then contraction of public enterprises, the growth and then stabilization of state expenditures, or the cycling of macro-economic policy 'fashions'), common outcomes frequently reflect quite different policy dynamics across countries. Underlying this empirical defence of using nation-states as the building blocks of comparative inquiry there are deeper implicit postulates, about the importance of sovereignty and the potential primacy of the political sphere.

Unitary explanations focus comparative political analysis on nation-states because they view some form of unitary actor assumption as an important mode of understanding variations across countries. Historically, 'national character' explanations provided an early impetus to cross-national research, a tradition which lives on in some contemporary society-centred theories (Nordlinger, 1981). Some state-centred theory focusing on differing 'policy styles' across countries also links with the 'national character' tradition. Unitary actor models of nation-state behaviour are also powerfully developed in 'black box' systems theory, international relations theory (Allison, 1971), game theory, economic models of rational decision-making

(Jackson, 1982), and a developing macro-level public choice stream (Levi, 1988) – all of which have influenced the development of comparative politics. There is no sense in which unitary actor models can be seen (as they were at the height of the 'behavioural revolution') as simply a kind of temporary short-hand, primitive first-approximation accounts which will ultimately be translated into detailed micro-level explanations as theoretical development and improved ways of gathering and analysing data allow. Instead this stream of explanation has proved too resilient for that, constantly recurring in different modernized forms. It seems clear that unitary actor models of countries' behaviour operate at a different level of explanation from disaggregated models, rather than competing directly with them.

Each of the four aspects of the institutional rationale for focusing on countries confronts some fairly well-known problems. First, although the common characteristics of 'statehood' are indeed substantial, there are considerable differences in the ways that different countries' arrangements instantiate these features, even among liberal democracies alone. The development of the European Union also seems to mean that its component nation-states no longer meet all eleven criteria set out above – for example, on control of entry and exit, and on monopolization of legitimate authority within the national territory. Indeed EU countries may move increasingly towards a 'regional state' pattern (Dunleavy, 1993).

Secondly, the argument from sovereignty confronts severe difficulties because of the existing variations in the scale and capacities of nation-states. Small countries' sovereignty is more theoretical than actual, especially in unfavourable economic or geo-political circumstances. And the behaviour of very large countries (like the USA) routinely demonstrates a practical policy stance which pays only lip service to the sovereignty of other countries (Krasner, 1978). The exercise of substantive sovereignty within a context of respect for other states' sovereignty is thus a feature only of medium-sized nation-states.

The apparently growing importance of transnational and international institutions and procedures in influencing policy development also poses problems for the sovereignty argument. The internationalization or 'globalization' of significant areas of governance, the formation of multi-country blocs, and cross-national policy standardization – all these trends or pressures imply a diminution of effective sovereignty at national level. If liberal democratic countries are differentially exposed to these trends and pressures, then the common characteristics of statehood are eroded. If countries are uniformly exposed to these shifts, then a pervasive hollowing out of 'sovereignty' is implied.

Thirdly, the public policy rationale for founding analysis on countries confronts as many similar difficulties as the sovereignty argument. Globalization, internationalization and policy standardization mechanisms will clearly erode the distinctiveness of the nation-state as a policy regime. In addition, however, even where each country remains a centre for unilateral decision-making, the contemporary period seems to be marked by faster and more extensive processes of cross-national policy learning, policy imitation and diffusion of innovations. There seems no easy way of determining either empirically or a priori the relative weight of national and transnational influences in shaping government decision-making, as the public policy rationale seems to require.

Finally, although unitary actor models are legitimate and discrete explanations, they cannot possibly exhaust the available field of interpretation – more disaggregated counter-interpretations are always feasible. Hence, unitary actor explanations cannot underpin the almost exclusive focus of comparative political inquiry on the study of patterns across nation-states. They offer an appropriate defence of a niche for cross-national research focusing on countries alone, but not of founding the whole field on such an approach.

Disaggregated comparisons

Because the experiential approach tries to measure people's experiences of democracy, and not how institutional power is controlled or determined, it focuses primarily on disaggregated indices. In large or medium-sized states there are actually relatively few political phenomena which people experience in a homogeneous way. Hence national statistics and data commonly represent averages of quite different underlying experiences and consequently can be severely misleading about the pattern such experiences form. By contrast, experiential measures try to identify areas which are meaningful for people's experiences. Disaggregated data are preferable for several reasons: they capture different experiences in component regions or areas of larger countries; they often have a clearer and less ambiguous meaning because they are closer to people's experiences; and they generate more cases to aid comparative analysis.

Once suitable disaggregate data are generated, there are two broad avenues of analysis open. One is to compare democratic performance across regions in different countries directly, looking for common patterns or threads which apply to many countries or groups of nations, and at the same time exploring those features which are genuinely distinctive to particular countries. A second variant is to create new national-level indicators of democratic performance, by reaggregating data in a distinctive experiential manner. Rather than taking a simple average of regional results, scores for the different areas of a country can be weighted by population size to construct a national mean which reflects the probability of a given voter in the country having a particular experience.

We apply this approach to the deviation from proportionality (DV), a well-known statistic in institutional accounts. Calculating the institutional version of DV is a simple matter: we simply add up the differences between political parties' shares of the national vote and their shares of seats in the legislature (discounting positive or negative signs here), and then divide by two. The institutional measure thus shows what proportion of members of a legislature are 'not entitled' to their seats in terms of their party's national share of the vote. Hence it is a measure of *party* overrepresentation in parliament. But, as we shall see, there is no necessarily close connection between the statistics thus produced and voters' experiences of how their vote is treated by the electoral system.

The alternative experiential approach to deviation from proportionality is to disaggregate national figures for seats and votes down to a regional or sub-regional level, in order to find out instead what proportion of *voters* found their preferences ignored or discounted by the electoral system in selecting members of the legislature (Dunleavy and Margetts, 1993). In order to reconstitute a single figure for the national DV, the experiential approach suggests taking a mean of the regional scores, with regions weighted by the size of their electorates. The resulting figure shows the overall probability of a given person's vote being ineffective simply because of electoral system distortions.

To see the difference which an experiential approach makes, consider Figures 7.1 and 7.2 which show data from seven liberal democracies – Sweden, Germany, the USA, Japan, Spain, Australia and Britain. Figure 7.1 plots the scores for the deviation from proportionality (DV) for component regions in each of these countries on the vertical axis, against the institutional measure of national DV on the horizontal axis. The individual regional scores appear as a set of squares in columns whose distribution along the horizontal axis is set by the national DV figures. Figure 7.2 again plots regional DV scores on the vertical axis, but this time against the *experiential* measure of national deviation from proportionality on the horizontal axis. The differences in the two figures are startling. In figure 7.1 Spain has the largest national DV score, and Australia and Britain are bunched together closer to the origin. But in Figure 7.2, Britain's national DV score is far and away the highest, while Spain's score places it well behind Australia. Similarly, the interrelationship

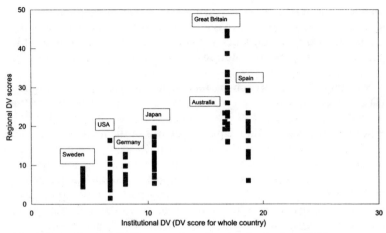

Figure 7.1   *Regional DV scores plotted against institutional DV*

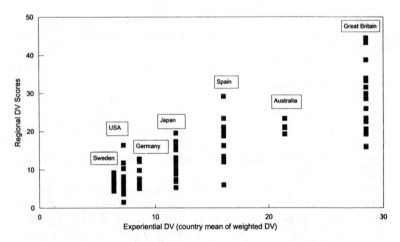

Figure 7.2   *Regional DV scores plotted against experiential DV*

between regional and national DV scores in Figure 7.1 is a complex one, while by contrast the pattern in Figure 7.2 has a straightforward intuitive interpretation – as the median regional DV increases, so the experiential measure of national DV increases. There are sharp variations in the spread of the regional scores apparent in different countries, but their association with the experiential measure of national DV is clear-cut.

The explanation for the superior performance of experiential measures in Figure 7.2 is simple. The institutional version of DV in Figure 7.1 is a largely bogus statistic. Britain's national DV score is far *lower* than the actual scores at a regional level, because in the aggregate party figures strong biases towards the Conservatives in some parts of the country are offset by strong biases to Labour elsewhere. In terms of parliamentary representation, the parties' fortunes even out. But this score has nothing at all to do with the proportion of voters who have their signals discarded or ignored by the electoral system.

Conversely, in Spain the institutional DV score at national level is *higher* than the level of distortion experienced by voters, because it is measuring also the degree of malapportionment in seat allocations between regions. Spain's system of list PR fairly allocates seats to votes, but the distribution of seats across areas of the country is considerably distorted to favour country areas over the main cities. This malapportionment is a conceptually separate factor which the experiential measure of national DV more effectively screens out. Voters in Madrid or Barcelona experience the electoral system as basically fair, even if they also experience severe underrepresentation in the legislature.

Using benchmarking to highlight what is unusual

A third possible audit approach is to define an absolute standard against which a country's performance can be assessed. In the past, political scientists have often assumed that liberal democracies' performance can only be measured in a relational way, that there are no such benchmarks which would be unanimously agreed or even endorsed by a consensus. In particular, the suspicion has been that possible indicators rarely have an unambiguous meaning, and hence that they cannot be sensibly relied on without extensive supplementary interpretation, whose importance in qualifying or shading numerical scores would belie the rationale for using benchmarks in the first place.

However, there may be many indices which would be widely accepted as always relevant at some level to assessing aspects of democratic performance. For example, the number of deaths due to political violence, or the number of wrongful imprisonments in serious cases, should ideally be zero in any country. In the audit approach, compiling a large number of such indicators may also mean that the limitations of any one index can be offset by the strengths of others – a common experience in the field of performance measurement for public sector organizations.

Beyond these considerations, there are wide differences between institutional and experiential approaches about comparing a country's democratic performance against absolute standards. The institutional approach generally rejects comparison with standards which are foreign to a polity's own aims or constitution. In their view only *ad hominem* argument is feasible. For example, proportionality is a relevant criterion for assessing the performance of a country with a PR electoral system, but irrelevant for countries with plurality rule or other supposedly 'majoritarian' voting systems (Reeve and Ware, 1991). Because these countries make no claim to achieve proportionality in the composition of their legislatures, then success or failure in approximating such an outcome carries no domestic political implications. And because performance here makes little or no difference to the ways in which political power is exercised, the institutional approach assigns it low or zero salience in developing indices.

By contrast, the experiential approach insists that it is useful to apply benchmarks for democratic performance across political systems, irrespective of their immediate political salience in the countries involved. The point of absolute standards is to prompt analysts to ask questions about apparently unusual or anomalous scores, to search for the roots of odd-looking comparisons, to highlight and throw into an objective perspective features which might otherwise be glossed over (usually in a system-biased way). In inductive, qualitative and aggregate accounts political scientists have a poor record of taking whatever recurrently happens to be 'natural', understandable, unexceptional. A good example was the notoriously unscientific discourse in British electoral studies about voting for 'class-typical' or 'natural class' parties.[1] Benchmarking combats the easy recourse to qualifying explanations, the 'Oh, that's normal' reaction, by insisting on taking an absolute standard seriously until a viable explanation of variations can be found.

We illustrate the usefulness of benchmarks in this role by looking at a further statistic which is closely related to DV – the index for 'relative reduction in parties' (RRP) (see Taagepera and Shugart, 1989: 270–7). It measures the proportion of parties voted for by the electorate but not effectively represented in the legislature. The countries we compare are the USA and Britain, in elections for the lower houses of their legislatures, the House of Representatives and the House of Commons. Whereas DV gauges the national representativeness of the legislature, RRP shows the extent to which the electoral system oligopolistically buttresses established political parties by excluding new or different competitors from representation.

The normal institutional version of RRP is computed in three stages (Taagepera and Shugart, 1989: 77–91). First, the effective number of parties represented in the electorate (N_V) is measured as one divided by the sum of the squared fractions of the national vote for each party:

$$\frac{1}{(V_1^2 + V_2^2 + \ldots V_n^2)}$$

Secondly, the effective number of parties represented in the legislature (N_s) is measured as one divided by the sum of the squared fractions of total seats held by each party in the national legislature:

$$\frac{1}{(S_1^2 + S_2^2 + \ldots S_n^2)}$$

Thirdly, we express the reduction in the effective number of parties in the legislature as a percentage of the effective number of parties voted for by electors:

$$\frac{(N_v - N_s) *100}{N_v}$$

The experiential version of relative reduction in parties is calculated in exactly the same way, but this time using *regional*-level votes and seats data for parties, rather than overall national totals. It measures the probability of any given alignment or organized viewpoint held by voters being systematically excluded from representation in each area.

The regional RRP scores for both countries are shown in Table 7.1 in stem-and-leaf form. Although Britain and the USA use a virtually identical plurality-rule electoral system dominated by two major parties there is a stark difference between them in RRP scores. The median regional score in Britain stands at 37 per cent, while that in the USA is only 7 per cent. In some British regions (such as Strathclyde or large parts of south-east England) the RRP scores touch 60 per cent, and scores in every single region exceed 25 per cent. But in the USA only two out of fourteen regional scores are greater than 9 per cent: the exceptions were the southern Atlantic states (excluding Florida) at 17.5 per cent, and Texas at 15 per cent. Six out of fourteen US regions have scores under 5 per cent, and four of these achieve levels effectively indistinguishable from zero-relative reduction in parties.

The RRP index has a restricted range. Theoretically it has a minimum of just below zero. Small negative scores are rarely found, but are technically feasible, as Table 7.1 shows. In a liberal democracy the RRP index has an effective maximum score of about 70 per cent, but the highest recorded scores at national level are between 50 and 60 per cent. Presumably the democratic ideal is a

Table 7.1   *Comparing regional RRP
scores in Britain and the USA*

Britain	Stem	USA
01	6	
9	5	
3	5	
99	4	
234	4	
55,777	3	
1,124	3	
59	2	
	2	
	1	58
	1	
	0	677,889
	0	1,234
	−0	10
Medians 37		7

Note: Stem unit is 10 per cent; leaf unit is 1 per cent

representative system scoring close to zero, one which does not
exclude any significantly mobilized view from representation in the
legislature. But in this case two similar plurality-rule election systems
produce very divergent scores against this supposedly absolute
standard. Does this divergence show that all such performance
indices need interpretation? Critics might argue that benchmarks
either generate wildly fluctuating scores, as apparently here, or can
only be interpreted as relative measures, for example judging any
country's performance against the background of liberal democracies' performances as a group rather than against the RRP scale.

However, like any other audit strategy, comparing against absolute indices involves an implied *ceteris paribus* clause. Divergent
scores from apparently similar systems direct our attention to the
possibility that some exceptional or particular factors may be
distorting the meaning of the index in that case. Here the suspect
score is definitely that for the USA: it is simply too perfect for words.
At 7 per cent, America's median regional RRP score is half that for
Germany's additional member system (14 per cent), normally
regarded as a PR system. The US score is also below the equivalent
figures for Sweden's hyper-proportional list PR system (10 per cent).

The proximate reason for the USA's performance is easy to
identify by comparison with Britain. In Britain voters' choices in 1992

meant that the number of effective parties ranged between 2.5 and 2.9 in England and Wales, and touched between 3.2 and 3.8 in Scotland. Yet the British electoral system converted voters' alignments into seats in a discriminatory way penalizing third and fourth parties with diffuse support, so that the number of effective parties in the legislature ranged mainly between 1.5 and 2.3 across regions. Indeed, in some areas, the voting system cut the number of effective parties represented in the legislature to the absolute minimum, just 1.1 or even 1.0 parties. (See also Dunleavy et al., 1992a, 1992b.)

By contrast, the number of effective parties at the level of votes was just 2.0 or 2.1 in every region of the USA, while the effective number of parties represented in Congress varied only from 1.9 to 2.0 parties in eleven regions. There are three minor exceptions where the two-party system in terms of votes was converted into regional scores in legislature seats slightly below 1.9: the south Atlantic states except Florida (1.6 parties), Texas (1.7 parties), and the east-south central states (1.8 parties). Plurality elections in the USA thus produce an almost perfect representation of parties in Congress because there are no significant third parties represented at the votes stage.

The two major parties' complete hegemony in Congressional elections reflects three main factors:

First, it is a reflection of US procedures for registering voters. Only 70 per cent of the eligible population are on the voter rolls, mainly because US law leaves the onus on the individual to come forward. Registering entails some significant costs, and is effectively controlled by the major parties, plus a few other political action organizations mostly linked with the main parties. In many states voters also have to register formally as a Republican or Democrat voter to take part in party primaries.

Secondly, numerous other devices in the American political system privilege the established parties and create high (almost impossible thresholds) for third-party challengers to surmount. US political finance arrangements mean that the costs of standing for election are very high, making personal wealth and party backing vital for success. In presidential elections the electoral college set-up means that third-party candidates have virtually no chance, for unless they win states they will end up with no electoral college votes at all. None the less, it is interesting to note that 'third force' candidates for the presidency are much more common than at the Congressional level, and elicit far more voter support, notably Ross Perot's 19 per cent share of the national vote in the 1992 election.

Finally, the US parties themselves are uniquely flexible and low-ideology operations. They are relatively permeable recruitment mechanisms because of devices such as primary elections. Republican and Democrat organizations at many levels have something of a 'shell organization' character, which can be taken over by whichever candidate emerges as the winner from quite open primary elections. Hence the parties provide 'brand-name' vehicles for élites from diverse sources to intervene in politics. Party ideologies vary flexibly across time. And across different regions of the country state parties' stances closely reflect the electoral centre of gravity in their state. While Democrat parties are more liberal than Republican parties in every state, none the less some Democrat parties (in conservative states) are more conservative than some Republican parties (in liberal states) (Erickson et al., 1989). Furthermore, party discipline in national institutions like Congress is relatively weak by European standards. All these features strongly reduce the incentives for dissident élites to create new parties.

The effects of the two-party monopoly at the voter level are specifically compounded in translating votes into seats in the legislature by a strongly entrenched form of US election districting known as 'bi-partisan gerrymandering'. American electoral law requires House seats to be apportioned strictly in accord with population, but implementation rests largely with state legislatures or other party-controlled bodies. Their characteristic response is to devise boundaries which strengthen each party's 'stronghold' seats, helping to maintain the very high re-election rates for incumbent Representatives. In most states bi-partisan districting practices partially offset the normal 'leader's bias' tendency under plurality rule where the leading party wins an exaggerated number of seats, further reducing overall RRP rates.

In the light of these features, the very low American RRP regional scores become understandable. They reflect the fact that the Democratic and Republican parties enjoy such a high level of oligopolistic insulation from any alternative competitors that virtually no other candidates present themselves. With the number of effective parties supported by the electorate already so low, and with a degree of party balance at the regional level plus bi-partisan gerrymandering, there is virtually no scope for even plurality rule elections to effect further reductions. Far from the low regional RRP scores reflecting robust good health, they provide grist to the mill of critics who see the USA as a sick democracy, marked by low levels of turnout and high levels of established party domination. For example, Vanhanen's (1990) index of democratization entails multiplying the proportion of the vote won by the largest party by the proportion of the eligible population actually voting. On this basis most European democracies in the early 1990s achieve scores around

35–38, Britain achieves 32, but the USA's score in legislative elections is just 17 – less than half the main European level.[2]

Tracking democratic experiences across time

Looking within a single country, the audit approach places a lot of emphasis on over-time comparison, between current democratic performance and the historical record. The advantages of historical analysis are primarily in taking full account of the traditions, characteristics and differences which separate each polity even from close-comparison countries. The appropriateness of cross-country comparisons can always be called into question on some grounds, but historical analysis relies on the *ad hominem* argument that what was achieved in a country's past can always be repeated (or improved on) in the present.

Institutional and experiential approaches adopt less differentiated approaches to over-time comparison. The institutional approach concentrates on changes or trends which significantly influence decision-making or power structures, so that information about more routine democratic performance may go uncollected or be discounted. At least some institutional studies have been characterized by a very episodic and ungrounded concern with historical data. For example, Heath et al. (1991) analyse survey data from successive British general election studies as a series of 'great books' which somehow stand outside time. Their meaning is ascertained in a context-free manner, with no reference to intervening evidence (movements of opinion polls, events or even leaders) that might shed light on the distinctive meanings of verbally similar responses at different points in time. The institutional premise underlying such work is, of course, the conviction that voters' opinions at times of decisions are somehow qualitatively different, better-formed or more important than their views in election mid-terms – a view which the experiential approach rejects. Although general election results have enormous institutional implications because they determine access to governmental power for a run of years, we have no clear basis for treating them as based on qualitatively superior voter experiences. Election results can express temporary or shallowly held configurations of the electorate's views – witness the dramatic collapse of the British government's popularity in autumn 1992, within a few months of the general election.

The experiential version of an audit strategy is committed to searching out long data runs and multiple indicators in historical analysis, rather than relying on overly simple pattern-seeking – which produces explanations framed in terms of golden age myths (all change is decline), linear progress myths (all change is improvement) and other forms of over-generalization. A more systematic effort to measure democratic performance over time will allow us to track complex patterns of change. By seeking for associations which endure through cycles or long trends, analysis can also better illuminate the causes of varying democratic performance. Focusing on multiple indicators also allows a clearer focus on interconnections between changes in apparently separate performance indicators linked by relationships of compensation, displacement, substitution and complementarity.

The benefits of the experiential approach can be demonstrated by examining methods of tracking the evolution of electoral system disproportionality over time. This kind of analysis has never been carried out systematically at a disaggregated level, even in Britain where its effects over the long term have been enormous. Of course, institutional authors are vaguely aware of some of the problems of relying solely on national-level indices such as those for DV and RRP discussed above. Fry and McLean warn that

> a nationwide index may conceal oddities in the regional distribution of seats. It is well known that when a plurality electoral system is used in a country such as the United Kingdom . . . where party strengths differ from region to region, the overall result may be more 'proportional' without the result in each, or any, region being so. (1991: 53)

And they go on to present data for DV by standard region for a single election, that of 1987, to demonstrate the occurrence of 'oddities'.

However, when we examine the evolution of regional level DV and RRP scores in Great Britain over a long period of time, as we do in Tables 7.2 (a) and 7.2 (b),[3] it is apparent that these alleged 'oddities', quirks or exceptional results recur constantly over time. By and large the distribution of regional DV scores has remained considerably more stable over nearly four decades than the national DV scores, which have grown enormously to reflect the swelling third-party vote for the Liberals/Alliance/Liberal Democrats (Table 7.2 (a)). There have been a few dramatic changes at regional level, especially in Scotland where a 1955 DV at 2 per cent (and 2 per cent lower than the national figure) grew to 29 per cent by 1992 (11 per cent above the national figure). But in other regions DV scores started off much higher than the national average and remained that way, the south-east moving from 35 per cent in 1955 to 43 per cent in 1992, East Anglia from 19 to 43 per cent from 1955 to 1987 and the south-west from 21 to 41 per cent in the same time period. Analysis suggests that there are complex patterns of association between regional-level DV scores over time and two other variables, the size

Table 7.2(a) *The evolution of regional-level scores for deviation from proportionality, Great Britain, 1955–92*

	1955	1959	1964	1966	1970	1974 Feb.	1974 Oct.	1979	1983	1987	1992
Institutional score	4	8	11	11	8	19	19	15	24	21	18
Regional scores											
South-east	35	39	37	30	39	42	37	40	41	40	43
East Anglia	19	26	23	12	41	40	27	26	39	43	34
South-west	21	28	31	17	30	34	31	35	40	41	32
Northern	15	28	26	21	20	23	29	31	32	29	30
Scotland	2	7	12	15	17	20	21	20	23	27	29
West Midlands (conurbation)	25	14	21	22	9	27	32	16	21	18	24
Yorkshire (conurbation)	9	12	17	23	21	34	31	25	22	27	24
Outer London	10	16	18	11	15	23	21	21	32	30	23
West Midlands (other)	6	19	19	12	16	18	20	27	37	33	23
Inner London	11	8	24	29	25	34	30	24	18	12	23
Wales	17	19	20	28	23	20	14	13	21	18	22
Yorkshire (other)	3	3	17	12	10	19	23	18	27	25	21
East Midlands	8	4	14	17	6	15	20	15	34	25	20
North-west (conurbation)	4	6	27	22	15	28	30	28	22	19	19
North-west (other)	2	3	22	25	12	19	19	19	30	31	16

Table 7.2(b)   The evolution of regional-level scores for relative reduction in parties, Great Britain, 1955–92

	1955	1959	1964	1966	1970	1974 Feb.	1974 Oct.	1979	1983	1987	1992
Institutional score	4	11	18	17	14	25	24	22	31	28	24
Regional scores											
South-east	45	51	49	40	51	54	49	55	55	55	58
East Anglia	16	30	30	15	49	50	35	37	53	57	49
South-west	26	39	41	21	42	44	41	49	53	53	42
Northern	16	32	34	29	24	32	42	41	40	40	42
Outer London	11	22	27	19	22	33	32	33	46	44	36
Yorkshire (conurbation)	8	10	22	30	27	44	46	35	31	40	36
West Midlands (other)	5	19	27	14	19	27	31	39	51	47	36
Scotland	3	7	15	19	24	21	18	29	21	34	33
Inner London	11	12	32	39	30	47	44	33	22	14	32
Wales	27	28	31	42	36	29	22	20	21	24	31
East Midlands	6	7	21	21	8	22	28	26	48	39	31
Yorkshire (other)	2	5	27	19	16	32	31	28	40	37	31
West Midlands (conurbation)	25	10	21	26	7	36	44	20	30	27	31
North-west (conurbation)	3	6	33	29	19	36	41	33	31	28	30
North-west (other)	0	5	24	23	16	27	27	29	44	43	25

of the third-party vote, and the largest party's lead over the second largest party (Dunleavy et al., 1993). At national level DV scores correlate almost perfectly with third-party voting, and much less well with the largest party's lead. But the same holds true only in about half the regions used in Table 7.2. Elsewhere the lead of the largest party is more important, and some regions' DV scores correlate hardly at all with third-party voting.

Turning to national and regional scores for relative reduction in parties, Table 7.2 (b) shows some similar divergences. The national RRP score grew steadily from just 4 per cent in 1955 to peak at 31 per cent in 1983, and then declined. This pattern was broadly followed in some regions (albeit with a larger range of variation over time in some cases). But elsewhere the RRP scores changed relatively little over the period, or showed no single trend. In the large south-east region RRP scores rose from a high starting level of 45 per cent to 58 per cent in 1992. In Wales the RRP score grew from 27 to 42 per cent in 1966, but then fell back sharply in the 1970s and 1980s. And in inner London RRP scores peaked at 47 per cent in February 1974 and then fell back to 32 per cent by 1979. At the other end of the scale, the rate of increase in Scotland's RRP score was much greater than that in national figures, rising from 3 per cent in 1955 to 33 per cent by 1992.

In every election since 1955 the regional levels of DV and RRP scores in all but a few regions of the country have exceeded the institutional scores for these indices, often by a very wide margin. In some British regions, such as the Conservative heartland in the huge south-east region, and the Labour heartland in central Scotland, DV and RRP levels have consistently been more than twice the institutional scores, not just in the odd election, but in every election, for decade after decade. The experiential approach's emphasis upon looking at long runs of data, disaggregating national statistics to capture voters' experiences, and taking benchmarking seriously all combine to throw important new light on neglected issues.

Capturing the overall character of democratic experiences

Institutional approaches to devising indices characteristically tend to focus on very segmented bits and pieces of political behaviour, and to neglect the *subjective* links which tie them together in voters' experiences. Because institutional approaches are unremittingly objective, grouping together only those phenomena which expert observers or those in political power agree are linked, they risk neglecting or misinterpreting other forms of common interconnection. By contrast, the experiential approach emphasizes the importance of devising overall indices, which capture the totality of people's experiences, in particular linking up seemingly disparate phenomena which ordinary citizens perceive as linked.

For example, explaining why people participate so extensively in liberal democratic elections is problematic from a rational-choice perspective because each citizen will tend to have a negligible impact on election outcomes, and will gain any 'collective good' benefits anyway, whether they vote or not (Downs, 1957). Yet in most liberal democracies, attitudinal data show that the vast majority of electors reject arguments from negligibility, and instead affirm the 'democratic myth' that their own individual participation can be efficacious.

Yet why should it be 'rational' for voters to expect to be pivotal in elections? Rational-choice accounts give no clear justification for assuming a priori that voters should adopt so demanding and unrealistic an 'objective' standard as the touchstone for participation. A more plausible starting point might be that individuals define an appropriate 'aspiration level' against which to judge their involvement, continuing to participate if this level is achieved, and dropping out if it is not. This argument was made for organizations by James March:

> Aspirations adapt to actual performance. Organizations learn what it is reasonable to expect by observing what they achieve . . . Behaviour that is associated with success tends to be repeated; behaviour that is associated with failure tends not to be repeated. Typically, however, such adaptation takes time (and, of course, performance also changes simultaneously). (1988: 190)

By analogy, an apparently more 'rational' criterion for people to use is simply to ask whether voting was successful for them in terms of whether or not they ended up on the winning side, and hence ended up with some 'stake' in the electoral outcome.

Being 'on the winning side' could entail the following:

1 It could entail supporting the party which won control of government nationally; or a party with ministers in the national government. In countries with separately elected legislatures and chief executives, where 'divided government' outcomes are feasible (as in the USA), voting for a party participating in the winning coalition in the national legislature would need to be included as an additional element to voting for the party controlling the presidency.

2 It could entail supporting a party which won seats in the local constituency at the national elections.

3 It could entail supporting the party which won control of government regionally; or a party with ministers in the regional

government; with separate recognition of support for a party participating in the winning coalition in the regional legislature if there is a regional-level separation of powers; or for the preponderant regional party in countries with no elected regional government structures (such as Britain).

4 It could entail supporting a party which won seats in the local constituency at the regional elections.

5 It could entail supporting the party which won control of the local authority, or control of different tiers of local government where these exist (as in much of Britain). Again, where 'divided government' outcomes are feasible at the municipal level (because of separate elections of mayors and councils), voting for a party participating in the winning council coalition would need to be included as an additional element.

6 It could entail supporting a party which won seats in the local constituency or ward at the local elections.

This list graphically demonstrates the complex ways in which citizens' participation might give them a stake in government.

No institutional study would even consider compiling an overall index of this kind. In the institutional approach each of these forms of stake-holding in democracy/majority rule is a completely separate item of behaviour. Since these behaviours do not cumulate in any institutionally significant way – across levels of government, or different institutions at each level, or the election of representatives for a given area – it makes no sense to try to measure them. But for the experiential approach what unifies these different items of behaviour is their joint contribution to shaping voters' perceptions of democratic participation itself. Influencing government in any of the ways listed above would be enough to sustain an individual voter's subscription to the democratic creed of individual influence.

Empirically, the experiential approach could produce rather different views of voters' experiences of 'success' in voting from institutional indices. Tables 7.3 (a) and 7.3 (b) look at plurality rule elections to the House of Commons in 1992, and measure success in just three of the many possible ways listed above:

1 voting for the party forming the national government;
2 voting for the winning party in the local constituency; and
3 voting for a party which is dominant in the region where the constituency is located.

Breaking down voters for the three main parties across these categories (as in Table 7.3(a)) shows that in 1992 Tory voters who

Table 7.3(a)   *Triple, double and single 'winner' voters shown as percentage of total voters in the 1992 British general election*

Category of voters	% of total Great Britain voters				
	Cons	Labour	Liberal Democrat	Other	Total
Triple winner	20.6	0.0	0.0	0.0	20.6
Double winner:					
National/local	9.9	0.0	0.0	0.0	9.9
National/regional	5.5	0.0	0.0	0.0	5.5
Regional/local	0.0	11.2	0.0	0.0	11.2
Single winner:					
National	6.8	0.0	0.0	0.0	6.8
Local	0.0	9.0	1.2	0.4	10.6
Regional	0.0	8.5	0.0	0.0	8.5
Any form of winner	42.8	28.7	1.2	0.4	73.1
Triple loser	0.0	6.5	17.0	3.3	26.8
Total	42.8	35.2	18.2	3.7	100.0

Table 7.3(b)   *Triple, double and single 'winner' voters shown as percentage of party vote in the 1992 British general election*

Category of voters	% of total Great Britain voters				
	Cons	Labour	Liberal Democrat	Other	All voters
Triple winner	48	0	0	0	21
Double winner	36	32	0	0	27
Single winner	16	50	7	10	25
Triple loser	0	18	93	90	27
Total	100	100	100	100	100

Note: 'National' means that the party voted for formed the government; 'Local' means that the party voted for won the local constituency; 'Regional' means that the party voted for was dominant within the region, defined as gaining 70 per cent or more of the seats. The regions used are those given in Table 7.2.
Source: House of Commons Library disk of the 1992 general election results

were 'triple winners' form the largest component part of the electorate, accounting for 20.6 per cent of voters. 'Double winners' included Labour voters in safe Labour regions, and Conservatives in non-Tory constituencies or regions. 'Single winners' were mainly

Tory voters in Labour heartlands, and Labour voters in constituencies outside their regions of strength. Liberal Democrat voters were very rarely single winners. The 'other' column includes the Green voters (all of whom were losers) and the nationalist parties in Scotland and Wales, who account for all the single winners in this column.

The pattern of partisan-skewed success charted here has considerable implications for the ways in which we think about the mainsprings of participation. The Conservative government was re-elected in 1992 by just 30.5 per cent of British voters (those in constituencies won by Conservative MPs), while a further 12.3 per cent supported the party in constituencies they lost. Yet overall Table 7.3(a) shows that 73.1 per cent of British voters were 'winners' at one level or another, a share more than double that of Tory voters in Tory constituencies. Table 7.3(b) shows the distribution of 'winners' and 'losers' across the parties. As to be expected, the scores show that a Conservative Party voter is most likely to be in an advantageous position and obviously no Conservatives are 'triple losers'. But it is interesting to note that a Labour voter's chance of being in some form of winning position is far nearer to that of a Conservative voter than that of a Liberal Democrat. Only 18 per cent of Labour voters were triple losers, compared to 93 per cent of Liberal Democrats. The distribution of winning and losing voters across parties also helps to explain why Labour has maintained an ambiguous position on electoral reform.

Obviously Table 7.3 gives only the simplest picture of multiple winners and losers. Applying a similar approach in a federal country with a plurality rule electoral system, such as the USA, might raise the proportion of voters with some level of 'success' from their vote, as would applying the same procedures in a proportional representation system, where the proportion of 'winners' at some level or another should be very high (above 90 per cent). Even at this speculative stage, Table 7.3 raises serious questions for the view that 'rational' voters should abstain. There is considerable potential for comparative and historical research to explore the linkages between the proportion of voters who count as 'winners', and levels and trends in turnout. People's experience of winning or losing in casting their vote may also have important implications for trends in partisan alignment in systems, like Britain, where a relatively high proportion of voters will end up as multiple losers.

Conclusions

While most political science work predominantly adopts an institutional approach to indices, we have argued instead for an experiential approach to auditing democracy, focusing on citizens' objective experiences of democratic involvement and participation. An experiential approach entails some radically different ways of constructing indices: disaggregating national indices down to areas which are meaningful for voters; comparing democratic performance against benchmarks; looking at long time series, not just institutionally significant periods; and devising overall indices of experiences composited across different institutional settings. Taken together with a commitment to develop multiple indices, this agenda is an extensive one. But since democratic interactions are at once so important and so controversial in the development of modern societies, the effort to systematize our understanding and generate more 'useable knowledge' about them (Lindblom and Cohen, 1979) seems worthwhile.

Notes

We are grateful to Stuart Weir for help and comments on the ideas in this chapter. This chapter forms part of the Democratic Audit of the UK, funded by Charter 88 Trust and the Joseph Rowntree Charitable Trust. The Department of Government at the LSE is developing systematic data sets for assessing Democratic Performance in the UK.

1 For example, Heath et al. argue for using odds ratios as a key index of class voting in these terms: 'If Labour (or for that matter the Conservatives) begins to draw relatively more support from *the opposing class* than from its *natural supporters*, then we are indeed seeing a far more interesting change in class/party relations' (1985: 31; emphasis added). The interest, of course, derives only from assuming that anyone is a 'natural' supporter of a particular party, or a member of 'the opposing class' to another party. People do not naturally vote one way or another, and while they may have a 'natal' class position, its political alignment is not set at birth.

2 The 1992 presidential election, when Clinton was elected with only 43 per cent of the vote, because Ross Perot polled 19 per cent, would produce a higher score on Vanhanen's index. The interesting issue here is why third-party candidatures are so relatively common at US presidential elections compared with senatorial or Congressional races.

3 Data for these tables were taken from the Nuffield Election studies by Butler and co-authors (1955–92), Appendix 1. Unfortunately, although this is the closest we have to a journal of record, the data available are inadequate (for example, numbers of voters are not given for several elections) so we supplemented these with *The Times Guide to the House of Commons* which contains regional breakdowns from October 1974 onwards.

References

Allison, G. (1971) *Essence of Decision*. Boston, MA: Little Brown.

Beetham, D. (1993) *Auditing Democracy in Britain*. Democratic Audit Paper No. 1. Human Rights Centre, University of Essex, Colchester/Charter 88 Trust, London.

Bollen, K. A. (1991) 'Political democracy: conceptual and measurement traps', in A. Inkeles (ed.), *On Measuring Democracy: Its Consequences and Concomitants*. New Brunswick, NJ and London: Transaction Publishers. pp. 3–20.

Butler, D. (1955, 1959) *The British General Election of 19...* London: Macmillan.
Butler, D. and King, A. (1964, 1966) *The British General Election of 19...* London: Macmillan.
Butler, D. and Pinto-Duschinsky, M. (1970) *The British General Election of 1970*. London: Macmillan.
Butler, D. and Kavanagh, D. (1974a, 1974b, 1979, 1983, 1987, 1992) *The British General Election of 19...* London: Macmillan.
Dowding, K. (1992) *Rational Choice and Political Power*. Aldershot: Gower.
Downs, A. (1957) *An Economic Theory of Democracy*. Boston, MA: Little Brown.
Dunleavy, P. (1990) 'Mass political behaviour: is there more to learn?', *Political Studies*, 18(3): 453–69.
Dunleavy, P. (1993) 'The state', in R. Goodin and P. Pettit (eds), *The Blackwell Companion to Contemporary Political Philosophy*. Oxford: Blackwell. pp. 611–21.
Dunleavy, P. and Margetts, H. (1993) 'Disaggregating indices of democracy: deviation from proportionality and relative reduction in parties'. Paper presented at ECPR Workshop 16, 'Indices of Democratization', University of Leiden, April 1993 (available from ECPR archive, University of Essex).
Dunleavy, P., Margetts, H. and Weir, S. (1992a) *Replaying the 1992 General Election: How Britain Would Have Voted under Alternative Electoral Systems*. LSE Public Policy Paper No. 3. London: Joseph Rowntree Reform Trust/LSE Public Policy Group.
Dunleavy, P., Margetts, H. and Weir, S. (1992b) 'How Britain would have voted under alternative electoral systems in 1992', *Parliamentary Affairs*, 45 (3): 640–55.
Dunleavy, P., Margetts, H. and Weir, S. (1993) 'The 1992 British general election and the legitimacy of British democracy', in D. Denver, P. Norris, D. Broughton and C. Rallings (eds), *British Elections and Parties' Yearbook 1993*. Hemel Hempstead: Harvester Wheatsheaf.
Erickson, R. S., Wright, G. C. and McIver, J. P. (1989) 'Political parties, public opinion and state policy', *American Political Science Review*, 83(3): 729–50.
Fry, V. and McLean, I. (1991) 'A Note on Rose's Proportionality Index', *Electoral Studies*, 10(1): 33–51.
Health, A., Jowell, R. and Curtice, J. (1985) How Britain Votes. Oxford: Pergamon.
Heath, A. with Jowell, R., Curtice, J., Evans, G., Field, J. and Witherspoon, S. (1991) *Understanding Political Change: The British Voter, 1964–87*. Oxford: Pergamon.
Jackson, P. (1982) *The Political Economy of Bureaucracy*. Deddington: Phillip Allan.
Krasner, S. (1978) *Defending the National Interest*. Princeton, NJ: Princeton University Press.
Levi, M. (1988) *Of Rule and Revenue*. Berkeley: University of California Press.
Lindblom, C. E. and Cohen, D. (1979) *Useable Knowledge: Social Science and Social Problem Solving*. New Haven, CT and London: Yale University Press.
March, J. G. (1988) *Decisions and Organizations*. Oxford: Blackwell.
Nordlinger, E. (1981) *The Autonomy of the Democratic State*. Cambridge, MA: Harvard University Press.
Reeve, A. and Ware, A. (1991) *Electoral Systems: A Comparative and Theoretical Introduction*. London: Routledge.
Taagepera, R. and Shugart, M. S. (1989) *Seats and Votes: The Effects and Determinants of Electoral Systems*. New Haven, CT and London: Yale University Press.
Vanhanen, T. (1990) *The Process of Democratization: A Comparative Study of 147 States, 1980–88*. New York: Taylor & Francis.

8

The Idea of Democracy in the West and in the East

Nikolai Biryukov and Victor Sergeyev

The parliamentary idea

There is a fundamental methodological problem as far as indices are concerned. Applying indices presupposes a normative model, and normative models involve values. If in our analysis of the transition to democracy we mean to compare a particular stage to some such model, the relevant values must be made explicit. But these values, though related to the notion of democracy, need not be identical to it. It may be more appropriate to speak of assessing implementation of *certain* democratic values (for example, human rights) rather than assessing 'the level of democracy' as such. 'Democracy' does not seem to have an obvious (intuitive) meaning shared by all. If one intends to analyse *actual* processes and *actual* behaviour of political agents, one has to describe *their* model of democracy before attempting to apply indices. The presence of competing models makes a typology (both institutional and cognitive) indispensable. This chapter seeks to illustrate the point by describing a model of democracy that is obviously different from the conventional Western one. This is not to say that all models are 'equally' good or 'equally' cogent. The one we speak of here does not have a particularly impressive record. Still, it seems that our understanding of democratization will not be facilitated if we ignore the way democracy is interpreted within the culture in question.

The problem of representative democracy emerged on the eve of the modern era as part of a larger task: the rational organization of society. Inspired by conspicuous success of mathematics and natural sciences, the greatest thinkers of the seventeenth century tried to understand not only the interrelations of human mind and nature, but the nature of human society as well.

There seems to be a close relationship between human attempts to understand nature and our attempts to rationalize social relations through giving *sense* to forms of social life. Just as the development of science and philosophy in the 'golden age' of Pericles was followed by waves of revolutions in Greek *poleis* that brought direct democracy into being, so the outstanding intellectual achievements of modern times gave birth to new forms of statehood: representative democracy and the separation of powers.

Of the various topics that are related to the problem of understanding the nature of society and inventing a rational system of its government, based on the ideas of 'natural' human rights and the initial equality of human beings, some appear to be of primary importance.

The first is the source of state sovereignty and the development of cooperation between egoistic individuals. If people are born equal and free, how can human commonwealth with its inherent hierarchy and power relations emerge out of the initial chaos of individual egoistic drives? How did civil society originate? The question was asked by Hobbes, who drew the following conclusion: civil society was created by a *social contract* between individuals who had renounced their rights in favour of a *sovereign* in order to put an end to the natural state of *war of all against all*. This idea of a social contract became the main topic of political debate in the next century – up to the French Revolution – and formed the theoretical basis of representative democracy, that is, a political system in which citizens invest their elected representatives with the legislative powers that belong to them by right of nature. A powerful and dynamic statement of this interpretation of democracy is to be found in the treatise by Rousseau with its constant emphasis on the necessity to represent and express *the will of the people*.

This served to introduce the next theme: how could one prevent tyranny on the part of the new, 'elected' sovereign? Its theoretical aspects had been discussed by Montesquieu, who had proposed the celebrated principle of *the separation of powers*, later to be implemented in the constitution of a new North American state.

Both principles – democratic representation and separation of powers – proved insufficient, however. This was made apparent by the tragic events of 1793–4 in revolutionary France where the democratically elected Convention, operating formally under conditions of separated powers and declared human rights, established and maintained a state of bloody terror. Many leaders of the democratic revolution, including members of that sovereign assembly, fell victims to it.

Political mechanisms that could safeguard society and its members against abuse of power on the part of those they had themselves elected emerged as the third main problem of democratic political theory. The solution came as a demand for *free political activity*, that is, freedom to create political organizations that might express and defend interests of various social groups.

These three ideas – political representation through free election, separation of powers and freedom of political activity – may be said to form the basis of modern democracy.

However clear these principles may have appeared to be after the debates of the enlightened seventeenth and eighteenth centuries, a problem of profound complexity has since been encountered, namely *transition to democracy*. Unlike theoretical interpretations of the nature of democracy – and we may still witness impressive insights[1] here – the problem of transition to democracy calls for descriptive (see, for example, *Transition*, 1991) rather than prescriptive studies. For differences both in the initial conditions in which various societies find themselves and in their subsequent development are so great that speculations (like the recent debate on the need for an authoritarian phase in the transition from totalitarianism to democracy)[2] will hardly yield anything more reliable than prophesies by an oracle.

Part of this problem is the close relationship between totalitarianism and the mass culture that developed in the course of the industrial revolution and its accompanying process of 'human standardization', the mentality of that 'man of the mass' to which Ortega y Gasset (1932) first drew our attention.[3] Although totalitarianism appears to be an outcome of a unique constellation of circumstances peculiar to modernity, 'the man of the mass' in whose psychology it is reputedly rooted is by no means a 'new' man – he is essentially a man of the traditional, 'pre-mass' culture. Which makes one wonder in what relation the traditional culture and the phenomenon of totalitarianism stand to each other.

Twentieth-century totalitarianism has always been at odds with the idea of parliamentary rule. It would be easy to rationalize this as a natural outcome of the conflict between the irrational 'mass consciousness', on the one hand, and the rational cooperation of the 'best' members of society, on the other. But this interpretation raises a series of uncomfortable questions, including, perhaps, the most 'awkward' one, namely in what sense may one regard elected representatives of the populace as indeed the 'best'? It would also involve a sound scholarly description (and conceptualization) of the process of their collective legislative activity.

Why should we think that 'one mind is good, but two minds are better', as a Russian proverb has it? And what about a few hundred minds that usually constitute a parliament? It is a point of common knowledge, well supported by everyday experience, that a crowd tends to be less rational than the individuals it consists of. This would make one doubt the validity of the proverbial assumption. Why should an assembly of elected representatives of the populace be more reasonable than a crowd of ordinary citizens? And if it would, what are the necessary conditions? And, finally, what does the expression 'a wise decision' mean when it is applied to a group?

It seems clear that for a great number of people to behave more or less reasonably they must interact in a rational, orderly way. They need some kind of organizational structure implemented in a set of rules of behaviour, that is, *a procedure*. When parliamentarians discuss their problems they interact, they argue, they exchange opinions and knowledge. This entitles us to treat parliamentary decision-making as essentially the same process of altering the structure of knowledge as takes place in the human mind, according to the latest findings of cognitive science and artificial intelligence studies, when it contemplates and makes its decision.[4] The difference is that in collective decision-making the transformation of knowledge is externalized. The 'program' that determines the process of contemplation is projected 'outside' and takes the form of procedures regulating the activities of the organization and the behaviour of its members. All organizations may indeed be viewed as some kind of 'artificial intelligences', except that their 'minds' are embodied in procedures, statutes and regulations rather than in computer processors (see Sergeyev, 1985). The problem thus becomes one of political culture. The bulk of the work is done in human minds, of course, but the stricter the rules, the more predictable (and the more manageable) the outcome.

With the help of this metaphor of artificial intelligence, one may venture to examine in what sense the activity of a parliament may be called 'rational'. Is a group of individuals cleverer than a single individual? Why do we need (if, indeed, we do) collective decision-making? While it is improbable that any group can be cleverer than a very clever person, when it comes to parliaments the stakes are different. An assembly of ordinary ('average') persons can, under certain circumstances, be cleverer than any one of them taken alone. The function of procedures is to provide for these circumstances. But what is, perhaps, even more important is the fact that the public character of debates makes 'the working' of this collective intelligence comprehensible to outside observers and hence subject to the conscious control by those who delegate the deputies. Which can hardly be the case if a single leader, however democratically elected, contemplates her/his decisions, more competent though they may be, in the silence of her/his office after private exchange of opinions with her/his advisers.

Populism and democracy

That the parliamentary idea was not always favoured by privileged minorities is hardly surprising. That it would sometimes come under attack from those who believed themselves to act in the best interests of 'the people' makes less sense. But whether populist critics of parliamentary democracy were misguided or not, 'democracy' and 'populism', one is forced to admit, are different notions.

For a contemporary Russian, 'populism' sounds unmistakably foreign and is just another '-ism'. But the concept behind the word is not unfamiliar. The political rhetoric of nineteenth-century Russia used to put great emphasis on the notion of *narodnost'*. *Narodnost'* is derived from *narod*, which stands both for 'nation' and 'people', the latter almost invariably understood as 'the common people' and opposed to 'the higher' or, as Leo Tolstoy would have put it, 'the educated' classes.

That interpretation might have belonged to the common stock of the European egalitarian/democratic ideology, but what formed a peculiar feature of the Russian political culture as it developed towards the end of the last century was the implication that the people were not just 'our suffering brothers', of whom their more prospering fellow citizens ought to take care and whose burden they were to relieve (if they were 'honourable men', that is); 'the people' stood for something immeasurably greater: it was a source, or rather *the* source, of ultimate truth and ultimate wisdom denied to representatives of the privileged classes despite the elegance of their life-styles and their superior education. Leo Tolstoy's *Confession* (1904a: 59–61, 79–80) would provide a glaring example of that attitude, while his Platon Karatayev has developed into a textbook illustration of a common man, a man of the people, from whom that sophisticated aristocrat, Pierre Bezukhov, still has something important to learn (see Tolstoy, 1904b: Vol. 8, 66 ff.).[5]

Applied to politics, however, this appeal to popular wisdom was indicative of, or bound to create, a belief pattern that must be distinguished from the notion of popular sovereignty as it had evolved within the European democratic tradition. The classical teachers of democracy had not based their arguments on the belief in the *dēmos* as the repository of unique political wisdom. The notion of the sovereign as the ultimate source of legitimacy would constitute a natural point of departure for any theory of delegated authority, while attribution of that status to the people, rather than to some other body social, would be justified by the people's natural right to choose their own destiny.

The line of argument used to substantiate this view can be traced to the nominalistic roots of the philosophical tradition to which the majority of the classical democratic thinkers belonged. Most of them, it will be remembered, shared a common, if broadly defined, empirical outlook. Within this tradition, any question as to whether this or that particular choice is 'true' or 'false' is utterly pointless, though it certainly makes sense to distinguish between 'right' and 'wrong'.

The traditional Russian political outlook is, by contrast, realist (in the sense implied by scholastic philosophy): it would identify a 'right' decision as the one that is objectively justified ('true' or 'correct') and it would expect a political actor to aspire to such a decision. This outlook is based on the ontological assumption that there is some ultimate reality, some objective social order to back up a 'correct' – and therefore 'right' – decision.

The classical democratic theory is pivoted on the idea of the people's will because it finds it appropriate for the right to choose to belong to those who are to be affected by the choice. There can be no other approachable authority above the people legitimately to question their decisions, display them as either true or false, much less to substitute them with its own judgement. The conceptual model we attempt to analyse here belongs to a political culture moulded in a different way, a culture that strives after answers that would be 'correct'. If it turns to the people, rather than to anyone else, it is because it assumes that the people possess the appropriate knowledge, not because it believes in their 'rights' or attributes any to them.

Regarded in the procedural perspective, the difference becomes crucial. If your primary concern is to know the people's *will*, you will seek to ensure that the will is really theirs, that it has not been distorted, falsified or misinterpreted in any way. You will try to invent and introduce a set of measures that would protect your sovereign people from being bullied or deceived. You will do your best to prevent any abuse of power over their bodies and minds. And you will ask for opinions not because you are looking for the correct one and, hence, believe that the more you have to choose from, the better your chances of finding it. You will do so because there is no other way to arrive at a solution that would be acceptable to all; and the reason it has to be acceptable to all, or at least to as many as possible, is that it is to be binding on all.

But if you are concerned with finding the one correct decision, rather than a generally acceptable one, just any opinion will not do: it will have to be the opinion of the best available expert. Turning to 'the people' for that expertise is of tremendous consequence, both ideologically and politically.

First, strange as it may sound, 'the people' gain very little from it as far as practical benefits are concerned. They may be acclaimed as 'true masters of life', but they are not allowed to become 'masters of their own fate'. They are not free to choose, for experts are asked for

advice, not for their choice. But 'the people' are not even experts in
the literal sense of the word. It would be more appropriate to call
them 'oracles', for the origin of their superior wisdom remains
somewhat mysterious. The political implications of this apparently
'demophilic' position have little in common with what the Western
political tradition would recognize as genuine democracy. Not only is
every dissident minority to be treated as a gang of heretics, which in
itself would be a violation of one of the fundamental principles of
democratic community; but the majority itself is not expected to
exercise any particular 'rights'.

Secondly, it is evident that anyone can make mistakes. Whomever
you choose to classify as 'the people' will be no exception. Moreover,
if you ask people for their opinions, you are sure to find that they
differ from one another. And if you still insist on retaining your belief
in the people's wisdom, it will have to take the irrational form of an
appeal to the people en masse. In that case, the people will no longer
be 'they' but 'it'. And the decision will have to be *its*, not *theirs*. The
resulting outlook is paradoxical. 'The people' taken as a single whole
does know 'the truth', while the empirical people, that is, the social
agglomerate that consists of (and hence is divided into) particular
groups and individuals, lack that knowledge. Within this outlook
and, it would not be out of place to observe, in full accord with the
spirit of scholastic realism, 'the people' as a whole acquires an
independent and peculiar ontological status to be distinguished from
those of empirical individual human beings, social groups or even
those very people regarded as a concrete socio-historic formation, for
example the population of a given country at a given time. The unity
of 'the people' pervades space and time and is considered a primary
bond, not to be doubted or denied, whatever the (empirical)
circumstances.

Thirdly, this type of political culture has no use for democratic
procedures, if by that name we mean a set of rules whose primary
function is to help find out and implement the will of the people.
Interests differ, and it takes much time and great effort to negotiate
an acceptable compromise.

But it would be a waste of time and effort to enter a debate, if the
result were already known. And it certainly would be ridiculous, not
to say immoral, to compromise over matters of truth and falsehood.
This would pose no particular problem as long as one were dealing
with objective reality, for objective reality does not need to be
recognized, nor does objective truth depend on whether people agree
to accept it or not. But when it comes to matters of public concern,
the situation is different. No decision may be justified by reference to
popular will as long as that will remains ambivalent. If, for some

reason, you choose to demonstrate that what is objectively true is also willed by the people, the procedures you need will be those that ensure the unanimity of decisions, rather than their universal acceptability. A representative institution to qualify for this task will have to differ from its counterpart in Western political culture, namely the parliament.

The problem is somewhat analogous to the scholastic debates over God's will. Some philosophers have argued that God is not free if His decisions are motivated by His knowledge, if that is independent of His will. Others would object that He is not wise if He goes against His better judgement. The solution would come in the form of some mystic harmony between His will and His knowledge. The populist myth calls for a similar harmony, and Russian political philosophy has a name for it – *sobornost'*. If this harmony does not come spontaneously, it has to be created; if it cannot be created, it is to be faked.

The idea of *Sobornost'*

The word *sobornost'* alludes to *Sobors*, representative institutions of sixteenth- and seventeenth-century Russia.[6] Throughout this chapter it is used to refer to a model representative institution, alternative to the British Parliament and its various counterparts in other Western countries. Whether historic reality will eventually justify this use of the term seems, from our standpoint, irrelevant. For it is the models, or what Max Weber would have called the 'ideal-types', that we deal with when we study political cultures, rather than actual institutions that did or do exist on the political scene. Still, choice of names should not be entirely arbitrary; ours is not, as the following effort to trace the ideal of *sobornost'* to its medieval roots will show.

To begin with, *Sobors* of medieval Muscovy were originally ecclesiastical institutions. The word is still used in contemporary Russian to refer to ecclesiastical councils and, more significant still, it translates the Greek *ekklēsia*: both mean 'assembly'. (This, incidentally, accounts for the word's other meaning: 'cathedral'.) Its connotations are thus peculiarly religious for the Russian ear. But what is relevant to the present argument is the fact that representative political institutions cannot be modelled on ecclesiastical councils without significant consequences. For underlying whatever polemics might take place at them is the notion of the ultimate truth to be attained. They are not convened to reach a balanced opinion that would suit anyone (or even the majority), and it will make little sense to negotiate a compromise over an issue at them or put it to the participants' vote. Neither procedure is appropriate, for what an ecclesiastical council, or for that matter a scientific symposium, seeks is the objective truth. Neither is expected to take care of the participants' personal interests, or interests of those they may be considered to 'represent'. Hence, neither will qualify as a 'representative' institution, much less a genuinely democratic assembly, for both are sure to fail in meeting the egalitarian standards of modern democracy.

A Russian medieval *Sobor* never presumed to do so, of course. Nor did any other European representative assembly, whether the Parliament of England, *les États généraux* of France, or the *Cortes* of Castile at the time they came into existence. The difference between the latter and the former is that Russian *Sobors* never had the chance to evolve into modern representative institutions. One reason was that their history was too short compared to that of their European counterparts: it was confined, indeed, to little more than a century.[7] And throughout that century they remained an irregular ad hoc institution. It was only at times of severe crises – little short, perhaps, of national catastrophes – that they were allowed to play a significant political role.

The latter circumstance was of major importance. Convened primarily to solve issues of an extraordinary nature and with little or no experience of 'normal operation' under stable conditions, the Muscovy *Sobors* were not considered assemblies whose members were to represent their electorate, or their parties, or even their social strata – regardless of the particular procedure used for their nomination. A *Sobor* was meant to represent the civil society as a whole. It was a symbolic deputy of the people in its intercourse with the government. Its primary function was to re-establish the union between the two lost through the hardships of fortune. As such, the *Sobor* would consider it most improper to attempt to play the role of opposition, or to tolerate any factions within its ranks.

The subsequent evolution towards unlimited autocracy left no niche for a representative institution in the political life of the Russian Empire. *Zemskie Sobors* (secular assemblies) fell into total disuse, and it was not until the nineteenth century that the idea of *sobornost'* began to play a significant role in Russian political philosophy. It was put forward by Slavophiles, a peculiar band of philosophers who managed to combine a liberalizing outlook with a fervent idealization of medieval Muscovy, and later elaborated by the great idealistic thinkers of what came to be known as the 'Russian Renaissance'. It stood for some mystic union of humanity and was opposed to the individualism believed to be a characteristic feature of Western (unorthodox) culture. *Sobornost'*, by contrast, was exemplified by the collectivistic totality of the Russian orthodox *mir* – a self-governed village community.

The philosophers did not 'invent' the idea, of course. It would be more appropriate to say that they 'elicited' it from the fundamentally religious culture of the masses. It was this culture that the triumphant victors of October would have to deal with and, in the long run, to rely on.

Sobornost' and the Soviets

One may wonder, however, how that culture could 'stomach' – moreover, so fast and so easily – what appeared to be the entirely alien ideology of Marxism. For, admittedly, Marx had little or nothing to say on the substance of problems that afflicted Russian society. The assimilation was doubtless facilitated by similarities in political rhetoric. Marx's 'Jacobin spirit', his fervent support for whatever he believed to be a revolutionary movement, made his theory appear relevant and attractive to revolutionaries throughout the world.

In the case of Russia, however, the decisive factor was of a different nature. Although the Marxist tradition in social thought is justly associated with the ideas of social stratification and class struggle, the stratification itself was invariably regarded by Marx and his followers as a social evil to be eliminated in the course of future development, while the much celebrated struggle between the bourgeoisie and the proletariat was expected to pave the way to a homogeneous (classless) society. It is not difficult to discern in this goal the ideal of *sobornost'* that has formed the basis of a peculiar national political utopia.

For all the differences in their *Weltanschauungen*, Marx and Russian ideologues of *sobornost'* agreed on one significant point: the wills of social agents were believed to be objectively determined – 'prescribed' – and those 'wills' would often fail to coincide with actual aspirations of individuals that comprised those collective agents. It is not surprising, therefore, that, different though these thinkers' social ontologies were, they tended to work in a similar manner when it came to political behaviour. And this, in turn, would account for the paradoxical syncretism created by superimposing the revolutionary outlook of Marxism on the religious culture of traditional Russia.

This taken into account, one should not be surprised to come across many traditional features in the political system that the self-professed grave-diggers of the old Russian society created on its charred ruins. Representative institutions were no exception.

The Bolsheviks never liked parliaments, and their hostility was, perhaps, justified – from their standpoint, that is. The whole project of socialist construction was bound to fail were it to depend on the outcome of this or that election or this or that vote. Their ideal of political representation was the system of Soviets.

The Soviets were conceived as an alternative to the 'bourgeois' system of separation of powers. They were to be endowed with both legislative and executive power[8] embodying the democrats' opium – the idea of direct popular rule.[9] However, the arrangement could not help paralysing the hierarchy of government. For since every Soviet was instituted as an agency of direct authority and was meant to possess what bourgeois political science would have called 'sovereignty', it was bound to find itself in permanent conflict with every other Soviet that had nominal jurisdiction over the same territory, that is, with every higher or lower Soviet.

The Soviet model of state power could only exist and operate as long as it had a kind of 'backbone' in it – inasmuch as there existed and operated behind the scenes an entirely different political hierarchy that was totally independent of the Soviets and could undertake to solve the problems and conflicts that proved beyond the capacity of the amorphous Soviet system.

Though used as the regime's official designation, 'Soviet power' was thus a singularly misleading name: it was not the councils of workers' deputies that ruled the state, but the party that operated within those councils and dominated them, as, for that matter, it did everything else in the country. It was the party hierarchy, acting over the head of the Soviets, that ensured that coordination of local and national interests, or rather the subordination of local authorities to central power, without which the country could not be preserved as a single whole.

The party itself was prepared for the task. Theoretically, the way was paved by *What Is to Be Done?*, a pamphlet written by Lenin as far back as 1902 (see Lenin, 1961). Its purpose was to ensure the party's leadership in the revolutionary movement of the time. Lenin's argument was based on the assumption that society and history are governed by objective laws and whoever knows these laws is likely to have his or her way. It took little effort to infer thence that scientific understanding of society entitled one to rule it. Though not easily swallowed by the sceptically minded intellectual élite, the idea seemed more alien in form than it was in substance. It was obviously related to the realist standards of the national political mentality, and it appealed to the masses who had come to worship all-powerful science, both natural and social, as they had worshipped the omnipotent and omniscient God only a generation ago.

It may be wondered, however, why this system of Soviet power based on the principles, albeit defective, of election and representation did not evolve, if not into genuine representative democracy then at least into some kind of moderate pluralism. Granted it proved ineffective; granted it could not help being ineffective in the circumstances; but why was there not a single attempt to improve? Why did it so slavishly acquiesce to serve as a cloak for party rule? To answer this question we must turn back to the model of *sobornost'*. For it was this model, somewhat modified, that formed the basis of the Soviet system.

The notorious triune formula of imperial Russia, 'Orthodoxy, Autocracy, Populism (*narodnost'*)', had often been subject to criticism and ridicule. Not all critics seemed to realize, however, how congruous it was in its own way or to feel the intrinsic agreement of its constituent elements. *Narodnost'* may be interpreted in different ways, of course, and so indeed it was. There were conservative populists in Russia, even reactionary populists, and there were revolutionary populists. Some populists would defend autocracy, some would conspire against it. There were even genuine democrats among them, although the latter would feel somewhat uncomfortable in the company. The idea of populism, we have already argued, is not identical with that of democracy. The difference between the two may account, to some extent, for the ordeals suffered by representative democracy under conditions of direct popular rule. As a matter of fact, however, the difference goes even deeper than that. It was not through historic fortune alone that the model of *sobornost'* turned out to be linked with unrestricted autocratic power: in fact, the former may be said to presuppose and generate the latter.

The Slavophiles seemed to sense this in their time, although their apologia for autocracy sounded somewhat artificial.[10] There are no mechanisms or procedures for collective decision-making, still less for collective action, within the unstructured totality of a *Sobor*, and by definition there cannot be. A *Sobor* as a body is able to approve or disapprove of a decision, but it has no means to work it out. And it certainly lacks the organs required to implement it. In order to acquire them, it would also have to acquire differentiated structures. Such a development, however, would be manifestly unacceptable since it contradicts the idea and ideal of *sobornost'*. It was not by chance that the majority of Russian thinkers who discussed the notion of *sobornost'* placed it within the spiritual sphere: it was certainly ill adapted to secular affairs. That is why political *sobornost'* – that is, *sobornost'* as a political ideal or rather a distinct type of political culture (and it is this meaning of the word that concerns us here) – cannot be embodied directly in a system of power agencies. It exists and functions as a spiritual background for power that is alienated from the people and opposed to them. The function of power is to act, whereas a *Sobor* is unable to act, for reasons given above. Since no organs of action can be instituted within the *Sobor*, they are instituted outside it.

It was, thus, not through their bad luck that the Soviets lost real power. They could hardly have retained it if the political culture within which they had evolved were to continue. The Soviet system was created by and for people whose patterns of political mentality would not resist development of power structures outside and above the Soviets, but would, on the contrary, presuppose them.

Populist rhetoric and totalitarian practice

So it was not long before the only function left to the Soviets was to dress the windows. But this was no trifling function. And it would be a mistake to believe that the decorative façade of the Soviets was intended for outward effect only, whether domestic or abroad. References to presumably democratic representative institutions might, of course, be used to beat off accusations of lack of genuine democracy. But it was scarcely possible that anyone would sincerely expect such arguments to be convincing. However, the invariable and unfailing demonstration of unity in voting – the phenomenon that would later be given the scathing nickname of '*approveh'm*' ('*odobryams*') – could not help influencing the mentality and behaviour of the deputies themselves.

It is hard to believe that in all the years of its history the USSR Supreme Soviet never had among its members a single individual who had reason or whim to vote just once against the majority. Such situations were bound to spring up, all the more so as the corps of deputies was by no means composed of mere puppets or extras admitted for the sake of observing the proprieties. There were influential persons among the deputies, truly influential: government officials, generals, top-rank party functionaries, well-known representatives of free professions – in short, the national élite. They could not always have been of the same opinion: that would have been ridiculous. But since there were different interests involved and different views held, there had to be some effort to achieve a consensus. But whatever was done to arrive at mutually acceptable decisions, it would take place outside the Supreme Soviet. If its deputies argued and quarrelled among themselves, that was always elsewhere. Within the Soviet, pathetic accord would invariably be displayed: the deputies seemed to be imbued with a desire to demonstrate their unity to the whole outside world, or perhaps to themselves. Even those who were contra would unfailingly vote pro. The Supreme Soviet was thus able to perform successfully its basic function, far more important, indeed, than any overseas propaganda might have ever been: to maintain the myth of the monolithic unity of the Soviet people rallied around the Communist Party in struggle for their common cause.

This unity, of the kind that would have been worthy of the ideal of *sobornost'*, was the embodiment of the deep-rooted understanding of what constituted the people and representation of the people. The word *sobornost'* was never heard, to be sure: it sounded 'pre-revolutionary' enough to be suspected of being 'counter-revolutionary'. But its functional substitute, the idea of a classless society, was proclaimed the Soviet Union's official goal. Marxism proved opportune again. From the standpoint of social theory, the Marxist paradigm stresses class contradictions. But it was not the theory, but the *myth* of Marxism that was the foundation of the Soviet political mentality: the myth of the proletariat that had nothing to lose but its fetter and that in pursuing its specific class interest would abolish itself as a class of the have-nots, and, with it, class differentiation as such. When class contradictions disappeared following the elimination of class distinctions, the ideal of popular unity would be realized and political institutions that embodied it would be legitimated.

Within the operational experience acquired in these institutions, disagreement with the majority is regarded not as a natural, albeit unfortunate, manifestation of divergent interests or beliefs, but precisely and fundamentally as an intentional demonstration of dissent and disunity. Such behaviour is inadmissible, for it threatens to undermine the sustaining myth of the political culture.[11] The deputy must realize that if he votes contra, he opposes not those who vote pro, but the whole people. In this, he exposes himself to be a secret 'enemy of the people' and a traitor. The myth demands the renegade be cast out. The ostracism might assume different forms and have different consequences for the outcast, but the depth of the roots the myth had put down was attested to by the fact that it took thirty-five years after the bloody repressions of the Stalin era had ceased before the Soviet parliament had occasion to witness a deputy who dared to break the rules of the game and express his disagreement by openly voting contra.

The idea of a representative institution that formed the basis of the Soviet model was thus radically different from the parliamentary idea. A Supreme Soviet's deputy was certainly a 'representative', but not inasmuch as he or she 'represented' his or her voters or, terrible to think, his or her party (the latter was altogether inconceivable since there was only one party, and it did not need to be 'represented'): the deputy was a 'representative' because he or she was a member of a body that 'represented' the people as a whole, and was the people's deputy in direct intercourse with the authorities. In this capacity, the Supreme Soviet, first of all, could claim no authority for itself. Secondly, it could not and ought not to be considered an arena in which particular interests were defended or reconciled and conflicts were settled or solved. It was the Supreme Soviet's task to presume there were no conflicts within the people and within the society.

The democratic idea, if and when it evolves within the political culture based on the notion of *sobornost'*, has little use for the three basic principles of the classical democratic theory as described in the opening section to this chapter. In the first place, democracy, even if duly defined as 'government of, for and by the people', is not justified by reference to citizens' *human rights*; nor does this doctrine imply that community is constituted by some sort of *social contract* between them. Every genuine and lasting community is a natural organism of which constituent parts can enjoy no rights as against the whole. Secondly, the *separation of powers* is not regarded as a safeguard against abuse of power; on the contrary, it is to be denounced as a vile attempt to weaken the power and thus deprive it of its *raison d'être*. The same is true of any other device whose function is to limit power or bring it under control. Last but not least, *freedom of political activity* is not seen and sought as a means to maintain a just social order; what is required to attain this goal is the superior understanding of the nature of social life. Hence it follows that politics is not to be profaned (nor the community to be endangered) by opening the way to ignorant ambitions.

Whether we call this democracy is a matter of definition. Various practices and institutions may qualify for it, though perhaps on different grounds. The old Russian village community with its long tradition of self-government, for example, may be called a democratic institution without stretching the definition too far. It does not seem fair to discard it as non- or pseudo-democratic simply because it does not wholly resemble the classical patterns of today.

The question, however, is whether this would automatically make it a feasible model for a modern democratic state. The present predicament of Russia's democracy may be due in part to lack of proper understanding of the paramount difference that separates a set of democratic practices cultivated by certain social groups under specific circumstances from a system of democratic institutions on state level, and to the resulting attempt to build the latter on a model that seems ill adapted for the task. Still, this is a natural endeavour, for where else can people's notions and ideas, expectations and phobias be rooted if not in their own social experience? And however scholars define democracy for their own scholarly reasons, it would hardly serve their purpose to ignore the ways democracy is understood by men and women who are involved in the actual process of democratization scholars seek to explain.

Notes

This chapter was written with the support of the Russian Foundation for Fundamental Research.

1 See classical works by Dahl (1982, 1985). For studies of political culture within which democratic institutions operate, see Aberbach et al. (1981), Putnam (1976), Verba (1987).

2 See Migranyan (1989). (For an English version, see Migranyan, 1990.) This controversial article caused an extensive polemic joined by a number of prominent political writers of the time. For this, see *Literaturnaya gazeta* 1989 (33, 38, 39, 42, 52: articles by E. Ambartsumov, L. Batkin, I. Klyamkin, A. Kron, A. Migranyan and others, in Russian), and Pospelovsky (1990).

3 The problem was later discussed by the social philosophers of the Frankfurt School; see Marcuse (1964) and, especially, Adorno and Horkheimer (1972), a work that was written during the Second World War but profoundly influenced contemporary 'postmodern' theories of society.

4 It is worthwhile noting here that the metaphor of 'a community' of individuals has proved fruitful in building models of intellectual activity (see Minsky, 1985).

5 'No, you cannot understand what it is I learned from this illiterate, foolish man', Pierre would later say to Natasha (Tolstoy, 1904b: Vol. 8, 323).

6 For the latest survey of historic data, see Cherepnin (1978).

7 The first *Sobor* met in February 1549; the last was convened at the end of 1683 and, having held no session, was dissolved next March (Cherepnin, 1978: 382–4).

8 Characteristic features of the Soviet system of state power were defined by Lenin as follows: 'Abolition of parliamentarism (as the separation of the legislative from executive activity); union of legislative and executive state activity. Fusion of administration with legislation' (Lenin, 1965b: 154).

9 'The socialist character of Soviet, that is *proletarian*, democracy . . .', Lenin wrote, 'lies in the fact that all bureaucratic formalities and restrictions of elections are abolished; the people themselves determine the order and time of elections' (1965a: 272).

10 They would infer the need for autocracy out of their semi-anarchistic condemnation of all politics and all power as sinful. Since, however, society cannot exist without government, they argued, it is more appropriate for this deplorable, albeit indispensable, job to be done by one rather than by many (see Berdyaev, 1947).

11 The notion of a political culture's sustaining myth was advanced by Tucker (1987: 22).

References

Aberbach, J., Putnam, R. and Rockman, B. (1981) *Bureaucrats and Politicians in Western Democracies*. Cambridge, MA: Harvard University Press.

Adorno, T. and Horkheimer, M. (1972) *Dialectic of Enlightenment*. New York: Herder and Herder.

Berdyaev, N. (1947) *The Russian Idea*. London: Geoffrey Bless.

Cherepnin, L. (1978) *The Zemskie Sobors of the Russian State in the 16th–17th Centuries* (in Russian). Moscow: Nauka.

Dahl, R. A. (1982) *Dilemmas of Pluralist Democracy: Autonomy vs Control*. New Haven, CT and London: Yale University Press.

Dahl, R. A. (1985) *A Preface to Economic Democracy*. Berkeley and Los Angeles: University of California Press.

Lenin, V. (1961) *What Is to Be Done? Burning Questions of Our Movement*, in *Collected Works, Vol. 5*. Moscow: Foreign Languages Publishing House. pp. 347–527. (Original work published 1902.)

Lenin, V. (1965a) *The Immediate Tasks of the Soviet Government*, in *Collected Works, Vol. 27*. Moscow: Progress Publishers. pp. 235–77. (Original work published 1918.)

Lenin, V. (1965b) 'Ten Theses on Soviet Power', in *Collected Works, Vol. 27*. Moscow: Progress Publishers. pp. 153–5. (Original work published 1918.)

Marcuse, H. (1964) *One-Dimensional Man*. Boston, MA: Beacon Press.

Migranyan, A. (1989) 'A long way to the European home' (in Russian), *Novy mir*, 7.

Migranyan, A. (1990) *Perestroika as Seen by a Political Scientist*. Moscow: Novosti Press Agency.

Minsky, M. (1985) *The Society of Mind*. New York: Simon and Schuster.

Ortega y Gasset, J. (1932) *The Revolt of the Masses*. New York: Norton.

Pospelovsky, D. (1990) 'Totalitarianism – authoritarianism – democracy?' (in Russian), in *Knizhnoe obozrenie*, 20.

Putnam, R. (1976) *The Comparative Studies of Political Elites*. Englewood Cliffs, NJ: Prentice Hall.

Sergeyev, V. (1985) 'Artificial intelligence as a method of studying complex systems' (in Russian), *Sistemnye issledovaniya. 1984*. Moscow: Nauka.

Tolstoy, L. (1904a) *My Confession*, in *The Complete Works, Vol. 13*. London: J. M. Dent. (Original work published 1879–82.)

Tolstoy, L. (1904b) *War and Peace*, in *The Complete Works, Vols 5–8*. London: J. M. Dent. (Original work published 1865–8.)

Transition (1991) *The Transition to Democracy: Proceedings of a Workshop National Research Council*. Washington, DC: National Academy Press.

Tucker, R. (1987) *Political Culture and Leadership in Soviet Russia: From Lenin to Gorbachev*. New York, London: W.W. Norton & Co.

Verba, S. (1987) *Elites and the Idea of Equality: A Comparison of Japan, Sweden and the United States*. Cambridge, MA: Harvard University Press.

9

Cultural Diversity and Liberal Democracy

Bhikhu Parekh

Such principles as equal respect for persons, equality before the law and equal civil and political rights of citizens are central to liberalism, and embodied in different degrees in the structures of all liberal-democratic states. The existence of cultural diversity in contemporary societies raises acute problems about how these principles are to be interpreted and applied. Their conventional individualist and culture-blind interpretation leads to much injustice, and casts doubts on the validity of the attempts to assess the democratic character of a society by simplistic devices based on mechanical notions of equality. No discussion of the definition and measurement of democracy today can be satisfactory unless it is grounded in and informed by a full appreciation of the inescapable reality of cultural pluralism.

Almost every modern state is characterized by cultural diversity, that is, by the presence of different and sometimes incompatible ways of life that seek in their own different ways to preserve themselves. As such, the state is confronted with such questions as the range of permissible diversity, how to accommodate differences without losing its social cohesion, how to reconcile the apparently conflicting demands of equality of treatment and recognition of cultural differences, and how to create a spirit of common citizenship among its culturally diverse members.

Cultural diversity in the modern state takes several forms, of which four currently arouse the greatest concern, First, the indigenous peoples, such as the Amerindians, the Maoris, the Australian Aborigines, the Inuits and other 'original nations', are anxious to preserve their distinct and largely pre-modern ways of life. Their ways of life are integrally bound up with land, to which they have a deeply spiritual relationship. Although they once enjoyed independence which they later lost to white colonizers, they do not generally seek to form themselves into independent states; their main concern is to recover or retain their land and to be left alone to lead their traditional ways of life within the framework of the existing states.

Secondly, there are territorially concentrated and politically self-conscious communities that wish to preserve their distinct languages and cultures, if possible within the existing states, if not by becoming independent. Such groups as the Francophones in Quebec, the Basques, the Bretons, the Tamils in Sri Lanka and the Muslims in Kashmir fall within this category. Unlike the first group, they are not opposed to the wider society's way of life and share its economic, social and political aspirations. The Francophones in Quebec, for example, do not reject the modern industrial way of life. But they have a distinct linguistic and cultural identity which they are anxious to preserve. They feel that they cannot do so within the framework of the traditional federal state granting them administrative autonomy and equality of status with other provinces. They therefore demand the right to control immigration, to impose measures designed to protect the French language, culture and ethos, and to remain a 'distinct society' within the Canadian state. They argue that since their cultural needs are different, they require rights and powers the rest of Canada does not need, and that there is nothing inherently unfair or unequal in an asymmetrical federalism. The demands of the Kashmiri Muslims, the Bretons and others are broadly of a similar kind.

Thirdly, there are territorially dispersed but culturally distinct groups who wish to preserve their ways of life. They include such groups as immigrants, indigenous ethnic minorities and religious communities. Unlike the first two groups, they neither demand to be left alone nor seek political autonomy. For the most part they seek the cultural space to lead and transmit their ways of life and an opportunity to make their distinct contributions to the collective life.

Finally, the demand for the recognition of cultural diversity also comes from groups of men and women sharing in common a self-chosen life-style. They include such groups as gays, lesbians and those opting for unconventional forms of living together, who demand not merely toleration but respect for what they consider to be not just unconventional practices but distinct sub-cultures. They are not distinct ethnic or cultural groups, and their ways of life are not radically different from that of the majority. What distinguishes them is the fact that they have evolved distinct sub-cultures within the framework of a shared common culture. Unlike the first three kinds of groups which differ in varying degrees from individualist liberalism, this last group is firmly committed to it and uses its freedoms and opportunities for purposes disapproved of by many of its adherents. They are unconventional liberals, and legitimize their unconventionality in the liberal language of individual choice.

These groups, and several others I have not mentioned, seek different kinds of diversity and forms of accommodation, and call for different modes of restructuring the cultural and political space. As such, they raise different problems, invoke different moral and political principles, require different responses, and generate different discourses. Arguments used to justify or reject the claims of native people do not make much sense when applied to those of, say, Francophones in Quebec, let alone Muslims in Europe. Much intellectual confusion is created by assimilating them all into a uniform and undifferentiated discourse on cultural diversity.

In this chapter I shall concentrate on the third kind of cultural diversity and analyse the problems posed by the presence of ethnic, cultural and religious minorities seeking to preserve their distinct ways of life. Most modern states have religious groups with their distinct ways of life. They also have immigrant groups who wish to preserve their traditional ways of life as far as is possible within their new environment. Many modern states also have such long-existing groups as the Jews who also cherish and seek to preserve their cultural identity. These groups wish to participate as equal citizens in the collective life of the community, but they also wish to preserve their way of life and demand recognition of their cultural identities. This raises the question as to how a liberal state should respond to their demands.

The question has received three answers, which for convenience I shall call assimilationist liberalism, cultural *laissez-faire* and cultural pluralism.[1] I shall reject the first two and endorse the third. I shall argue that while the first two fall squarely within the dominant strand of the liberal tradition, the last stretches the tradition to its limits and both retains its central insights and goes beyond it.

Assimilationist liberalism

The assimilationist liberal argues that the liberal state presupposes and is a custodian of a way of life centred on such values as personal autonomy, freedom of choice and independent thought.[2] Minority ways of life, which are based generally on different sets of values, deny their members freedom of choice, prevent their children from growing up into self-determining adults, able to prosper in a competitive individualist society, and threaten the integrity of the liberal way of life. Being self-contained communities, they also prevent their members from fully integrating into the wider society. Furthermore, their demand for the recognition of their differences is incompatible with their demand for equality. In asking that their special needs and circumstances be taken into account or that they be exempted from certain requirements, they ask to be privileged over their fellow-citizens. To treat people equally is to treat them in more or less the same way, and that entails adopting a culture-blind or difference-blind approach. If the state started taking differences into account, they could easily become the bases of unfair discrimination and injustices, of which apartheid – existing until very recently in South Africa – is a salutary reminder. The assimilationist liberal argues that for these and other reasons, the liberal state has both a right and a duty to refuse to recognize the claims of cultural diversity and to do all in its power to integrate the minority communities into the liberal way of life. He or she contends that if the minority communities gave a serious thought to the matter, they would themselves see that assimilation was also in their own long-term interest. So far as the immigrants are concerned, the assimilationist liberal advances the additional argument that since they have migrated and decided to stay on of 'their own choice', they have implicitly or explicitly agreed to adopt the dominant liberal way of life.

Assimilationist liberalism is right to insist on the importance of common citizenship, social cohesion, a shared system of meanings, the limits to a society's ability to tolerate cultural diversity, and the dangers of being too sensitive to cultural differences. However, it takes an exceedingly narrow view of these values and additionally violates some of the central principles of liberalism. First, the liberal is committed to equal respect for persons. Since human beings are culturally embedded, respect for them entails respect for their ways of life. One's sense of personal identity is closely bound up with one's language, characteristic modes of thought, customs, collective memories, and so on, in a word with one's culture. To ignore the latter is to denude individuals of and reject what constitutes them as particular kinds of persons and matters most to them, and that is hardly a way of showing them respect. In abstracting away their differences, the assimilationist liberal reduces them to uniform and attributeless atoms, and shows respect not for the individual in all his or her uniqueness but for an indeterminate abstraction, which he or she is not. Assimilationist liberalism respects the abstract or basic humanity, but not the concrete or historically articulated humanity, and de-personalizes the individual. This does not mean that a way of life may not be criticized any more than respect for a person exempts him or her from criticism. But it does mean that we ought to make a sympathetic attempt to understand a way of life from within, be open to differences in beliefs and practices, and discourage or fight its specific features only after its adherents have failed to give a satisfactory defence of them.

Secondly, the assimilationist liberal mistakenly equates equality with uniformity, and fails to appreciate that otherwise different individuals are treated *unequally* if subjected to uniform treatment. Jews are not treated equally if they are required by the law to close their shops on Sundays. For Christians Sunday is a holiday, not for Jews, who are therefore reduced to opening their shops only five days a week. Muslim women are not treated equally if required to wear trousers at work. Since they are culturally forbidden to expose their bodies in public, the requirement virtually renders them jobless. To exempt them from this requirement is not to privilege them but to ensure them equality of treatment. It is true that differential treatment can become a basis for unfair discrimination, but so can uniform treatment. What is needed is to find ways of being discriminating without becoming discriminatory and of guarding against misuse of differences.

Thirdly, the liberal rightly values cultural diversity and pluralism on moral and epistemological grounds. As he or she argues, cultural diversity increases the range of available options, expands imagination and sympathy, and enriches life; it also encourages a healthy competition between different ways of life and deepens our knowledge of the nature and possibilities of human existence. Since this is so, the liberal cannot consistently privilege and protect the liberal way of life and conduct an assimilationist campaign against those that differ from his or her own. To do so is to assume that the individualistically defined liberal way of life alone is 'true' and represents the last word in human wisdom, a view that is not only arrogant and illiberal but one which the liberal cannot justify without incurring the change of circularity.

As the liberal should know, no way of life, however rich it might be, can ever express the full range of human potentiality. Since human capacities and aspirations conflict, to develop some of them is necessarily to neglect, suppress or marginalize others. Every way of life cherishes and highlights some human capacities and forms of excellence, and in so doing it necessarily marginalizes, ignores or suppresses others. Different ways of life therefore correct and balance each other and restrain each other's partialities. They should therefore be judged not only on the basis of what they are in themselves, but also in terms of their contribution to the overall richness of society. Even if a culture is judged 'poorer' than another, it might nevertheless play a vital role in preserving values and aspirations ignored by the latter. Once the long-established ways of life are destroyed in the dogmatic belief that the autonomous way of life alone is valuable, they are lost for ever. If the liberal way of life were to run into unexpected difficulties, as it is beginning to do today, we would have no resources left from which to draw new inspiration and strength. Even if aesthetic, moral, spiritual and other considerations did not weigh with us, prudence alone would require that we should not dissipate the inherited cultural capital and invest all our hopes in one cultural enterprise.

Finally, assimilationist liberalism sometimes has opposite consequences to those intended by it. When it declines to accommodate the demands of cultural minorities, the determined minorities refuse to give in, and exploit such spaces as liberalism itself provides to legitimize their demands. For reasons which we cannot here examine, liberalism is extremely sensitive to religion and anxious not to appear intolerant of deeply held religious beliefs and practices. Minorities are naturally tempted to take advantage of this, and demand recognition of their differences on the ground that these are an integral part of their religion. The Sikh's turban no longer remains a cultural symbol, which is what it largely is, and becomes a religious requirement. The Hindu's refusal to eat beef, the Muslim's use of loudspeakers to call the faithfuls to prayer, the Rastafarian's dreadlocks and so on also come to be presented in similar terms. The morally embarrassed liberal more often than not concedes these demands.

The long-term consequences of this are unfortunate for all concerned. Minorities are increasingly led to define their identity in religious terms, and their religion monopolizes their culture. Lacking the restraining influence of the non-religious elements of their culture, the religion becomes narrow and dogmatic. Contingent cultural practices acquire the status of mandatory religious requirements, and pressures are mounted for their rigorous enforcement. With the religionization of the culture, religious leaders become its sole authentic spokespersons and acquire undue religious and cultural authority. Assimilationist liberalism unwittingly not only arrests the natural growth of a community but also paves the way for some form of fundamentalism. It is not often appreciated that fundamentalism is often provoked by liberal intolerance, and that once it arises, liberalism feels mortally threatened and unwittingly takes over many of the characteristics of is enemy.

Sometimes when the religionization of their demands does not work, minorities legitimize their demands as part of their ethnic identity, and insist that the liberal refusal to concede them amounts to a violation of the latter. Cultural practices get ethnicized and are given a pseudo-natural grounding. The same process that occurs in the case of the religionization of culture is repeated here with appropriate modifications, and with similar results. If cultural differences were accepted as legitimate, and if the demands based on them not dismissed out of hand, those involved would not need to ground them in something as intractable and non-negotiable as religion and ethnicity. Religious and ethnic differences would still remain, but there is no need to add to their number.

As for the assimilationist liberal's argument that immigrants have implicitly committed themselves to the liberal way of life, it is deeply flawed. Some immigrants come to escape persecution and to preserve their way of life. To tell them that they have committed themselves to the dominant liberal way of life is to misconstrue their intentions. Some others migrate because the host society badly needs their labour and recruits them by offering all manner of incentives. It could therefore be argued that in recruiting them in full knowledge of their way of life, the liberal society implicitly undertakes to respect this. The assimilationist liberal misinterprets the act of immigration, which is basically a bilateral relationship involving consent and commitments on both sides. To insist that immigrants must accept the liberal way of life or leave is both to ignore the host society's implicit commitment to them, and to treat them as second-class citizens entitled to enjoy equality only on condition that they surrender their cultural identity.

Cultural *laissez-faire*

Some liberals such as John Gray (1993: chs 18, 20) have argued for cultural *laissez-faire*.[3] Extending the liberal principles of choice and competition to the realm of culture, they insist that every individual should be free to choose his or her way of life in a fair competition between several of them. In a truly liberal or rather libertarian or free society, the liberal way of life should compete with others on equal terms. It might win the competition, or it might not. A good liberal should accept the outcome without regret or recrimination. In order to ensure fair competition, Gray insists that the state should observe strict neutrality and not throw its weight behind the liberal way of life. It should be a purely formal and procedural institution requiring nothing more of its members than acceptance of its authority. Gray also rules out state education, the traditional liberal means of cultural homogenization, and would replace it with vouchers and tax deductions, leaving each family free to make its own educational provisions. He wants the government to eschew social, cultural or economic goals as well, and to confine itself to creating the conditions of order and civility and protecting individual choices.

There is something to be said for Gray's proposal. In almost all liberal societies, the state embodies and encourages the liberal way of life. Other ways of life suffer from structural disadvantages and are subjected to considerable official and unofficial pressure. As a result they are unable to flourish, and the liberal state's claim to respect or even to tolerate them equally remains hollow. While Gray is right to highlight this problem, his 'postmodern liberal conservatism' goes nowhere near solving it.

First, Gray postulates culturally unattached individuals freely choosing their way of life in a kind of cultural supermarket. Such a view misunderstands both the individual, who is of necessity a cultural being, and culture, which cannot be 'chosen' except from within a specific culture and which cannot therefore be chosen in the manner of material goods. As Gray himself sometimes admits, his society presupposes an individualist moral culture and is therefore structurally biased against those ways of life that discourage or lose their integrity and wholeness in a climate of individual choice.

Secondly, since Gray's society rests on an individualist moral culture, the state cannot remain indifferent to the latter. As he is led to admit, the government has a vital role in 'preserving, or repairing, the framework of practices and replenishing the fund of values on which individuality depends for its successful reproduction' (1993: 281). He nowhere explains what such cultural engineering involves, but he clearly assigns the government a considerable educational and cultural role. Like the libertarian project of economic *laissez-faire*, Gray's cultural *laissez-faire* presupposes an authoritarian state constantly attending to its necessary background conditions and correcting its unacceptable outcome. Such a state is hardly neutral. It also sits ill at ease with Gray's privatized education, for it is not clear how the state can replenish individuality without controlling education.

Thirdly, even if cultural competition were not to be rigged in the way Gray suggests, it would still remain deeply biased. Thanks to the two centuries of domination and state patronage, the liberal way of life is embodied in all the major legal, economic, political and other institutions and enjoys enormous political and economic power and cultural prestige. In a competition with it, non-liberal ways of life start off with severe material and psychological disadvantages. The outcome is predictable. In order to ensure genuine competition Gray's state would initially at least have to practise a policy of positive discrimination in favour of them, and that raises awkward questions for his libertarian theory of the state.

Finally, Gray's idea of a morally neutral state is logically incoherent. Every state has a specific structure of authority or constitution, and it makes laws and policies. Neither can be morally neutral. The state can be constituted in several different ways, each embodying a specific conception of the good life. It might be secular, theocratic or a mixture of the two. If secular, it might be based on universal franchise or on one limited by race, class or gender. The universal franchise might be equal or weighted in favour of the intellectual élite, as J. S. Mill argued. The system of elections might be direct or indirect, and might represent individuals, as the liberals advocate, or corporate groups, as Hegel and others have urged. The state might be based on the separation of powers, as the liberals insist, or it might concentrate all authority in one organ, as Marx and the communists have argued. Whatever its structure, the state is inescapably grounded in and biased towards a specific way of life.

The laws and policies of the state cannot be morally neutral either. Should it allow slavery, polygamy, polyandry, incest, public hanging, euthanasia, suicide, capital punishment, abortion, violent sports involving animals, marriages between first cousins, coerced marriages, divorce on demand, unconventional sexual practices, lesbian and homosexual marriages, rights of illegitimate children to inherit 'parental' property, and so on? If it does not legislate on these matters, it indicates that it does not consider them sufficiently important to the moral well-being of the community to require a collective, uniform and compulsory mode of behaviour. If it legislates, it takes a specific stand. In either case it presupposes a specific view of the good life. A morally neutral state, making no moral demands on its citizens and equally hospitable to all human choices, is logically impossible. And since every law and policy coerces those not sharing the underlying values, a morally non-coercive state is a fantasy. As we shall see, some states can be morally less partisan and narrow and hence less coercive than others, but no state can be wholly free of a moral bias and of the concomitant coercion.

Cultural pluralism

Unlike assimilationist liberalism, cultural pluralism welcomes cultural diversity on several interrelated grounds. It argues that human beings are cultural beings. As self-reflective beings they develop distinct cultures in the course of coming to terms with their natural and social experiences and giving meaning to their lives. All human beings share several distinctively human capacities in common, but these are defined, structured and developed differently in different cultures. Since human beings are culturally embedded, and since cultures are human creations born out of the human search for meaning, respect for human beings implies respect for their creations and sources of meaning.

As we saw earlier, no culture can ever exhaust the full range of human possibilities. It develops some capacities and sensibilities, but not others, and is necessarily limited. Unless human beings are able to step out of their culture, they remain imprisoned within it and are unable to appreciate its strengths and limitations. And they cannot step out of it unless they have access to alternative visions of life offered by other cultures. Cultural diversity is therefore a necessary condition of the human search for freedom and critical self-understanding. Human beings lack a master Archimidean standpoint from which to look at themselves and their cultures, but they do have available to them several mini-Archimidean standpoints in the form of a plurality of cultures. They can use each to view the others from the outside, and to tease out their similarities and differences. And they can also use their knowledge of them to uncover the full range of human capacities and achievements. We need access to other cultures not so much to increase our range of 'options', for cultures are not options, as to appreciate the singularity as well as the strengths and limitations of our own. This means that cultural diversity is valuable not so much because it expands our choices of ways of life but because it extends our sympathies, deepens our self-knowledge, and enables us to enrich our way of life by borrowing whatever is attractive in others and can be integrated into our own. Cultural diversity both institutionalizes human finitude and offers a moderate release from it. In so doing it encourages such worthwhile intellectual and moral qualities as humility, modesty, self-knowledge, objectivity and self-transcendence. It is therefore an objective good, a good whose value is not derived from human choices but from its being a necessary condition and component of human well-being and growth.

Cultural diversity, then, is a collective good.[4] It both gives the individual a sense of rootedness and creates the conditions of a collectively enriching dialogue. As we saw, it cannot be safeguarded by a policy of cultural *laissez-faire*. Since it is a valuable public good and since it cannot be left to the vagaries of a distorted cultural market, the state needs to play an active part in promoting it. Promoting cultural diversity involves *both* respecting and valuing different cultures and encouraging a dialogue between them. As we saw, the two are closely related. We should respect other cultures because we owe respect to our fellow-human beings whose creations and sources of meaning they are, and also because we hope thereby to generate a climate in which different cultures feel confident and stimulated enough to enter into a creative dialogue with each other.[5]

Respecting and promoting cultural diversity requires action at several levels. It requires that cultural minorities should be protected against conscious or unconscious discrimination in socially significant areas of life. In all societies, including and, one might even say, especially, the liberal, there is a persistent tendency to assume that there is only one proper way of being rational, reasonable or moral, only one proper way of constituting the family, finding sexual self-fulfilment, conducting interpersonal relations, behaving in public, leading a good life, and so on. As a result we tend to interpret and evaluate human actions in terms of a single set of criteria, causing much injustice to those guided by different criteria. A few examples from Britain will illustrate the point.

It was recently discovered that ethnic minority candidates for jobs and examinations were systematically underscored by their white interviewers, because their habit of not looking the latter in the eye led the interviewers to conclude that the candidates were shifty and unreliable. In a court case involving a black defendant, two white judges gave him a longer sentence than a white defendant guilty of exactly the same offence, because they thought that his repeated tendency to avoid their gaze proved him to be shifty, evasive and unreliable, and cast doubt on his evidence. When their black colleague insisted that this was the defendant's way of showing respect for the authority of the judges, the white judges were intrigued and unmoved. An orthodox Jew contesting police evidence was disbelieved by the magistrate because, though religious, he refused to take oath. The man was convicted on the basis of false police evidence. It was too late when the judges realized that some devout Jews do not take the oath for fear that they might inadvertently say something wholly or partially untrue and offend God. A Sikh defendant was thought to be making an unreasonable demand and was distrusted when he asked to wash his hands before taking an oath on the Sikh holy book. In many schools head teachers could not understand why their Hindu and Muslim pupils preferred to starve rather than eat beef or pork.

In these and similar cases, the party involved suffered discrimination and disadvantage because of the failure to take account of cultural differences. Those in authority abstracted their acts from the systems of meaning in which they were embedded, and uncritically interpreted them in terms of conventional categories and norms. Not surprisingly they wholly misunderstood the acts and ended up treating their agents both unequally and unjustly. Individuals are unlikely to be treated equally if their relevant differences are not taken into account. Two examples will indicate how justice can be done against a background of cultural difference. In Holland a Turkish woman's unemployment benefit was discontinued by a government officer because she refused to accept a job in which she would have been the only woman in a group of male workers. On appeal the Dutch Central Court of Appeal ruled that the discontinuation of benefit was unjust, as the woman's refusal to accept the job in culturally and religiously unacceptable conditions was fully justified.

A white woman's appeal in a similar situation would have received a different treatment. The two women are treated differently but equally, the equality consisting in the fact that they are judged *impartially* on the basis of the *same* criterion of what constitutes reasonable or acceptable working conditions for each.

Difficult situations do of course arise. In Britain a Nigerian woman scarred the cheeks of her 14- and 9-year-old sons in accordance with her tribal customs. This went against the norms of British society and she was convicted. However, since the woman was following her cultural practice, and since the cuts had been made in a ceremonial atmosphere and were unlikely to inflict permanent damage on the children, she was granted an absolute discharge. The judgment reconciled the demands of the two cultures, and avoided the dangers of both abstract universalism and naïve relativism. The Nigerian woman was first judged on the basis of the universally acceptable principle of not causing harm to others. Her culture was then brought in to elucidate the context and reinterpret the nature of the harm and to annul the consequences of the application of the universal principle. On the abstract universalist view, she should have been convicted and punished. On the relativist view, she should not have been convicted at all. On the culturally mediated universalist view, which the court took, she was convicted but not punished. The court's judgment indicated to the woman and to the minorities in general that while the British courts respected cultural diversity, they would only do so within certain limits and subject to certain conditions.[6] We shall consider later how these limits and conditions are determined.

The liberal tendency to reserve the public realm for the shared or common culture and to confine cultural differences to the private realm also tends to weaken cultural diversity and needs to be reassessed (see Modood, 1992). In this view, cultural differences are seen as a private matter for the minority communities and not as a valued part of the collective cultural capital of the community. The liberal culture remains the official culture of the community and enjoys all the concomitant prestige and glamour, whereas minority cultures diffidently survive on the margins of society. Not surprisingly, minorities tend to feel nervous and shy about their cultural identity and increasingly lose their cultural self-confidence. Almost all minorities, including the Jews in Europe, and until recently in the USA, tell stories of how they felt deeply embarrassed when their parents spoke their languages, wore their national dress and practised their religious rituals in public, or pointed to their special needs, and how over time they either suppressed all but the most banal features of their way of life or modified it at least in public to suit the majority taste. The burden of difference is not easy to bear, and becomes virtually unbearable if difference is resented, mocked, privatized, penalized and denied a public presence. It is hardly surprising that many minorities take the easy path of conformity and cultural euthanasia. Since cultural diversity is a vital collective good, we should ask not only the ideologically loaded question as to how much diversity a society should tolerate without losing its cohesion but also how much homogeneity it should tolerate in order not to become suffocating and bland.

The state can also encourage and sustain cultural diversity in a variety of other ways. There is no reason why public funds cannot be provided for the teaching of minority languages, cultures, religions, and so on, and for supplying appropriate bilingual educational material. In so doing the state shows its respect for minority languages and cultures, accepts them as part of the community's collective heritage, and exerts a measure of public discipline on them. The school curriculum could also reflect the diversity of society, and stress both its shared history and culture and the inheritances and settlement experiences of minority communities. Some countries such as Britain have gone further and provided for thousands of state-funded schools for Catholics, Jews and Anglicans as well as scores of single sex-schools. These so-called separate schools have often aroused liberal wrath mainly because of the fear that they create a divided society and militate against common citizenship. There is no evidence to justify the fear. Catholics, Jews and Anglicans have had their schools for decades, even centuries, and there is no evidence that their pupils have failed to integrate into mainstream society or that Britain has been reduced to a chaotic conglomeration of mutually incomprehensible groups. In fact many widely admired citizens, political leaders and administrators are products of such schools. One could go further and argue that these schools have contributed to the richness and variety of Britain by producing men and women who have brought their diverse talents, sensibilities and ways of thought and life to different areas of British life. The Roman Catholic Bishop of Leeds recently put the point well:

> The experience of my own community, which had been a persecuted minority, is that having our own schools within the state system helped us to move out of our initial isolation, so as to become more confident and self-assured. The effect of separate schools for us has been integration, not divisiveness. (*Bradford Telegraph and Argus*, 3 January 1991)[7]

Such schools do of course tend to become divisive in divided societies or when run by dogmatic and 'fundamentalist' communities. The answer then would lie either in requiring such schools to meet nationally prescribed and periodically inspected requirements on syllabus, pedagogy, examinations, norms of conduct, forms of discipline and so on, or better still in developing genuinely multicultural schools reconciling the demands of cultural diversity and a shared body of values. Since different societies have different histories and face different problems, no single formula suits them all. But the general principle guiding their search for appropriate educational systems should remain the same, namely how to sustain cultural diversity and stimulate intercultural dialogue within the framework of a shared body of public values, sentiments and loyalties.

The state can also sustain cultural diversity by recognizing the cultural needs of minorities and involving the latter in finding the best ways of meeting them. It can adopt group-related welfare policies and invite minority communities to participate in planning community centres, housing associations, urban development programmes, health and social services and so on. The state might patronize minority religious and cultural functions, fund museums displaying the contributions of different communities, and offer tax exemptions, subsidies or matching grants for activities designed to affirm cultural diversity and intercultural cooperation. By adopting a suitable cultural policy involving these and other measures, it nurtures the self-confidence of the minorities, draws them into the mainstream, opens up the public culture to their influences, and helps create a rich and lively community of different but equal citizens.

Some minorities have a rich and flourishing communal life. There is much to be said for the state encouraging self-governance among them and becoming a community of communities. This reduces its administrative and moral burden, encourages a sense of community and collective responsibility among the minorities, creates a participatory ethos, and helps them become self-regulating. Decentralization has many virtues, and there is no obvious reason why it should be based only on territorial and occupational and not on communal grounds as well. Similarly there is no reason why active participation in communal life should be considered less valuable than in the conduct of local affairs. Theorists of participation make the mistake of concentrating only on the territorial units and ignoring the increasing importance of communal life. In a society in which neighbours have only limited contacts with each other and are bonded by limited common interests, it is unwise to put all our hopes in neighbourhood communities.

In Britain the state grants considerable autonomy to Jews and does much to reinforce the authority of their representative institutions. Jews may open their shops on Sundays without being in breach of the

Sunday trading laws provided they obtain an appropriate certificate from the Board of Deputies of Jews. This acknowledges and reinforces the authority of their representative institutions. The Rabbinical courts, to which the Jews may take their disputes if so they wish, are recognized by the state and their verdicts are binding on the parties involved. On matters relating to their community, the Board of Deputies is invariably consulted and its views are treated with respect. Thanks to all this, the Jewish community has a collective presence in British public life. While a Jew remains free to leave his or her community and to disagree with its collective pronouncements, those who remain attached to the community respect its democratic structure of authority and are subject to its moral and social pressure. When crime or divorce rate rises within the community or when the family unity declines, they are widely discussed in synagogues and community newspapers, and appropriate actions are demanded and often taken.

Similar tendencies are also evident among other minorities in Britain, France, Germany and the Netherlands. The French who for long frowned on and refused to recognize ethnic and religious organizations are now beginning to stress their value as 'vital social tissues'. Since they are relatively new, the minority organizations lack the cohesion and the democratic structure of their Jewish counterparts. However, they are beginning to develop them. There is no obvious reason why the state should not encourage and sustain this process. To be sure, its job is not to *protect* minority cultures, for if they lacked the required will and capacity they would not survive and the state's protectionist measures would only arrest their natural evolution. Nor is it the state's job to *institutionalize* the relevant communities into bureaucratic corporations and throw its authority behind them. That is the way to social fascism in which communal corporations, enjoying the patronage and subject to the manipulation of the state, oppress their members, build up vested interests and freeze the inescapable process of cultural change.

What I am proposing has very different implications. Communities that are cohesive, have democratically accountable self-governing institutions and allow their members a right of exit play a vital role in giving their members a sense of rootedness, harnessing their moral energies for common purposes and sustaining the spirit of cultural pluralism. Rather than seek to dismantle them in the name of abstractly and narrowly defined goals of social cohesion, integration and national unity, the state should acknowledge their cultural and political value and grant them such support as they need and ask for. They do not threaten its cohesion and unity; on the contrary, they give it a moral and cultural depth. There is nothing inviolable about the traditional liberal separation between state and society. Conducting the affairs of a complex society is too important a task to be left to the state alone. It requires partnership between the two, and encouraging cohesive communities to run their affairs themselves under the overall authority of the state is an important dimension of that partnership.

Limits of permissible diversity

We have so far talked about the value of cultural diversity and the various ways of sustaining it. No society can tolerate every practice, thus raising the question as to how a liberal society should determine the range of permissible diversity. Liberals have paid insufficient philosophical attention to this question. In practice most liberal societies have summarily banned such practices as polygamy and the withdrawal of girls from schools before the statutory age. And although Britain has not banned so-called arranged marriages, its immigration policy is designed to discourage and even penalize them. None of these decisions was preceded by a serious public discussion, and many of them were deeply resented by the communities involved.

By and large, liberals have invoked three principles in deciding which cultural practices not to permit. First, some have appealed to what I might call the autonomy principle.[8] They argue that liberal society is centred on such values as individual autonomy, independent thought, choice and uncoerced self-determination, and cannot permit minority customs and practices that flout them. It might initially rely on educational, economic and other measures to discourage them, but if these fail it should ban them with a clear conscience. This is a standard assimilationist argument, and we have already said enough to indicate why it is flawed.

Secondly, some liberals have appealed to the no-harm principle. If a practice harms others, it should be banned. If it does not, the state should leave it alone, however strongly the society at large disapproves of it. Some liberals define harm in narrowly physical terms, others define it broadly to mean damaging the capacity for autonomy or to lead a good life. The no-harm principle is largely unproblematic when harm is defined in physical terms, but it is then too limited and narrow to allow us to ban such practices as incest, polygamy, polyandry and euthanasia which almost all liberal societies forbid. The no-harm principle runs into difficulties when harm is given a broader definition. If it means damaging the capacity for autonomy, the position is no different from that of the assimilationist liberal, and open to the same objections. If harm is defined in terms of the good life, acute problems arise for there is no consensus on the latter within the majority community itself, let alone between it and the minorities.

Thirdly, some liberals have appealed to the so-called fundamental or core values of their society, and argued that customs and practices incompatible with these may rightly be banned in a liberal society.[9] While there is much to be said for this view, it cannot be accepted without considerable redefinition and qualification. The concept of 'fundamental' or 'core' values is too elusive to be of much use. If it refers to values that constitute the foundation of society such that their rejection would spell social disintegration, the list is too long and vague and also too contentious to be helpful. If the term fundamental values refers to values shared by all the members of a specific society, it is difficult to think of suitable candidates. As individuals we do have such values, but they vary from person to person, and hardly any of them are common to all the members of a society. To talk of the core values of a society is to reify the latter and to impose on it an unacceptable degree of homogeneity. Is equality a value shared by all in a liberal society? Racists, sexists and many religious people would disagree. It is certainly an important liberal value, but not all the citizens of liberal society are liberals. Is respect for persons such a value? Racists, fascists and others would disagree, and many others agree only because it is so weakly defined as to make no moral demands. Is monogamy a fundamental value? One would not have thought so. Many men and women in our society set up loose alliances or 'open' marriages that are designed to excuse them from the demands of sexual loyalty. Even conventionally married people are not always immune to the temptations of adultery and some of them feel little guilt. The recent government proposal in Britain to grant 'no-fault' divorce implicitly removes the social stigma from adultery. Given the high rate of divorce, there is perhaps some truth in the Muslim complaint that monogamy in a liberal society is really serial polygamy and that their 'more honest' and 'open' polygamy does not deserve all the opprobrium that is heaped upon it. It is also worth noting that such monogamy as remains and is valued in modern society is a weak version of its traditional form.[10]

Although the term 'fundamental' or 'core value' is problematic, we can give it an acceptable meaning by redefining it. A society has a body of values which are enshrined in its constitutional and political institutions and structure the conduct of its collective affairs. Not all its members need or do as a matter of fact believe in them. But that does not detract from the fact that these values inform their collective life and that in that sense they are all publicly and as a community committed to it. They might disregard them in their personal and interpersonal lives, and might even seek to change their society's

commitment to them. However, so long as the prevailing constitutional and political institutions remain unchanged, the society is
officially committed to them. They constitute what I might call its
'operative public values'. Operative public values are values because
society collectively cherishes and seeks to live by them; they are
public in the sense that they pertain to the conduct of its collective
affairs; and they are operative because they are not abstract ideals
but embodied in its institutions and practices. Operative public
values are the moral and political anchors of a society that guard it
against understandable temptations and pressures, and their violation provokes deep unease and even outrage. So far as liberal
society is concerned, these values are not easy to determine.[11] By and
large, such values as respect for human dignity, equal respect for
persons, secure spaces for self-determination, freedom of dissent and
expression, and the pursuit of collective interest as the central *raison
d'être* of political power would seem to fall within this category.[12]

Operative public values are not always mutually compatible and
sometimes pull in different directions. They are not static either,
although they only change over a long period of time and in response
to major moral and cultural changes in the society at large. Since they
define the collective self-conception of the society, they permeate
downwards and influence other areas of life. But they may not, and
are no less significant for being confined to the public and collective
life of the community. Although all liberal societies share the same
operative public values, they define, relate, limit and cherish them
differently, and therein consists their identity. Not all groups in a
society accept the way it defines and relates these values, and their
disputes form the subject matter of its politics. While the minorities
have an obligation to accept the values, they remain at liberty to
participate in their redefinition. As the controversy surrounding the
Rushdie affair in Britain showed, Muslims successfully reopened the
debate on the nature and limits of free speech, the state's relation to
religion, and the nature of equality. In so doing they added a distinct
perspective to the ongoing discussion about British society's operative public values.

I suggest that the operative public values of a liberal society
provide the only acceptable principle for delimiting the range of
permissible diversity, and that a society may legitimately ban
practices that violate these values.[13] The values do not represent the
best let alone the only rational or 'truly human' way of organizing
human societies, but they are central to the historically developed
moral self-conception of the liberal society and represent the way it
has chosen to live as a community. They are not sacrosanct and
immune to change. But until such time as society remains collectively

committed to them, the minority has an obligation to respect and uphold them. The obligation is not moral in nature, for the minority does not have to believe in these values and accept them *in foro interno*. All that is required of it is that it behave in conformity with them. Insofar as it *does not believe* in them, there is a regrettable but unavoidable hiatus between its beliefs and conduct, and the minority in question is subjected to coercion. But since it *does not have to believe* in them, the coercion is not moral in nature. Its integrity is inviolate and no moral enormity is committed against it.

Although liberal society's operative public values are related to its laws and cultural practices, the relationship is not as close as is often claimed. Take the equality of the sexes, one of the operative public values in a liberal society. It requires that if men enjoy certain rights and liberties, women should enjoy them too. It does not entail monogamy; all it entails is that if men are allowed polygyny, women should be allowed polyandry. Monogamy is a product of a different cultural tradition and requires a different justification. That it is separable from the principle of equality of the sexes is evident in the fact that those who depart from it do not generally reject the latter. Even the law which insists on the equality of the sexes neither bans adultery and taking mistresses nor punishes 'illegitimate' children.

This means that monogamy is not as central to the liberal way of life as the equality of the sexes. If the majority of people in a liberal society were to practise and demand legal recognition of non-monogamous relationships, it is not unlikely that monogamy may disappear. This is how the centuries-old ban on homosexuality came to be dropped. This is not at all to say that polygamy should be permitted; but rather that the ban on it needs a stronger and better-argued justification than a mere appeal to the principle of the equality of the sexes. What is true of polygamy is also true of several other minority practices. If they can be shown to be in clear violation of operative public values, they may legitimately be banned. But when this is not the case, a greater sensitivity must be shown to minority beliefs, and only such decisions should be taken as are based on a broad consensus arrived at after a sympathetic intercultural dialogue. Every society has a specific set of operative public values, and thus a distinct moral character. It is therefore logically and morally impossible for it to grant *full* equality to all its cultural groups. But it can and ought to grant them as much free cultural space as is compatible with its operative public values, and it ought also to bear in mind that the values are a product of historical consensus and need to win the allegiance of and be revised to meet the legitimate grievances of new groups.

Theorizing liberal practice

It might be asked if the kind of pluralist society I sketched above can properly be called liberal. The answer is a qualified yes. The culturally pluralist society respects the individual, is tolerant, welcomes dissent, limits the role of the government, does not turn cultures into ontological super-subjects enjoying the right to subordinate and oppress their members, and so on. In that sense it is liberal in character. However, it also departs from much of mainstream liberal thought in several significant respects. It views individuals as culturally embedded beings, defines them in communal and non-individualist terms, and locates their choices and autonomy within a wider and richer framework. The pluralist society also revises the traditional liberal mode of separating private and public realms. It rejects the conventional liberal concern to abstract the state from society, and reintegrates and establishes a creative partnership between them. It also redefines the traditional liberal views on the nature and functions of government, and gives the latter a socially constitutive role. The government does not merely 'govern' society but also nurtures its moral and cultural resources and helps it become cohesive and self-regulating. The pluralist society de-absolutizes liberalism, cherishes the so-called non-liberal ways of life and institutionalizes a dialogue between them. It is characterized by diverse ways of life: some secular, others religious; some individualist, others communitarian; some liberal, others non-liberal; and each in turn nurturing its own diverse forms. In these and other respects the culturally pluralist society is not liberal as the term is currently defined by such influential writers as Rawls, Raz and Dworkin. We might therefore say that liberalism is *aufgehoben* in such a society. Its central insights are teased out, its weaknesses rejected, and the former are absorbed and preserved in a richer social framework.

If we look at the practices of societies we call liberal, we see that this is broadly the direction in which they are themselves moving. As we saw, their laws take account of cultural differences, and their courts of law apply them in a culturally mediated manner. Their governments follow policies which sometimes take account of the special needs of cultural communities and adjust their ideas of equal opportunity accordingly. Some of them also support minority languages, cultures and communal institutions, and permit and even fund minority schools. Although liberal societies have still a long way to go in the direction of cultural pluralism, and although their journey is sometimes marked by nervous self-doubts, they are nevertheless increasingly moving away from and in that sense transcending the narrowly individualist liberal doctrine.[14]

We might see their practices as regrettable deviations from 'true' liberalism under the influence of political expediency, electoral politics and seductive 'illiberal' doctrines. Although there is some truth in it, such a view is deeply mistaken. It essentializes and homogenizes a rich tradition, sets up abstract and ahistorical norms that are not grounded in and cannot therefore guide political practice, and denies liberalism a vital opportunity to interact with other bodies of ideas. The better way to view the practices of liberal societies is to see them as morally sensitive attempts to articulate central liberal values in an increasingly plural world and to deepen and enrich them by drawing on both the neglected principles of liberalism itself and the values of other traditions. Rather than excogitate abstract principles *ex nihilo* and insist on their ideological purity, liberals need to reflect on and theorize the practices of liberal societies. They need to develop not *liberalism* but a critical theory of liberal practice, based not on the divergent and subjective intuitions of liberal philosophers but on the agonized legal and political judgements of liberal institutions.

Notes

I am most grateful to John Crawley, Tariq Madood and David Beetham for their helpful comments on this chapter.

1 Assimilation is not distinctive to liberalism. Communitarians and socialists can also be assimilationists. In this paper I concentrate on the liberals.

2 In its extreme form, assimilationist liberalism is intolerant of all departures from what are taken to be the constitutive principles of liberalism. In its moderate form, it tolerates them if confined to the private realm. The distinction is not easy to draw and many liberals directly or indirectly advocate the extreme variety. My argument in this section is directed at the extreme form of assimilationist liberalism. I criticize the moderate form in my discussion of cultural *laissez-faire*. In either form, assimilationist liberalism is advocated, among others, by Raz (1986) and Barry (1991). I have argued elsewhere that assimilationism has been a central and abiding feature of the liberal tradition. See Parekh (1994).

3 Gray's views are shared by several libertarian writers in Britain.

4 For a further discussion, see Parekh (1991). Throughout this chapter I talk of cultural diversity rather than cultural differences. Differences remain isolated, episodic and transient unless they form part of a practice and are patterned and integrated into a more or less coherent framework. I use the term diversity to describe such socially structured and legitimized differences. I am interested in cultural diversity, and a culture is by definition a reasonably coherent way of life.

5 Will Kymlicka (1989: chs 8, 9) offers a perceptive analysis of how liberalism can accommodate cultural diversity. He sees cultures as contexts of choices, and argues that they need to be protected when disadvantaged by factors beyond the control of their members. Although he advances ingenious arguments in support of his thesis, I do not find them persuasive. As I argue in this chapter, cultures are not just contexts of

choices, and such an individualist account of them misses out their important features. Kymlicka sees cultures only from the standpoint of their members and not that of the society at large. Although his distinction between choice and circumstance is useful, it is not free from difficulties. And I am not sure why cultures need protection only when they are disadvantaged. Galston (1991) provides another way to accommodate cultural diversity within liberalism.

6 For a discussion of these and related cases, see Parekh (1991).

7 Religious education has given much trouble to liberal societies and evoked different responses. In such countries as Switzerland and Austria, people pay clearly earmarked religious taxes to be entitled to religious education. In France the religious education of immigrant children has to be funded by their home governments. In Germany the Turkish government sends fully paid Muslim teachers to teach Islam to Turkish immigrant children during school hours. These ad hoc measures at least partly owe their origin to liberal society's lack of clarity and consensus on the public role of religion.

8 This seems to be the view of Raz (1986). His subsequent writings reflect a different view.

9 Liberals and communitarians sometimes arrive at different lists of fundamental values. In recent years both have begun to invoke the elusive concept of national identity to determine the permissible range of diversity. By and large, they mean by it little more than what others call fundamental or core values. In several countries governments have appointed committees or commissions to define the fundamental values of their societies. For one such attempt, see Australian Government (1989). This is a report of the Committee set up to advise the government on the principles that should guide Australia's immigration policies and determine the kind of commitment that can legitimately be expected of the immigrants. It rejects 'core values' but sees no difficulty in setting out the 'basic institutions and principles' of Australia. These are largely liberal-democratic in nature (Australian Government, 1989: 4f.).

10 Traditionally monogamy, which, etymologically means sexual intercourse with one person only, ruled out premarital sex as well.

11 This is so because we are concerned not with what values *liberalism* has traditionally espoused nor what values different *philosophers* have stressed, but with those that liberal societies as a matter of historical fact cherish and seek to live by. That requires a careful analysis of their structures, practices and political discourse.

12 The list is necessarily tentative and vague. Each of these values would need to be carefully unpacked and its different forms and meanings distinguished in order to uncover the sense and form in which liberal societies generally define and cherish them. For example, we would need to explore what they generally mean by dignity and respect in order to identify the specifically liberal mode of respect for human dignity, as different from, say, the socialist or the conservative or the religious. Respect for human dignity, equal respect for persons, etc. are all values that the modern individual cherishes, and there is nothing distinctively liberal about them. The distinctiveness of liberal societies lies in interpreting them in a specific way.

13 The operative public values of a society might be outrageous as in the case of the Nazi Germany, the apartheid regime in South Africa and the Stalinist Soviet Union. Since I am here concerned with liberal society, I ignore the ways in which the values of these regimes can be criticized. The communist regimes did espouse great values, but these were not *operative*.

14 It is therefore becoming increasingly inaccurate to call them liberal. To call them post-liberal, however, is to ignore their liberal features and just as inaccurate.

References

Australian Government (1989) *Immigration: A Commitment to Australia*. Canberra: Australian Government Publishing Service.
Barry, B. (1991) *Liberty and Justice: Essays in Political Theory 2*. Oxford: Clarendon Press.
Galston, W. A. (1991) *Liberal Purposes*. Cambridge: Cambridge University Press.
Gray, J. (1993) *Post-Liberalism: Studies in Political Thought*. London: Routledge.
Kymlicka, W. (1989) *Liberalism, Community and Culture*. Oxford: Oxford University Press.
Modood, T. (1992) *Not Easy Being British*. London: Trentham Books.
Parekh, B. (1991) 'British citizenship and cultural difference', in G. Andrews (ed.), *Citizenship*. London: Lawrence and Wishart. pp. 183–204.
Parekh, B. (1994) 'Decolonizing Liberalism', in A. Shtromas (ed.), *The End of 'isms'?* Oxford: Blackwell. pp. 85–103.
Raz, J. (1986) *The Morality of Freedom*. Oxford: Clarendon Press.

Index